The Inner Restoration
of Christianity

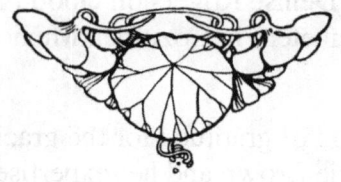

by
Efstratios Papanagiotou

Preface by
Theodore J. Nottingham

Second Edition
2013

The Inner Restoration of Christianity

Second Edition
© 2013 by Theosis Books

Cover: Photo of the Christ at Sunrise
taken by Denise Rogers on Good Friday
in a cemetery in Cozumel, Mexico.

A special expression of gratitude for the gracious assistance
of Kathleen Marie Brown and her expertise in bringing
polish and ease of reading to you who pick up
this masterful book.

ClipArt by FCIT

Holy Ghost Flower

All rights reserved.

ISBN 978-0-9859074-0-2

Printed in the United States of America.

TABLE OF CONTENTS

Preface by Theodore J. Nottingham	v
Prologue	ix
Introduction	xi
Metamorphosis	1
Egoism	3
False Belief	17
Trials	27
Self-Knowledge	39
The Spiritual Life	45
The Meaning of Life	61
Remembrance of Death	69
God	81
Atheism	91
Remembrance of God	101
The Love of God	107
The Love of Man	113

Forgiveness	125
Prayer	137
The Will of God	163
The Bitter Cup	177
Unseen Warfare	187
Hope	199
Humility	205
"God Be with You"	223
"Along with Athena, Move Your Hand"	227
Jesus Christ	233
The New Testament	263
Guidance	271
Steadfastness	281
Patience	289
Pain	293
Fear	299
Evil	307
Happiness (Or Good Fortune/Luck)	317
Strength	321
Consolation	327
Hesychia (Stillness)	333

Silence	345
Loneliness and Solitude	365
Fullness	375
"What Shall be Able to Separate Us from You?"	383
Freedom	391
Perfection	395
Work	401
"For Your Sake"	415
"Why Don't You Cry, My Heart?"	421
The Lost Paradise	431
"To Be My True Self"	433
"You... and We"	437
Epilogue	443
Acknowledgments – Bibliography	445

The Inner Restoration of Christianity

Preface

By Theodore J. Nottingham

In this important work, the reader will find a treasure trove of ancient spiritual wisdom from the Christian East. Still little known to the Western world, the first thousand years of Christianity taught transformational, psychotherapeutic theology which has been virtually lost to our part of the world. Only the great Christian mystics managed to keep contact with that living Truth which goes back to the very source of these teachings. In the West, John Cassian was a disciple of the Desert Father Evagrius and later Meister Eckhart's mentor was Dionysius the Aeropagite.

The author's exceptional breadth of knowledge and scholarship in the field of Eastern Orthodox spirituality offers the reader direct contact with the spiritual Masters who were the Grace-filled light-bearers of this universal Truth originally made known by Yeshua the Anointed One. The reader will find countless citations – pearls of wisdom – gathered here in a unique fashion, along with the author's own profound understanding of these teachings that have immediate impact on daily human life and the power to awaken and transform the consciousness of every human being.

The reader will find here a depth of understanding that transcends cultures and creeds, and which re-aligns a hopelessly fragmented religion with its true intent. This work could not be more timely as churches are rapidly disintegrating and emptying, spiritual guides are almost impossible to find, and the foundational truths of this great revelation of Light to humanity has been betrayed and distorted in so many ways.

The Inner Restoration of Christianity

As an example, one of the many lost teachings from the transformational wisdom of early Christianity is the idea of *hesychia,* or "inner silence" which is at the heart of the earliest expressions of Christian practice and faith. This way of being has been a fundamental spiritual practice in the traditions of Eastern Orthodox Christianity going back to the first centuries after the appearance of the Anointed One in the hill country of Judea. The term *hesychia* can be translated as "inner tranquility" or "inner silence" and a complex psychological teaching and set of practices has grown up around it, involving some of the great figures of eastern Christianity such as Saint Gregory Palamas, John Cassian, and many others. Hesychasm is a quality of conscious presence that combines constant inner awareness and prayer with deep stillness. It requires a profound self-knowledge, attentiveness to each breath of the body, and commitment to the reality of the sacred at the heart of life. A synthesis of this teaching can be found in a revered book known as "The Philokalia" (translated as "Love of Beauty" or "Love of the Good") which is central to Orthodox spirituality.

The teaching on "hesychia" is modeled in many ways by the actions of Jesus as recorded in the Gospels, but especially in the strange scene presented in Luke 4:28-33, after Jesus had revealed his mission to the people of his hometown: *"All the people in the synagogue were furious when they heard this. They got up, drove him out of the town, and took him to the brow of the hill on which the town was built, in order to throw him down the cliff. But he walked right through the crowd and went on his way."*

In the midst of violent attack, he maintained an attitude of extraordinary inner peace – as he would later on the way to the cross – and responded to the hatred and fury with silence and a detachment that mystically saved him from harm. Though particularly evident in the humility and inner grounding of the Christ, "hesychasm" is a universal concept. Its parallel can be found in other ideas related to spiritual evolution, such as detachment, freedom from desire, inner peace. The results of this effort are seen in the presence of sages and saints in all times and places.

Inner silence ultimately means self-transcendence. It requires us to overcome a fundamental self-interest that guides everyone's life, in order to accept the difficulties of passing circumstances and to remember the greater context in which our lives are taking place. Accomplishing such inner freedom which leads to inner silence is no passive effort. It in fact demands "inner warfare" as we seek to become liberated from all that is connected with the inherent selfishness in which we are born, which includes the self-absorption of relentless thoughts, most of them based on self-interest. This condition is part of our natural make-up, as basic to us as the instinct to survive. The paradox we all must face is that spiritual and psychological survival requires the opposite of this natural instinct. The maturing of the human character means turning one's attention to something greater than oneself, which then offers a basis for inner stability, independence from externals, and a peace that "passes all understanding."

To be without this inner silence founded on the spiritual consciousness of a greater reality is to literally lose ourselves in the stimuli of the outside world and in the hallucinations of our imaginations, fears, daydreams, and vacuous illusions. The serenity that is witnessed in the sages and saints of the past is not meant to be some rare or unique nobility of character. It is right alignment with reality, an achievable state for all of us and no less than our birthright, if we are willing to struggle for it.

This inner freedom has nothing to do with emotional disconnection, lack of compassion or disinterest in what is going on around us. In fact, to be rooted in an active state of inner silence gives one the widest scope of vision and makes possible a new awareness and a capacity for unconditional love. Certainly, this is very difficult work, the true "spiritual warfare," as anyone will quickly discover upon making efforts to overcome the noise of our relentless and random thoughts and feelings. It demands moment by moment remembrance of our true purpose in this world, and a constant check on our automatic reactions based on acquired habits and imitations of those around us. The "hesychastic" way calls us to take the state of calm found in deep meditation and carry it with us into the noise and tumult of daily life.

To follow this way of inner silence requires the capacity to accept necessary suffering, a fact that everyone must deal with in one way or another. To experience inner pain without falling victim to self-pity or despair is a sign of a new maturity of will and understanding. At the apex of this way of being is the ability to find joy and gratitude for the gift of life even in the face of great turmoil, injustice, or tragedy. Living in that paradox creates a new quality of Self which transcends the ever-shifting scenery of temporal life. This inner silence is the groundwork of unity, constancy, and true freedom.

This is but one example of the great value, significance, and timeliness of this epic spiritual book. May you rediscover the origins and authentic power of the teachings of the Christ expressed by the ancient traditions whose wisdom for human life are deeply healing, renewing, and timeless.

Prologue

At first reading, this book may seem rather "harsh" to the reader. This may be due to the fact that it deals with very subtle matters which concern and trouble us all. Its main focus is based on the One Truth that *"God is Love"* (1 John 4:16). So no matter how difficult things are presented concerning human beings and our irreconcilable enemy – egoism – in our depths, all is good, beautiful and peaceful.

Because God Is Love.

What is it that prevents us from living through this Depth of our being, acknowledging and constantly experiencing this Truth? It is, of course, our egoism.

And that is why Jesus, the personification of Love, states rather strictly, *"Think not that I am come to send peace on earth: I came not to send peace, but a sword"* (Matthew 10:34). This Divine Sword is destined to separate us from our most intimate and "beloved" possession, our egoism, and in this way to set us free from our worst oppressor.

In the beginning, God's Love might even seem harsh. Yet, as soon as He proceeds in His healing work, His Goodness and His Beauty are revealed.

This book deals with egoism, pain and Love, so, inevitably, it may seem harsh, but its hope is that, with God's Grace, it will be beneficial to the reader.

This book does not claim "infallibility" and it does not seek to develop "theories." Rather, it speaks through experiences, personal and otherwise.

The Inner Restoration of Christianity

If there is anything real in it, then this comes from the New Testament. If there is anything false, then this comes from human weakness and inadequacy.

In short, everything valuable in this work is due to God.

"For Thine is the kingdom,

and the power,

and the glory,

forever,

Amen"

Introduction

"Christianity is the doctrine of Christ our Savior. It is comprised of the practical, the natural, and the theological."

(Evagrius of Pontus, *Praktikos*, Chapter 1, p. 97)

Christianity still exists. It exists in the Holy Scriptures, in the Fathers, in the Mysteries and the Liturgies of the Church, in monks and in laymen, but essentially it has been lost inside of us. Many of us say that we are Christians, but our Christianity is lukewarm to non-existent. Even more of us say that we are not Christians, and we declare either atheism or profess we belong to other religions, traditions and spiritual paths.

Those of us who say we are Christians, if we want to be honest, may have to acknowledge that our Christianity occupies a very minimal place in our lives. It doesn't exist in our relationships, our work, our interests, our entertainment and our recreation, our aims and our efforts, it doesn't exist in our thinking and it doesn't exist in our hearts.

Even when Christianity plays a part in our existence, we still adjust it to our own standards, so it won't trouble us, and it won't be an impediment to our other activities.

How far do we stand from the exhortation of Christ to seek first the Kingdom of God and then everything else? How far do we stand from having Christianity as our first and main concern, and on this effort, build every other effort?

Perhaps all these facts do not apply to everyone, perhaps they do not apply to the others, but they surely apply to *us*.

The Inner Restoration of Christianity

The proper restoration of Christianity should be basically an inner one. We could say metaphorically that the conversion of the Apostle Paul is an inner restoration of Christianity. After persecuting Christianity on the outside, he acknowledged it on the inside and it took its fitting place.

The outer restoration of Christianity might be necessary, but it is of secondary importance, whereas *the inner restoration of Christianity* is requisite and of foremost importance, and in the long-term could also bring about the outer restoration. It is the same with the Apostle Paul, who preached Christianity after he experienced it inside him.

Metamorphosis

The Christian way is a way of *metamorphosis* that leads from *egoism* to *Love*. The way of metamorphosis is a difficult way, rough and lonely: *"Because strait is the gate, and narrow is the way, which leadeth unto life, and few there be that find it"* (Matthew 7:14).

It is the way of trial, revilement and persecutions: *"Blessed are ye, when men shall revile you, and persecute you, and shall say all manner of evil against you falsely, for my sake"* (Matthew 5:11); it is the way of temptations: *"Then was Jesus led up of the Spirit into the wilderness to be tempted of the devil"* (Matthew 4:1); it is the way of the cross: *"And he that taketh not his cross, and followeth after me, is not worthy of me"* (Matthew 10:38); it is the way of self-denial: *"If any man will come after me, let him deny himself"* (Matthew 16:24). It is a hard way: *"This is a hard saying; who can hear it?"* (John 6:60); it is absolute: *"Be ye therefore perfect, even as your Father which is in heaven is perfect"* (Matthew 5:48); and it asks everything from us: *"If thou wilt be perfect, go and sell that thou hast, and come and follow me"* (Matthew 19:21).

It is the way of the few and the chosen: *"From that time many of his disciples went back, and walked no more with him"* (John 6:66); *"For many are called, but few are chosen"* (Matthew 22:14); but it is also a universal way: *"God our Savior; Who will have all men to be saved, and to come unto the knowledge of the truth"* (1 Timothy 2:3-4).

It is a way of humility: *"Who then can be saved?"* But Jesus beheld them, and said unto them, *"With men this is impossible; but with God all things are possible"* (Matthew 19:25-26).

But one promise is being given: *"And your reward shall be great, and ye shall be the children of the Highest"* (Luke 6:35).

So we realize that in this way *our pain is not in vain.*

It may be a difficult way, but it is, as we said, a way of metamorphosis: *"The God of all grace, who hath called us unto his eternal glory by Christ Jesus, after that ye have suffered a while, make you perfect, stablish, strengthen, settle you"* (1 Peter 5:10); and along with our metamorphosis, the *way* is transfigured as well, and becomes a way of rest: *"Come unto me, all ye that labor and are heavy laden, and I will give you rest"* (Matthew 11:28); it becomes a pleasant way: *"For my yoke is easy, and my burden is light"* (Matthew 11:30); a way of joy: *"Ye shall be sorrowful, but your sorrow shall be turned into joy"* (John 16:20); *"And your joy no man taketh from you"* (John 16:22); of freedom: *"The truth shall make you free"* (John 8:32); of courage and real strength: *"Let not your heart be troubled, neither let it be afraid"* (John 14:27); *"But be of good cheer; I have overcome the world"* (John 16:33); of fearlessness: *"Fear not them which kill the body, but are not able to kill the soul"* (Matthew 10:28); of mercy: *"Be ye therefore merciful, as your Father also is merciful"* (Luke 6:36); of compassion: *"Lord, save me." And immediately Jesus stretched forth his hand, and caught him"* (Matthew 14:30-31).

It is the way of life and spirit: *"The words that I speak unto you, they are spirit, and they are life"* (John 6:63); of Light: *"God is light, and in him is no darkness at all"* (1 John 1:5); of Love, *"Beloved, let us love one another: for love is of God; and every one that loveth is born of God, and knoweth God"* (1 John 4:7).

It is the way of God: *"God is love; and he that dwelleth in love dwelleth in God, and God in him"* (1 John 4:16).

So let us continue with strength and courage, and with the help of God, face our worst fear...confront our worst enemy...our egoism.

Egoism

"The cause of all evils and root of all sins is egoism."

(St. Theophan the Recluse, *Guidance in the Spiritual Life*, p. 137)

"There was a wise teacher who knew the cure for the disease of egoism. Wanting to pass on his knowledge, he thought that he should address people with the biggest weaknesses so after their healing they would be a living witness of his words.

He found the biggest egoist of the world and told him with kindness: "Follow me and I will help you to defeat your egoism." His immediate response was: "Who do you think you are? I don't need your help, let alone following you. You are crazy, I am fine, and I don't need anybody's help."

The wise teacher left a little bit disappointed and searched for the second biggest egoist of the world. He told him nicely: "If you follow me, I promise you that I will help you get rid of the disease of egoism."

But he answered him, without much thinking: "I don't think I need your help... ok, I might have some egoism, but you can't call it a disease. Anyway my egoism is so little that it doesn't require any help. On the contrary it is rather YOU who needs help, because your presumptuousness and arrogance are beyond limit. You go around and assume that you can help people. Sick arrogant... egoist...."

The wise man, even more disappointed, kept seeking someone to pass on his knowledge to, but as much as he searched among the people and whatever the degree of their egoism was, no one accepted to become his disciple.

After having searched all the earth without having found one man willing to get rid of his egoism, he met the only saintly man whom he hadn't addressed, because he knew that he was the only human being that was cured from the disease of egoism.

Upon discussion, the saint asked him why he looked disappointed and the wise man answered honestly: "Because I know the art of getting rid of egoism but I can't find even one man to teach."

The saint, as if he could not believe his ears, fell on his knees with tears in his eyes and said: "Finally I meet you. It has been years since I've been looking for someone to teach me how to get rid of this disease. Please, I would be eternally grateful to you if you would take me as your disciple."

Our basic psychic disease is egoism.

Egoism can be removed and die only through hardship, tribulation, humiliation, trial, disapproval, mockery; only through painful means.

Egoism resembles cancer in its properties. And like cancer, its cure hasn't been fully discovered and it is very difficult to treat. In no way should we treat it with tolerance or endearment, because it spreads radically. It needs unrelenting warfare, without retreat. We need, of course, to show the necessary strategic prudence so our organism can endure the battle, but we should uproot it from the depths, because if there are any roots left, it will find a way to grow back. There could be a metastasis and the next time it could strike more forcibly.

So our fundamental psychic disease is egoism.

> "The gravest sin among all the sins is pride, self-opinion, self-confidence."
>
> (St. Ignatius Brianchaninov, *The Arena: An Offering to Contemporary Monasticism*, p. 93)

In its initial stage, egoism seems innocent, relatively insignificant, and maybe even cute or interesting. Perhaps it looks like a sign of authority, power or even love (as when it is manifested in the form of jealousy).

But immediately, in its next stage, it becomes tiring, annoying, monotonous, unpleasant and irritating – a source of tension, disagreement and misunderstanding.

In its subsequent stage, it becomes possessive, threatening, irrational, cunning, calculating, insidious, revengeful, resentful, malicious, unbearable and suffocating.

In its final stage, it becomes lethal: self-destructive or other-destructive, or both of them simultaneously.

With mathematical precision, the initial stage will lead to the next stage. Very often, the second stage will lead to the third. And more rarely, the third stage will lead to the final and more extreme stage. Usually we don't remain very long at this final stage because it is equivalent to total destruction. So the duration of our stay in this stage is short either way: either we destroy and are destroyed, or we recover.

The fall into the last and worst stages of egoism is exhausting and devastating. That is why we don't last long in them and after we exhaust all the supplies of our psychic energies, we return empty, as it were, to our everyday egoistic state.

We return to an initial stage of egoism, feeling much better, much healthier – and often thinking that we have been cured and released once and for all from our egoism – until we start sinking again into the worst stages... and everything starts all over again.

Generally, we come and go between these stages of egoism, either with our thinking, with our words, or with our actions.

So to heal from egoism, there are three basic requirements:

1) We have to understand its nature and its working;

2) We have to be taught its cure; and

3) We have to, of course, desire and apply it.

These three conditions interact and apply to every case. And since egoism is a deadly and severe disease, that should be its treatment as well.

> "Anyone who wishes and longs to be healed is obliged to endure whatever the doctor offers in order to be delivered from the illness. Indeed, no patient is happy to suffer an amputation or cauterization or to be cleansed with enema. Rather, every patient thinks about such things with disgust. Nonetheless, that same patient is convinced that it is impossible to be healed of his illness without them. He surrenders then to the doctor, knowing that in return for a little disgust, a great deal of healing will result for an unhealthy condition and chronic illness."
>
> (Abba Zosimas, *The Reflections of Abba Zosimas*, p. 5)

But this healthy severity and adamant determination, combined with deep knowledge, prudence and subtlety on the level of surgical precision, are characteristics *only* of God's Love.

Only God can carry out this operation in our soul when we have been affected, more or less, by the disease of egoism.

Only God is the true Doctor of souls.

Now, egoism needs special food in order to remain alive: approval, admiration, confirmation, achievements, accomplishments, and the *attention* and interest of others. All these constitute its favorite foods.

Egoism constantly believes that it has rights. It never puts itself in the other person's shoes; it just looks at things from its own point of view and that's why it always justifies itself.

It always thinks that it is an exception, "In my case things are different...." It feels very relaxed with other people's cases – "It's not such a big deal" – and very vexed with its own, "Nobody understands what I am going through...."

Egoism is deeply *unconscious*.

It is hidden in the *dark* and cannot stand the light.

And the more it is fed, the hungrier it becomes; as much as it is sustained, the more inflated it becomes. Egoism is greedy, it wants and it wants and it wants, all the time. When it says, "This is the only thing I want and nothing else," it *always lies*. It will always ask something more and it will always say, "This is all I want, really, and nothing more, this is the last, honestly...."

Egoism is *never* satisfied if it doesn't have its own way. It turns every desire, every situation, into a matter of life and death, and it is always anxious, "If this doesn't happen or if that happens, if I don't get this or if I lose that... how will I go on?"

Egoism wants everyone to suffer when it suffers or when it thinks it suffers. It wants the worst for other people in order to feel good about itself. It is shut in a small box and it tries to shut everything in there with it. It never rejoices with other people's joy; it is indifferent or distressed with their happiness. It cannot understand how it is possible for its friends to be well without it, and in that way it *essentially* wants their misery. It pretends that it cares for them and that it wants what is best for them, but in reality, its only concern is how to limit them in its narrow limits. It constantly strives to devour the objects of its interest and of its "love."

Egoism remembers very clearly whatever seemed to threaten it. It has registered every possible thing that might turn against it: words, faces, gestures, looks, jokes, situations, and all kinds of events. And every moment it seeks to bring all these into the forefront and capture us in their remembrance and their recollection. If it manages to do that... then it is inflated.

Egoism can see even best friends as enemies. It lives in absurd, imaginary situations where it distorts everything that happens, all that it sees and everything that exists.

Egoism is the darkest thing that we contain, and it makes us sick. It keeps us outside of the Kingdom of God and inhibits God's miracle, God's Will, His gifts and His beauty. It is the exact opposite of the God-centered state of being.

Egoism considers nothing sacred; it hates even its own self, which is why it is so self-destructive. It is as self-destructive an illness as cancer. In that way, every *self-destructive* tendency is, in *essence,* egoistic.

And of course, egoism is *moved* as well, it cries, it sheds tears, it hurts…

The pain of egoism "breaks" our hearts; it tears us up, it is immobilizing and freezes us up. It can drive us crazy, it blurs our mind, it encircles us and it shuts us up towards everything except the object of its interest. It is blind, deaf, incurable, sweeping, it doesn't take anything into account and it doesn't respect anything.

The pain of egoism is *insufferable*.

But in reality, it is untrue and *illusory*. And it often disappears as suddenly as it appeared, as long as we feed it with what it longs to devour. It is very clear that egoism *never cares for anyone or anything but itself*, no matter what it says to prove the opposite, because it always claims that what it does is out of love. It swears that it loves even to the point of death. Lies! *This is not Love.*

Wherever there is Love, there is no egoism and wherever there is egoism, there is no Love. Love and egoism are mutually exclusive.

And of course, egoism rejoices as well…

The joy of egoism is distinguished by an imperceptible aggressiveness, a certain insecurity *in case it is lost*. It is characterized by some strange *agitation* and by an excessive enthusiasm. It is accompanied by a narrowing of the heart, something that forebodes its consequence, the pain of egoism, with which it is bound together since it constitutes the other side of the coin.

Now, whenever egoism hears a discussion about itself, it feels that for some reason it doesn't concern it at all. The phrase, "It's a public secret" describes very well our relationship with our egoism and also the way it perceives itself.

But egoism and Christianity are two completely incompatible things. As long as we are egoists we cannot truly be Christians.

Christianity, though, can heal us from the disease of egoism. But Christianity consists of an intensive treatment because it is a way of Love. And Love doesn't consider Herself; She is not interested whether She will be popular or liked, or if someone will think well of Her. She cares only for the ultimate well-being of the one She loves. And when the person She loves is sick, like the man who is affected by egoism, She will do *everything* to heal him.

> "We should put egoism to death, this malefactor. And if you don't put it to death, then the Lord will, sending one blow after another. And this He will do not out of cruelty but out of love."
>
> (St. Theophan the Recluse, *Guidance in the Spiritual Life*, pp. 136-137)

The surgical operation for the removal of egoism is painful, but as soon as we start to recover, we feel healthier, happier and *free*; we see life differently, we perceive beauty and miracle, and things have *meaning*. We can now truly love.

This procedure is an open *heart* surgery without anesthetic so we will feel it, we will experience it; otherwise, if it doesn't finish its work, we will let our heart be affected by it again, to be made unclean and to be carried away by the foreign "loves" of egoism and not of God's Love.

The duration of the treatment is important as well for the removal of egoism. It cannot be removed in a couple of minutes, or in a few days. It is a long-term process.

But *we should never believe* that egoism is all-powerful, because this would give it incredible force and therefore power over us. It just needs a drastic treatment before it spreads; because as it spreads, its treatment becomes all the more difficult.

Egoism is very cunning and it will fight hard until it dies; it won't stay passive. If it is exposed, it will assume other ways to survive, like acknowledging itself. It might declare: "I am a big egoist," "I have a lot of egoism," and in this way it derives a bizarre, sick joy.

It might even want to undertake its treatment! And of course, it always believes in quick results. Egoism always states that it has got rid of egoism once and for all!!!

Egoism is very devious and wicked. Even the "best intentions" can spring from it. We worry over something we did, we want to apologize, but the reason beneath this desire is that we fear the opinion of the other person.

So egoism employs powerful self-protective mechanisms. It always tries to remain hidden, which is why it surrounds us with situations that feed it – friends, family, relatives, jobs, relationships – making sure it won't be exposed to anything that offends it, and usually, in order to succeed, it degrades and lowers everything that could threaten it.

It has innumerable, indiscernible expressions; it shows even a sense of importance for present or past sins that we might have regretted bitterly. It remembers them with a certain nostalgia and conceit, "You cannot imagine the things I have done...."

It always defends itself with great mastery so that it won't be perceptible, "If you want, I can explain..." and in the rare cases that it doesn't do that, it is because it feels a sense of superiority, "It isn't worth the bother...." *Egoism has many legs.*

Great vigilance and real honesty are needed in order to start realizing all its possible and impossible expressions, because it has the greatest ability to hide behind the most deceptive facades. Since it constitutes the root of our psychic maladies, it is very deeply hidden and its outer manifestations can easily mislead us. For example, we often consider people who are excessively preoccupied with themselves as creatures too sensitive and fragile for this cruel and egoistical world!

We could trace another example in the so-called panic attacks, big or small, that we all go through sometimes. We could perhaps call them egocentric attacks because, in essence, they consist of an extreme reaction of our organism towards a real or imaginary threat to *our* integrity. But if, in that moment, we could free ourselves from this sense of importance which tells us that whatever happens to us is extremely significant, whereas when it happens to others, "It's ok, everything passes..." then we could immediately relax and the panic or the egoism would subside. If we looked deeper into the matter, we would probably realize that all these panic or ego attacks are mostly related to an *excessive* preoccupation with ourselves.

The truth is that we don't realize deeply enough how many of our psychic problems are due to the disease of egoism; how many of our depressions, our insecurities, our weaknesses, our addictions, all eventually lead back to our *egocentrism*.

Even our body cannot be unaffected by the existence of egoism, since it responds to the dispositions of our mind and heart. In time, it develops the corresponding rhythm, the corresponding tendencies, and demands what we taught it to demand. Therefore we have the consequences of egoism: gluttony, obesity, voluptuousness and many more. All theses unpleasant events are essentially results of the psychic disease of egoism, which means an excessive desire to feed *our own* organism with surplus physical or psychical energy.

We don't realize that even ordinary sorrow (στενοχώρια – narrow space) can be a result of egoism. When we are sorrowful (στενοχωρημένοι – in a narrow space), our heart doesn't breathe, it is squeezed. And that happens because she doesn't have enough space, she is narrowed and limited. But Love cannot fit into a narrow heart; Love needs space so She can dwell only in spacious, big hearts.

Egoism closes our heart, limits it and we become small-souled. Love opens our heart, enlarges it and we become large-souled. That is why egoism is defeated *only* with Love.

Love is the means, Love is the weapon, Love is the way.

So the best medicine for the disease of egoism is Love.

Very useful indeed for our cure from egoism would be the prolonged exposure to the influence of healthy (holy) people who have transcended their egoism. In this way our own egoism would probably start to weaken and atrophy. But soon it would be necessary to make our personal contribution and efforts of transcendence. It is known from the lives of the saints (those people free from egoism) that they had to use harsh means in order to help with the treatment (catharsis) of their fellow-beings. And the people who received the harsh and painful treatment eventually acknowledged the deep Love of those holy men and praised their holiness (their purity).

To sum up, egoism is essentially something foreign to our nature. It is acquired, a stranger to our True Self, which has taken an existence of its own inside of us and claims control of our life. It professes that it knows better how we should live our lives, and naturally it promises every joy if we obey it. It maintains that it knows the way to Paradise. So in the beginning we are carried away by its whispers, and then by its loud and clear voice, and we give it a place inside us, thinking that it will truly lead us to everything good.

But we should eventually realize that our egoism doesn't serve us in anything and, despite its sweet promises, it leads nowhere except toward the edge of a cliff. And it constantly throws us down the cliff. But still, when we manage to climb back up, we gullibly allow ourselves to be carried away again by its seductive words.

> "When our spirit, with Grace's action, is awakened, it turns completely towards God. Our egoistic mind, however, remains alive and claims its rights. [...] So what should we do in that case? We should always ally with the spirit and resist the demands of the egocentric, carnal man. This is exactly what constitutes the spiritual warfare."

(St. Theophan the Recluse, *Guidance in the Spiritual Life*, p. 92)

We should speak to our "self" and tell him clearly:

"Ok, you had your own way. You had your satisfaction. And what happened? You fed your egoism. You made another step towards self-destruction, towards your hell, your prison.

You satisfy your egoism for a couple of minutes, for some time, and you ensure your constant condemnation, aside from being deprived of all true satisfaction and all true joy. And not to mention that you create disharmony, problems and troubles.

You deny the Voice of God inside you, and follow the voice of your egoism, and you believe its promised "paradise." But reflect... how many times did it tell you the truth? How many times did you find what it promised, and how many times did it throw you off the cliff?

Whereas, whenever you heard the Voice of Love... did She ever deceive you? Did She ever lie? When will you stop giving Her second place? Should you always exhaust every path of your egoism before you turn to the Love that is calling you inside? To God, who is knocking on the door of your heart? Who is offering you everything marvelous as long as your heart is pure to receive it?

May the moment come when we declare, with strength, inside us: "*I am fed up of my egoism. It disgusts me. It doesn't serve me well in anything. I want to get rid of it, I want to be healed, I want to be freed.*"

So the treatment can begin...

Two angels, one old and one younger, who is learning the job, are sitting in the secretariat of God's office. A human shows up and asks directions.

"How could we help you?" asks the experienced angel.

"I would like the Kingdom of God."

"Down the corridor, seventh door to the right...."

A second human arrives.

"What you would like?"

"I would like to have Love."

"Down the corridor, seventh door to the right...."

A third person arrives.

"How could we be of service to you?"

"I would like to be a Saint."

"Down the corridor, seventh door to the right...."

Then the younger angel, puzzled, asks:

"These people were asking different things, why have you sent them all to the same place?"

"They were all asking the same thing in different words."

"And where did you send them?"

"Ah, to the surgery... there egoism is removed."

False Belief

We must make a distinction inside us.

We have to distinguish our egoism, that is our false self, from our Real Self. We have to distinguish our essence from our surface; the Self that God has bequeathed to us, from our counterfeit acquired "self" that has been created in this life and wants to substitute for the Truth inside us. Unfortunately, we have difficulty in making this inner distinction (separation) because we are unfamiliar with our inner world and we rarely turn there to see what is really going on.

They say that the greatest deception of the devil is to convince people that he doesn't exist so he can work undisturbed, and this is very valid in relation to our inner world. We have inside us an inner devil, our egoism, our false self, and its main activity is to constantly, and in every way, convince us of its non-existence!

A characteristic example of its cunning, especially when we undertake an inner war against it, is to pretend that it died, that it is ok…we overcame it. And then it lurks so it can claim us back and enslave us when, as a result of not being vigilant, we become content with our feeling of freedom. That's why it always tries to hide from us, since its very existence is threatened. Nevertheless, we have to be skillful in its detection after we learn to recognize it inside us, and we have to *distinguish it altogether* from our essence, from our Real Self, from our divine Self. But first we have to be convinced of its existence: the inner devil is egoism.

The inner devil is constantly elevating itself, and in that way it doesn't allow God's light to penetrate. *It believes only in itself*, it knows very well the idea of *self-confidence* and fights for it, but it is totally unaware of the idea of *God-confidence*. It seeks and cares only for its own. It is impatient, it worries, it is frightened, it is anxious, it is agitated, it gets angry, it takes offense, it is suspicious, it gets disheartened, it despairs, it compares, and it creates inner accounts. It is the one who *opens the door* to let in *every* outer devil and it always reserves a place for them inside us.

Nevertheless, our inner devil is something foreign to our nature. It is of no use to us, it just harasses and tortures us. It promises us "paradise" and grants it for awhile (however, it is a *false* paradise), but most of the time it holds us in Hell and fights to keep us there.

It has been said that the outer devil has as much strength over us as God allows him to have. But the inner devil has as much strength over us as WE allow it to have. So we have to die to our inner devil in order to transform. After we recognize it by its fruits inside us and are convinced of its existence, we have to instantly disassociate our self from it and never consider, even for one moment, that *we* are it.

Next, we have to assign it to its proper place inside us. What does that mean? It means that we should never give it the place of God. That is, we should never believe that it is all-powerful, that it can control us and that we are at its mercy. The truth is that we are at the mercy of God alone, and only God is all-powerful. If we ascribe, even unconsciously, the attribute of all-powerfulness to the devil, to the inner one or the outer one, then, whether we realize it or not, we worship the devil and not God (Matthew 4:8-10).

This fact leads inevitably to one conclusion: that the more faith we give to the devil, the more power we grant it over us. The more we believe in our false self, the more real it becomes inside us, because we feed it in that way.

When we say "faith" we don't refer to faith in its existence, but faith in its power, its abilities and its substance. Our inner devil belongs to the surface of ourselves and that is why it can be removed, it can be destroyed. But if we feed it with our faith, that is with our power, then we let it grow roots inside us and fortify it, when in fact it has nothing to do with the depths of ourselves which concern only God and constitute God's place inside us.

On this point, it is worth noticing how all these apply to our interpersonal relationships. It is true that our inner devil hides skillfully all the time from us, but it is equally true that it cannot hide, whatever we do, from the eyes of other people. And others as well cannot hide their inner devil, their egoism, their false self from us. No matter how skillfully we hide from our fellow human beings, sooner or later, they will perceive the beast that we hide inside us. But we ourselves can spend our whole life without ever seeing this inner beast.

Nonetheless, if our faith in the devil is stronger than our faith in God, if our faith in evil, lying, deception, deceit, hypocrisy and self-interest is strong, then our faith in good, beauty, selflessness, compassion and virtue will fall ill.

We will be unable to perceive the depths of every human being and his real essence, which is created by God in His image. We will see only his superficial part, his false, egoistic and acquired part, which we will consider to be his essence, his Real Self. And how is it possible to forgive such people? How is it possible to love them? Or trust them?

"Christ's commands might sound lovely and ideal, but they are completely utopian and unattainable" whispers our inner devil, and we nod approvingly.

That is why we must be converted. We must remove our faith from the devil to God, from egoism to Love.

Love *"believeth, hopeth, thinketh no evil"* (1 Corinthians 13:4-7). This means that She doesn't believe in the false part of man, She doesn't see the devil inside man saying "that is you...that is your real self." She sees God in man saying "This is You...this Is your Real Self." She *doesn't* believe in evil inside man. She might recognize it, but She doesn't perceive it as our essential being; She perceives it as unessential. She doesn't conceive it as real or as strength, but as a weakness, and as something superficial without deep foundations. She doesn't perceive it as the Truth of man, but as his delusion.

Love inside of us, God inside of us, is the source of our real essence, our Real Self which is always immanent and latent within. He just needs our attention, our energy, our feeding, in order to blossom, to bring his fruits to the surface, setting aside the tares which are trying to grow roots inside us. *Our Real Self, the created image of God, has his residence deep within us and tries to manifest on the surface while our false self, our personal devil, lives on the surface and tries to penetrate our depths by growing roots inside us.*

The food for both of them is the same; it is our strength, our faith, our attention. Whichever concerns us more, this is the one we feed. Whichever we pay attention to, whichever we preserve and consequently live by, this is the one we sustain.

So our false self must atrophy inside us. We must stop making so much of it and considering it so "real." We must consider it as something completely foreign and separate from us that is born superficially and constantly trying to penetrate deep inside us so it can substitute for our essence, our Real Self.

And here we must be absolutely unshakeable, because if we allow ourselves to assume, even for a minute, that this is not the case, in that minute we position the devil inside of us, in the dwelling place of God. We give our faith to the devil. And we should have the same attitude towards everyone else as well. Let's stop considering the false inside of them to be their Real Self. Let's stop giving our faith to their inner devil and let's start *separating them in our perceptions.* Surely we should perceive the inner devil, the destructive egoism of other people, as well as ours, but we should have discernment, that is, we should distinguish their false self from the Real One and we should keep the appropriate feelings for each one: Love *"rejoiceth not in iniquity, but rejoiceth in the truth"* (1 Corinthians 13:6).

So we need discernment. But we must be very careful here. Who inside us can have discernment? Only our Real Self can have discernment. Only the Self that exists in our depths can perceive his essential self and the false "self" at the surface as well. On the contrary, the false self at the surface can perceive only itself. And residing on the surface, it only sees the corresponding "self" of other people. Our superficial self isn't capable of any discernment and sees only the surface of things. Our Real Self, however, can and should make this distinction between the surface and the essence. That is what discernment means. To perceive only the false, the devil inside us or others, is a lack of discernment. But seeing only the Real, the Love, in other people or inside of us, disregarding the egoistic surface, perhaps also indicates an incomplete discernment.

So we should make this distinction, both in us and regarding others, and perceive both God and the devil; Love and egoism; the false and the Real. And then we should of course have faith as well, and worship God – Love, the Real – working at the same time against the devil – egoism, the false – with caution and carefulness, and *without giving them* God's place inside us. Because belief in the false means unfaithfulness to God.

That is why the devil must lose its glamour inside us. We can have true Love for all and everything as Christ exhorts us to do only if we realize that the evil of every man – his egoistic part, his inner devil – is not real. We could say it is illusory, like a dreamy veil that "covers" Love inside us, that "kills" Love, that crucifies Love.

"Father, forgive them; for they know not what they do" (Luke 23:34).

But if we identify with it, then it assumes a real substance for us. That doesn't mean the devil doesn't exist, but as we stated, belief in the false provides it with a different substance. It makes it more "real" than it is, in the sense that it grants it the nature of *essence*, of *Being*. We believe that other people or we *are it* – this ugly and hideous, egoistic being. We should learn to see the Good that exists deep in others and then acquire the ability to bring it out by giving our faith to their Real Self, to the Love inside them.

When a human being manifests with his false, egoistic part towards us, if we react to it, we strengthen it. If we "forgive his debt" then we weaken it. And if we want to be honest with ourselves, we will easily observe that the only thing that reacts inside us to the false self of others is our own false self. Only the false believes in the false. The truth is that our false, egoistic selves are the ones that fight. Only they are the ones that quarrel, misunderstand, hate, contend, are bothered and destroy each other.

So let's start turning our attention to our interior to discover what we contain, and quickly we will ascertain that the only cause for every conflict with our neighbor is the interaction of egos. Any kind of egoistic self that might be manifested by our fellow-men cannot really affect us if we don't contain the corresponding egoism.

One aspect of life in which we can observe all the aforementioned at work is the one of friendship. All of us think from time to time that our friends are, or rather, *become* egoists. And that is why we often say, "Don't be egoist." And the truth is that it's very difficult to have egoistic friends. But what does it mean to have an "egoistic friend?"

A friend is one who loves. And one who truly loves cannot be egoistic because Love *"seeketh not her own"* (1 Corinthians 13:6).

So how can the notion of Love be reconciled with the one of egoism? Friendship with egoism?

Egoism is related to our false, acquired part, and the same goes in the case of our friend. It is related to his false part and not to the Love inside him. Now, if his false part has been strengthened; if it has grown roots and claims his depths; then it will be very difficult when it manifests not to believe in it and not to consider it as his real self, even if we know deep inside us that our friend contains also his Real Self, the one that loves us and has a friendship with us.

But here again, we should realize that it is our false self that cannot see and remember the essential part of our friend. Only our egoistic self cannot forgive. And even if we can manage not to charge our friend with his debts, it will hasten to remind us of them, to enlarge them and dig up the past in order to find more past debts, even the discharged ones, so it can support its case.

Perhaps we can now understand more clearly why it is so difficult to love our neighbor, let alone our enemies. It is very difficult not to react egoistically to the egoism of others, because our egoism is still very strong. We have let it grow roots in us and surround our heart. That is why Christ's command to love seems unfeasible, especially when it refers to our enemies; even if our enemies usually turn out to be our best friends or our beloved ones.

Here also comes the notion of forgiveness. Forgiveness has a neutralizing nature; it doesn't succumb to the law of action-reaction. It isn't related to our surface, but constitutes a product of our depths, so it isn't such an easy matter as we often think. It isn't just a matter of personal choice, because there are certain conditions necessary for it to become possible and truly existent.

Often we think we have forgiven things that have happened, and in that way feel good about ourselves and other people. In the course of time, however, we find out that many of the things we considered forgiven have accumulated and we reach, as we say, "the end of our tether." Why does this happen? Why are the things we feel we have assimilated and transcended, actually accumulated? Perhaps the answer can be found in the *distinction of the selves*. What is important is where we attribute all this negative data. We have to learn not to attribute it to "You." We have to "say" to our neighbor, or even better, *feel* about him that:

"*You* haven't ever done anything, but your false self has done a lot for which I don't charge you. It is not *your* fault, it is *its* fault. Therefore I forgive you, I cancel your debts because they were never there, they all belong to the false self that neither *You* nor *I* want to forgive. We can accept it as a weakness or as an imposed evil, but in reality both of us want its extinction."

So this first necessary condition of separating the selves, is followed by a second necessary condition for the possibility of forgiving: the necessity of *remembrance*.

We have to *remember*. We must remember who the other one is and what his false self is. Only in this way do we manage to not be negative with him. When we forget his real identity, his essence, there is no way we won't be negative towards him. And *we won't be able to get out* of this unpleasant state of negativity, no matter how much we try, unless we remember again who he truly is. Only then will we be able to forgive him anew, that is, to discharge him from his otherwise unjust accusation and transfer it to the real guilty party: his egoistic part.

And here comes the third necessary condition for the possibility of forgiveness. In order to remember "who the other one is" we should remember "who we are." Because if we forget who we are and we become our false self – often without realizing it – then it is impossible to remember who the other one is. Only when *we remember who we are* (and who we are not) will we be able to *remember who the other one is* (and who he is not).

In this entire procedure for the treatment of egoism, it is very important to realize its nature and see it as something distinct from ourselves; as something harmful and lethal that is needless and should be removed from us.

In every case, this false self has acquired multiple elements of reality and will affect our lives to a greater or lesser degree. It can entirely control every one of our actions, or it can manifest only rarely as a reaction to our neighbor's egoism. Every case is different, so the gravity of the disease is also different. But in every case we should know that the treatment is possible, and we should never consider the disease of egoism – the existence of the inner devil – as an incurable disease, because this kind of attitude comes near to blasphemy, placing the devil in the same (or even higher) place with God. Any kind of egoism in man can be cured: *"All manner of sin and blasphemy shall be forgiven unto men"* (Matthew 12:31).

But certainly no person can be cured against his will. No man who denies categorically his treatment for egoism, who keeps on admiring, protecting and worshiping his inner devil and consequently denying the spirit inside him (and in this way the Spirit outside him) is in a position to be cured: *"But the blasphemy against the Holy Ghost shall not be forgiven"* (Matthew 12:31).

When we remove our faith from the false, from the devil, then our faith in God, in Love, will be strengthened. Therefore our hope in God will be strengthened as well. Realizing the illusory strength of the devil, of the false, our hope in God becomes unshakeable. We understand that God is above all and that when we count on God we can prevail over the false.

In this way we can tread more decisively on our inner path, claiming back the strength that the belief in the false, in egoism, was stealing from us all this time without our knowing it. We stop thinking of egoism (ours and other peoples') as an insurmountable impediment. We realize that the treatment of egoism might look, and be, painful and hard, but it is completely *feasible*. Because the false, the egoism, the devil, moves on the surface and is, in *essence,* something nonexistent while the Truth, Love, God, exists in the depths and is the only *essential* Reality.

Trials

*"When the path of our life is strewn with flowers,
we can hardly save our souls."*

(St. Theophan the Recluse, *Guidance in the Spiritual Life*, p. 19)

A trial is a situation that imposes a question upon us:

In what will we believe: in the false or the Truth, in the surface or the essence? How do we want to live? Full of weaknesses, insecurities, negativities, fears, ugliness and darkness? Or full of Strength, Beauty, Light and Love?

Which path do we want to follow? The path of egoism or the path of Love?

And this question might be posed in a grandiose manner through great events or at any moment, quickly and fleetingly, through *seemingly unimportant* situations.

It is a question that we will constantly be facing in the course of our life and one which will demand a pressing answer.

It is a positive question which has no wrong answer; it has to do only with a choice: Do you want to live on the surface or in the depths, in essence?

So there is the view of the surface and the view of the depths.

If we lived in the depths of ourselves and saw things from there, if we looked at the surface from deep inside without being confused by considering it as our depths, certainly this question wouldn't be posed.

But we live on the surface of ourselves, on the surface of life, and therefore every one of our views is completely distorted, random and egoistic. We constantly seek the outer, superficial causes and responsibilities for everything that happens.

That is why we need to be careful!

Let's not blame anything or anyone!

Let's turn our attention to ourselves!

Everything is related to ourselves, always. Let's not be carried away from the events (imaginary or real) which try to convince us that freedom is something that is related with things outside of ourselves.

Events operate on the surface – the things we remember, that are happening and that we are expecting. As long as we believe in them, we will fight in vain with the outer conditions, thinking that if this or the other happened, if things were that way or the other, we would be happy, we would be whole, we would be free.

Trials call our attention exactly to this issue.

They upset the outer conditions, the surface, so they can make us turn to the essence, to the depths.

The essence and the depths are within us, not outside of us; they do not belong to the kingdom of this world, *"The kingdom of God is within you"* (Luke 17:21).

On the one hand, trials awaken us (sometimes perhaps rather abruptly, depending on how soundly we sleep) with the upheaval they produce and on the other hand they pose a choice to us:

Which kingdom do you want? The kingdom of this world or the Kingdom of Heaven?

The one is out there on the surface and the other deep within us.

With every trial we are given an opportunity to go deeper within ourselves; to seek the inner freedom from our "self," from our deceptions, our pettiness, our false loves and our imaginary hatreds.

If we find the inner Kingdom of Heaven, then we will be able to perceive also the outer Paradise of God.

As long as we remain entrapped on the surface, in the froth of life, we cannot penetrate into our depths, and consequently into the depths of things. We cannot connect with the essence of life because we don't have the right means for this connection. We do not live with our essence. We live with this little, fearful, unsatisfied egoism which constantly wants and worries, and distorts everything that happens.

There is no event or situation that can harm our essence, God within us. The only thing that any event can cause us, the only harm that we can be subjected to, is our disconnection from our depths, our shifting to the surface.

But the events are not responsible for this shifting. We are responsible because when the choice that the trial poses to us appears, we give an affirmative response to the surface, we give our faith to it. We refuse the call from our depths and turn our attention outside us.

The real strength that we are called to manifest towards any trial is our inner faith to Love, to God, by resisting our inner enemies, our inner devil, our egoism, that calls us pressingly to come up to the surface because we are in danger… that's what it tells us. But the truth is that if we listen to it, if we are carried away, then we will be truly in danger, because if we come out to the surface we will be prey to everything.

Again, let's repeat that the events which challenge us are not to blame. It is our fault that we are listening to our egoism, our false self, our surface self, and we side with it instead of turning ever more deeply inward and showing more persistence toward God.

Trials are a gift because they upset the towers that we have built on sand; the beautiful constructions in which we feel safe. And often, they can be very harsh with us in order to make us turn to the depths of things, of life, of ourselves. They can overturn situations that we consider to be a *given*, that we think of as our life or as our paradise.

They can deprive us of our beloved ones, of our possessions; they can threaten even our own existence. The story of Job is very instructive in connection with this and its lesson is simple. Job is called to remain faithful in his depths, the depths where he meets God. He is called to keep his attention turned to God, and not to the surface where all has collapsed.

Trials are not meant to torture us, they are meant to free us from our entrapment at the surface. The pain that we experience in relation to them is due to our attachment. *The stronger we hold to the surface,* the more painfully we experience our detachment from it.

Trials are a means of salvation, not of damnation and hardship. They take place *for our own sake,* not for the sake of God; so we can be freed from the enchantment of the surface and plunge toward the real beauty of the depths. They want to remove us from the surface's hell, where even if everything is going well, there is a constant worry lurking, an anxiety, a fear that all could be lost; we have a sense of unrest which doesn't allow us to deeply enjoy anything, and which will accompany us even to the last moments of our life. They want to save us from this *hell* and lead us to our beatitude, to the Paradise within which no one and nothing can harm, to the *"treasures in heaven, where neither moth nor rust doth corrupt, and where thieves do not break through nor steal"* (Matthew 6:20). They want to lead us to God, to the depths, where whatever happens is welcomed and experienced completely differently than when we lived on the surface.

There are three ways, three attitudes, with which to face a trial. The first attitude is one of groaning. The second is one of patience, and the third is one of gratitude.

In the stage of groaning we haven't yet perceived the difference between the surface and the depths. We fight for the surface, we struggle for it, we believe in it. We are not particularly related to God, and if we have some kind of relationship, we probably think that God is unjust to us; we complain to God. And that is because we still believe in the surface of things; we haven't realized the existence of essence. Even if we had once perceived something essential, even if we had deepened to some degree, in this moment of trial we forget everything and are transported entirely to the surface, where we suffer.

In the stage of patience, we have realized the existence of the surface and the essence, we don't lose our relationship with the Truth, nor do we deny it, but the surface is still exercising a strong effect on us. So we might not feel unfairly treated, but we feel perhaps, punished for something. We cannot easily grasp that the reason for our pain can be found in our attachment to the surface and not in the event itself. As long as the trial is there, we cannot remain in our depths. We don't forget them entirely, but we are shifted from them and just wait patiently until our return there.

In the stage of gratitude we are not removed from our depths, but due to our attitude we are all the more connected to it perhaps even without knowing it. With every challenge of the surface we go deeper because of our resistance to it, and we are more tightly bound with God.

We might suffer and feel some kind of pain due to the surface's challenges – which might attack us with diseases, deaths, injustices, accidents, hardships, betrayals, negativities of every kind – but it is of a very different quality. We experience the pain of catharsis, of going deeper, of dying towards everything false, superficial and vain.

When we feel gratitude during the trial and thank God for it, at the same time – with the pain – we experience the abundant resources of the depths. We experience moments of freedom and detachment from anything, good or bad, that might keep us captive to our self's surface. We conceive trials as what they truly are: a *gift*.

We remain connected with God and thank Him because through the gift of our trial we are given the opportunity to strengthen our relationship, our connection.

In the stage of groaning, trials are meant to awaken us:

> "If we never came up against any difficulties,
> then we would fall into spiritual hibernation."

(St. Theophan the Recluse, *Guidance in the Spiritual Life*, p. 149)

In the stage of patience, trials are meant to teach us:

> "Every affliction discloses the passions hidden in the heart and puts them into motion. Until trouble comes, a man imagines himself calm and peaceful. But when trouble comes, then passions of which he was unaware rise up and make themselves felt, especially anger, sorrow, despondency, pride, unbelief."

(St. Ignatius Brianchaninov, *The Arena: An Offering to Contemporary Monasticism*, pp. 101-102)

And in the stage of gratitude they are meant to strengthen us:

> "When the Christian surrenders himself to the will of God, denies himself and casts all his cares on God, he thanks and glorifies Him for the cross. Then the extraordinary power of faith suddenly appears in his heart; Jesus seals the disciple who has accepted His call with the Spirit – and earthly sufferings become a source of delight for the servant of God."
>
> (St. Ignatius Brianchaninov, *The Arena: An Offering to Contemporary Monasticism*, p. 99)

Overall their aim is to set us free:

> "He who resists troubles and tries to escape the hard way, is acting against his own salvation and is striving in his blindness to frustrate the order and plan of salvation appointed by God for all His servants."
>
> (St. Ignatius Brianchaninov, *The Arena: An Offering to Contemporary Monasticism*, p. 125)

The moment *we deepen even a little* and leave the surface, our thoughts, our pictures, our views, *everything is immediately changed* to such a degree that often we cannot remember exactly what we were thinking or what we were seeing while we were on the surface. We cannot remember what was bothering us so much. When *we go deeper, everything is immediately transfigured.*

Depending on the trial's duration and kind, the surface might try to carry us again outside of our depths; to lower us down from our heights; it can pull us with great strength by creating additional events or attacking with more force so we become tired and give in to it.

But the truth is that the stronger it pulls us, the greater is the possibility we are given to turn to our depths, to surrender even more decisively to God. The more it attacks us, the deeper we can go. The more persuasive it gets, the more faith in God we can acquire.

Whenever we observe an agitation, an upheaval, a tension inside us, we should see it as a trial and immediately give thanks for it. We must shift to the attitude of gratitude and side with our depths. In that way its value will start to reveal itself, and as we perceive its benefits, the more gratitude we will feel and the deeper we will go.

Trials teach us our prisons, the sides of life's surfaces which enslave us, frighten us, seize us…death, diseases, accidents, being left alone, rejection, injustice, suffering, love affairs, our desires, our needs. Which one of these can entrap us at the surface, in appearances, and make us lose our connection with the essence, with Love, with God?

Trials do not only manifest with a negative face, in the form of difficulty, but also in the form of comfort, of easiness. A pleasant occurrence can equally pull us towards the surface of ourselves, towards the surface of life, just as an unpleasant one can.

Either in a nice and enchanting way or in an ugly and hideous way, trials always pose the same choice:

Do you want the kingdom of this world or the Kingdom of God?

The first one is ephemeral, changeable, aimless, one moment pleasant and the next unpleasant, most of the time dark with its luminous spots being very dim – it is intense on one hand, and destructive on the other.

The second one is deep, real, beautiful, qualitative, essential and meaningful, with aim, duration and Light.

Pick and choose...

The first one serves only our little, insignificant "self" and the second one serves our Real Self and God, and the Total of Everything.

So trials tell us, "Choose: Do you want to «live» or to Live?" In other words, the question they pose to us is this: "Do you want to be freed from your «self»?"

There is no trial in the sense of punishment.

"*God is Love*" (1 John 4:16), He forgives.

There is no trial in the sense of proving something to God. "*God knoweth your hearts*" (Luke 16:15); He is omniscient, "*Lord, thou knowest all things*" (John 21:17). Trials exist essentially for *ourselves* to acquire certainty in relation to our stability. The struggle and the efforts are taking place so we can prove to ourselves *what we really want* and which is our true destination.

They are taking place so that the tares inside us can be uprooted; the ones that are seizing the ground where God's seeds should grow. And in that way we are preparing our soul's soil in order to be receptive to the seeds of His Love.

Trials are taking place for *us* to appreciate the Spirit's gifts in order not to underestimate them and consequently reject them, since otherwise we will have acquired them easily and effortlessly.

They are taking place in order to enable us to be devoted to Love; not to be prodigals again; not to worship idols; not to sell our souls; not to crucify Love inside us again, mocking and scoffing Her.

Trials are meant clearly for our own sake.

Not because God needs evidences.

God is Love. He forgives us and accepts us; He runs to us as soon as we decide to return to Him, *"But when he was yet a great way off, his father saw him, and had compassion, and ran, and fell on his neck, and kissed him"* (Luke 15:20). He doesn't need proof.

But we need it. So the struggle *is taking place for us*. Because in the storm of trials, what *we already know deep within us is confirmed*.

When we walk God's way, the returning path to Him, whatever happens takes place in order to solidify our resolution so that when we return to Him, when we unite with Him, nothing will be able to shake us anymore and nothing can come between us.

So let's be grateful for all the difficulties, for all the trials, all the disappointments, because without them it wouldn't be possible to ascend to God. All these are steps on God's ladder.

> "No one is yet to be found who climbed up to heaven without labor, uneasiness, trials, sorrows and strong temptations."
>
> (St. Theophan the Recluse, *Selection of Letters*, p. 63)

Each *trial* means that we are ready for a *breakthrough*.

It is an honor, so let's acknowledge it as such and let's adopt this truly positive perception.

> "The fruit of troubles, which consists in the purification of our soul and its rising to a spiritual state, should be guarded as a precious treasure. This fruit is guarded when, on

being subjected to temptation and rebuke, we take all care at the time to abide by the commandments of the Gospel, without being seduced by the passions which are exposed and stirred by temptation. Between the cross and the commandments of the Gospel there is a wonderful relationship!"

(St. Ignatius Brianchaninov, *The Arena: An Offering to Contemporary Monasticism*, pp. 103-104)

All the unpleasant situations are offerings of Love.

"He sends for example a calamity sometimes to educate us, sometimes to awaken us spiritually, sometimes to save us from some bigger harm, sometimes to raise our heavenly wages, sometimes to relieve us from some passion, etc."

(St. Theophan the Recluse, *Guidance in the Spiritual Life*, p. 29)

The more unpleasant a situation is, the more Love we can derive from it. And the more difficult it is, the more progress we can achieve in the knowledge and remembrance of God.

"It was the most difficult thing he had ever done; but that day, for the first time, he felt the presence of God. He was no longer alone, and as he walked on he thought about God, and he talked with Him every minute of the way."

(Mersine Vigopoulou, *From I-ville to You-ville*, pp. 75-76)

It is true that our life is hanging by a thread. But this thread is in the hands of God; and God holds the thread of our lives safely in His hands, "*Are not two sparrows sold for a farthing? And one of them shall not fall on the ground without your Father. But the very hairs of your head are all numbered"* (Matthew 10:29-30).

So let's thank Him for all the trials, for all His gifts, because He purges us, He teaches us, He elevates us and He deepens us. Let's beg Him to keep us in the heights of our Real Self and in that way to raise us to His heights. Let's be eternally grateful to Him for all His Love.

"God is faithful, who will not suffer you to be tempted [tried] above that ye are able; but will with the temptation [trial] also make a way to escape, that ye may be able to bear it" (1 Corinthians 10:13).

Self-Knowledge

"You want to know God? First know yourself."

(Evagrius of Pontus, *Maxims 2*, Maxim 2, p. 230)

We do not know ourselves.

In order to start walking in the path of self-knowledge we must start turning our attention to ourselves.

Yes, we can and should observe people, events, nature and everything else around us, but we should also learn to turn within, not only outside us.

We should learn to look at ourselves in the same way we look at everything else outside us. In that way, we will gradually and increasingly ascertain the necessity of turning and sustaining our attention to our self; because this is the only way to know ourselves.

We are lost between the various contradictory pictures and ideas of ourselves which, according to circumstances, we are either ready to defend to the death or willing to completely abandon.

We don't know who or what we are.

Sometimes we feel important, other times insignificant; sometimes we feel real and genuine, other times completely false; sometimes we feel worthy of everything, and other times of nothing. We feel like gods and we feel like devils. One moment we believe we have managed something in our lives and the next we feel incompetent and worthless.

We fight constantly between overvaluation and devaluation of ourselves. The moment we gain some self-confidence, the same moment we lose it.

One of our basic issues is *self-confidence*; the confidence, that is the faith, to our self. But to which self? To our willing, helpful, compassionate self or to our reactive, abrupt, indifferent self? To our dynamic, assured, stable self or to our weak, insecure, miserable self? To our tolerant, large-hearted, patient self or to our small-hearted, suspicious, merciless self?

Which one of these selves are we? What are we in conclusion?

In order to get out of this dead end, we declare hurriedly, "I am all these things... I have many aspects, I am not just one thing... besides that would be so boring." And for awhile we rest assured, but the truth is that deep inside us we remain unsatisfied by this convenient answer and naturally we remain very far from any sense of real self-knowledge.

Our daily routine is more or less tragicomic. Whatever ideals we believe that we stand for in our lives – ideals related to Love, beauty, strength, magnanimity, forgiveness, aid to our neighbor – are certainly rare to our everyday life and refer only to moments of our lives. Other than that, we go around daily with various tempers, behaviors and attitudes which are often contradictory, opposed to each other and even disprove each other.

That is why we are constantly wondering in relation to those around us, "Who are you eventually?" And more rarely we turn the attention inward to wonder of ourselves, "Who am I eventually?" "What am I in the end?"

The daily routine is like a big, sweeping river which carries us away and even though it brings us constantly up against ourselves, in essence it is not interested in our reactions and in our attitude towards our self. In this river there is not enough time and space for questions like, "Who am I?" "Where am I going?" "What do I want?" "What am I doing?"

The daily routine directs *us*, we do not direct it.

And that is happening for one reason: because *we* do not know ourselves, we do not know who we are, what we are, where we want to go and why. How then is it possible to give any direction to our lives?

So we are abandoned to the river of life to carry us wherever it wants to. The only way to acquire some awareness in relation to our direction would be to have at our disposal a boat with oars in that river.

Self-knowledge is that boat with oars.

Now, what does self-knowledge mean?

Self-knowledge means to see and know all the aspects of ourselves, from the most superficial to the deepest, the most false to the most real, the acquired ones and the essential ones.

It means to know who we *aren't* in order to know who we *truly* are.

> "When you want to know yourself as who you are, do not compare who you were, but what you have become from the beginning."

(Evagrius of Pontus, *Maxims 3*, Maxim 10, p. 232)

We have to know what we *think* we are but aren't, and what we *are* but don't know that we are.

A very appropriate example of the chaos which prevails inside us is the following: We think we are self-reliant and independent, while in reality we are extremely insecure and have built a façade of "strength" in order to hide our sense of weakness from others, but mainly from ourselves.

At the same time deep within us we contain a real sense of Strength which doesn't need to show off or be validated. It stands far from any thought of insecurity and weakness, yet, to a great degree we do not recognize it, and whenever we feel its call, we reject it, thinking of it as a weakness! When, for example, this sense of Strength appears in the form of sensitivity and compassion, our response to its call might be, "Yes, compassion is good, but I won't be taken advantage of!"

And then we believe our false "strength," that is, our cruelty. And we tell ourselves we are strong, while in reality we are dominated by a terrible weakness, turning our back to our sensitivity, which is our real Strength.

This is the chaos in which we live.

Or, more accurately, the *ignorance* in which we live; the ignorance of our self.

So until we get to know that which is in front of us, that which we are, how can we expect to know anything else, let alone God?

We must first acknowledge our surface in order to begin to know our depths. We might have a sense of our depths, but we don't know them in their totality, and consequently we don't live through them.

Our surface prevents us from being aware of our depths. It is as though we are wearing filthy rags which are stuck to us because we have worn them for a long time. We perceive them as a part of ourselves, as our skin; we feel them as *us*.

That is why we refuse to separate from them, and that's why we become hostile when someone refers to them. We feel threatened instead of being grateful for our eyes to be opened.

If we *felt* these filthy rags alongside a sense of our clean skin, our Real Self, then we would look forward to getting them off of us, to getting rid of them. That is why we must know both our surface and our depths in their totality.

When we acknowledge our depths one-sidedly, and refuse to also acknowledge our negative, ugly surface, we become full of conceit, pride and arrogance.

When we acknowledge our surface one-sidedly, and can't feel our depths behind it, we become full of despair, hopelessness and self-pity.

True self-knowledge, however, means knowledge and definition of each side. What is there, and what is what.

Which of the things we discover in relation to ourselves are our own and which are not? What must remain and what should go? And of the things that must remain, what can and should be developed and cultivated, and what shouldn't be? Which of the things that must remain are everlasting and essential, and what is ephemeral and useful only for this life?

We should sort out the things of the surface in order to be directed to our depths. And when we start to know our depths, we will begin to realize what the phrase means, "Man's soul is an abyss." The deeper we go within, the more astonished we will be. And there will come a moment when we will grasp that the deepening has no end, because *at the point where our depths stop, the depths of God are starting.* We are faced with an abyss, with fathomless depths. At this moment we will begin to understand the meaning of the saying:

"The kingdom of God is within you" (Luke 17:21).

Spiritual Life

"The spiritual world is open to him who
lives within himself."

(*The Art of Prayer – An Orthodox Anthology*, p. 161)

Whoever walked the path of self-knowledge truthfully to the end, there he met God. God calls us to the path of self-knowledge and stirs inside us the desire to walk in it because He knows that only through this path will we be able to discover Him, to know Him and to unite with Him.

The path of self-knowledge is outlined within us from Him, its destination is Him and we can tread it only with His help. It consists of an inner, spiritual journey which is not anticipated to be easy and strewn with flowers; there are many dangers, and that is why we need His help, *"Though I walk through the valley of the shadow of death, I will fear no evil: for thou art with me"* (Psalms 23:4). We will be constantly inclined to return to our usual "self," to turn back, *"But his wife looked back from behind him, and she became a pillar of salt"* (Genesis 19:26). Or we will meet obstacles that try to convince us to step backwards to the ordinary "life," to the surface, *"And they said unto Moses, because there were no graves in Egypt, hast thou taken us away to die in the wilderness? Wherefore hast thou dealt thus with us, to carry us forth out of Egypt? [...] For it had been better for us to serve the Egyptians, than that we should die in the wilderness"* (Exodus 14:11-12).

The objective aim of the path of self-knowledge is to know the spirit within us, "the spirit, which is the soul of our human soul" (St. Theophan the Recluse, *The Spiritual Life*, p. 64), in order to be in communion *through* our spirit, with the Spirit outside us, the Spirit of God (which we meet inside us).

Many of us understand the significance and the necessity of knowing ourselves, but few of us realize the true essence of self-knowledge.

Most of us think that finding our self has little or nothing to do with the question of God.

> "If you know Him by whom you were made, you will know yourself."
>
> (Select Sentences of Sextus the Pythagorean, Sentence 92, p. 61)

And in the same way, many of us think that we can find God without finding our self:

> "It is said that he who does not first reintegrate himself with his own being by rejecting those passions which are contrary to nature will not be reintegrated with the Cause of his being - that is, with God."
>
> (Saint Maximos the Confessor, *Various Texts*, 40, Second Century, p. 196, Vol. 2, Philokalia)

The truth is that in order to find ourselves we must find God, and finding God cannot be done without finding ourselves. And that means knowing who we are, to know our spirit and become our self, or more accurately, *be* our self. Then we will also be able to grasp the reality of God, of the Spirit, who is the Creator of our spirit. Whenever we are related to our spirit, whenever we will *be* ourselves, we will be related to God, we will *be* with God. Whenever we are lost, we will also lose God.

And most of the time we are lost.

That is why we are called to this journey of self-knowledge, which is a *spiritual* journey. That means we are called to live a spiritual life which doesn't refer to an intellectual life, but the life of spirit and Spirit.

The questions, "Who am I?" "Why do I exist?" "What is all this? The universe, man, life?..." are not "theoretical," that is, intellectual questions, but they are deep *spiritual* questions.

That is why they can be answered only from the spirit: *"For what man knoweth the things of a man, save the spirit of man which is in him?"* (1 Corinthians 2:11), which is taught from the Spirit: *"God is Spirit"* (John 4:24).

When we pose these questions to ourselves with *solemnity* and *honesty,* then everything stops. Every thought, feeling and sensation stops and we encounter God. In this kind of inner spiritual search we meet, inevitably, God, the Spirit.

> "So after disengaging oneself from all that is outside of oneself and from the body itself, one must gather oneself and enter within, and examine everything briefly and decide: Just what are you, matushka, my dearest?"

(St. Theophan the Recluse, *The Spiritual Life*, p. 70)

Along with these questions which emerge from time to time imperatively demanding answers, we must willy-nilly pose to ourselves another difficult question: "What is there inside us which is worthy of passing into eternity? Which part of us could be destined for eternity?"

Our random thoughts, our changeable feelings, our annoyances, our worries, our interests, our material achievements, our job, our pleasures? What?

What is worthy, beyond this life, to last forever?

We would be willing to abandon most, if not all, of the aforementioned, even in this life in order to make "a new start," as we like to say. But even if all these things which are filling our lives are extremely beloved and precious to us, do we honestly think them worthy of passing into eternity?

The answer to this question is given in the words of Christ: *"Thou art careful and troubled about many things: But one thing is needful"* (Luke 10:41-42).

This answer is given to Martha who "was cumbered about much serving" when she complains that her sister Maria has left her all alone and simply sits at the feet of Jesus listening to His word. It constitutes an answer which is not immediately understood. It is the most real and simple answer, but because of its simplicity we misinterpret and misunderstand it.

This answer doesn't refer to a simplistic worship, to a superficial religiousness, and for this reason Christ says somewhere else: *"Not everyone that saith unto me, "Lord, Lord," shall enter into the kingdom of heaven; but he that doeth the will of my Father which is in heaven"* (Matthew 7:21).

It refers to a whole way of life: *"Why call ye me, Lord, Lord, and do not the things which I say?"* (Luke 6:46).

"First God," we hear, "and then everything else:" *"Seek ye first the kingdom of God, and his righteousness; and all these things shall be added unto you"* (Matthew 6:33).

That means the Spirit first because God is Spirit (John 4:24), and then everything else. Only this part in us, the *spirit*, is worthy of passing into eternity, but first it needs to live, to grow and give fruit, applying the Word of Spirit in this life.

That is why Christ tells us the only thing that really matters is the relationship with Him; that is, the relationship of our spirit with His Spirit until this relationship becomes unbreakable, and we become One with Him and are able to say like St. Paul: *"Not I but Christ liveth in me"* (Galatians 2:20).

This process, however, is long and arduous. It is not enough to serve the Spirit with our outer parts as pious as they may be, like Martha, but we must be related with the Spirit Itself. We must unite with It. And the only part in us which is really worthy and able to unite with the Spirit is our spirit.

If we call upon God from any other part inside us, saying: *"Lord, Lord, have we not prophesied in thy name? And in thy name have cast out devils? And in thy name done many wonderful works?"* (Matthew 7:22), the answer will be: *"And then will I profess unto them, I never knew you"* (Matthew 7:23), because the Spirit recognizes only the spirit. Just as only the spirit can investigate the things of the Spirit, *"For the spirit searcheth all things, yea, the deep things of God"* (1 Corinthians 2:10).

In this point it would be useful to briefly examine the possible structure of man. We could roughly say that man consists of body, soul and spirit.

"And what is man's place in God's creation?

'I pray to God that your whole spirit and soul and body may be preserved blameless until the coming of our Lord Jesus Christ' (1 Thessalonians 5:23). Here St. Paul mentions the three elements or aspects that constitute the human person. While distinct, these aspects are strictly interdependent; man is an integral unity, not the sum total of separable parts.

First, there is the *body*, 'dust from the ground' (Genesis 2:7), the physical or material aspect of man's nature.

Secondly, there is the *soul*, the life-force that vivifies and animates the body, causing it to be more than a lump of matter, because it also possesses a soul, and so perhaps do plants. But in man's case the soul is endowed with consciousness; it is a rational soul, possessing the capacity for abstract thought, and the ability to advance by discursive argument from premises to a conclusion. These powers are present in animals, if at all, only to a very limited degree.

Thirdly, there is the *spirit*, the 'breath' from God (Genesis 2:7), which the animals lack. It is important to distinguish 'Spirit' with an initial capital, from 'spirit' with a small 's' The created spirit of man is not to be identified with the uncreated or Holy Spirit of God, the third person of the Trinity; yet the two are intimately connected, for it is through his spirit that man apprehends God and enters into communion with him."

(Bishop Kallistos Ware, *The Orthodox Way*, pp. 47-48)

The body has to do with all the natural functions of man which might include also his lower emotional and intellectual functions when these are related with simple biochemical processes. These are functions completely mechanical and consequently carnal. These might include, for example, the "love" that we feel for a food.

The soul has to do with that which vivifies the body, but basically, with the psychological functions, which don't belong to the carnal sphere. Here we have to do with the higher emotional and intellectual functions responsible for all the human ideals, for all the human wisdom and all the human inspirations. These kinds of psychological functions are not a result of having eaten or slept well, or of good or bad weather. The soul may be related to the highest *human* insights, and exists in a deeper level inside of man. Here we might include the love that we feel for man.

The spirit is the seed of God, of Spirit, in us; it is what has been created *"in His image, after His likeness"* (Genesis 1:26). It is God inside us, or more properly, it is what renders us Sons and Daughters of God: *"The Spirit itself beareth witness with our spirit, that we are the children of God"* (Romans 8:16). With our spirit we can *find* God and unite with Him:

> "With his soul (*psyche*) man engages in scientific or philosophical inquiry, analyzing the data of his sense-experience by means of the discursive reason. With his spirit (*pneuma*), which is sometimes termed *nous* or spiritual intellect, he understands eternal truth about God or about the *logoi* or inner essences of created things, not through deductive reasoning, but by direct apprehension or spiritual perception – by a kind of intuition that St. Isaac the Syrian calls "simple cognition." The spirit or spiritual intellect is thus distinct from man's reasoning powers and his aesthetic emotions, and superior to both of them."
>
> (Bishop Kallistos Ware, *The Orthodox Way*, p. 48)

Without the spirit we can only speculate about God, either rejecting Him or accepting Him (or standing in between these two positions), but without knowing Him. To the spirit belongs the Love of God and consequently, love of all and everything, when we acknowledge in them the Divine element.

The body and the corresponding carnal mind belong to the surface of our self. We could say that the soul and the corresponding psychological mind are related to an intermediate part inside us. The spirit is related to our real and farthest depths.

> "Sometimes the Fathers adopt not tripartite but a twofold scheme, describing man simply as a unity of body and soul; in that case they treat the spirit or intellect as the highest aspect of the soul. But the threefold scheme of body, soul and spirit is more precise and more illuminating, particularly in our own age when the soul and the spirit are often confused, and when most people are not even aware that they possess a spiritual intellect. The culture and educational system of the contemporary West are based almost exclusively upon the training of the reasoning brain and, to a lesser degree, of the aesthetic emotions. Most of us have forgotten that we are not only brain and will, senses and feelings; we are also spirit. Modern man has for the most part lost touch with the truest and highest aspect of himself; and the result of this inward alienation can be seen all too plainly in his restlessness, his lack of identity and his loss of hope.
>
> Body, soul and spirit, three in one, man occupies a unique position in the created order."
>
> (Bishop Kallistos Ware, *The Orthodox Way*, pp. 48-49)

The body is our animal self.

The soul is our human self and is able to connect the spirit with the body. It intermediates in order for the spiritual reality to manifest in the material sphere.

"What happened to the soul as a result of its union with the spirit, which is from God? From this union, the entire soul was transformed from being an animal soul, which it is by nature, into a human soul [...]. The human soul, being such as has been described, displays aspirations above all this and rises a step further, because it is an inspired soul."

(St. Theophan the Recluse, *The Spiritual Life*, p. 52)

The spirit is our Divine self:

"It is the force [the spirit] that draws that person from the visible to the invisible, from the temporal to the eternal, from the creation to the Creator."

(St. Theophan the Recluse, *The Spiritual Life*, p. 51)

So the soul is our human aspect and the spirit our Divine aspect which is meant to search the things of the Spirit, to be related to the Spirit and generally to lead us:

"It is not the purpose of the soul to deal with such things. It is the purpose of the spirit, while the soul is exclusively devoted to the structuring of our temporal – that is, earthly – existence. And its knowledge is entirely built on the foundation of that which gives experience, and its activity is devoted to the gratification of the needs of the temporal life, and its senses are engendered and persist only from its visible states and conditions. Anything that is above this does not concern it. To be sure, some things occur in it which are above what has been said, but they are guests which drop in from a higher realm, the realm of the spirit.

Just what is the *spirit? It is that force which God breathed into man when He created him.* The earth bore all the species of earthly creatures by God's command. From the earth also came every kind of living creature's soul. The human soul, although it resembles the animal soul in its lowest part, is incomparably superior to it in its highest part. That it is this in man is because of its bonding with the soul. The spirit, breathed by God, combined with it and raised it far above every nonhuman soul. That is why we note within ourselves, in addition to what we see in the animals, that which is peculiar to the spiritualized soul of man, and even higher, that which is peculiar only to the spirit.

The spirit, as a force which has come from God, knows God, seeks God, and in Him alone finds rest. With a certain innermost spiritual feeling attesting to its coming from God, the spirit feels its complete dependence on Him and acknowledges itself as obliged to pleasing God in everything and living only for Him and by Him."

(St. Theophan the Recluse, *The Spiritual Life*, pp. 46-47)

But in order to accept the things of the spirit, our soul must be clean and *turn* to the spirit by turning away from the things of the flesh, from the surface. She must have as her priority the Life of the spirit, that is the Kingdom of Heaven and not the life of the world, that is the biotic cares and the worldly pleasures.

Our soul, our human self is tainted when she turns to the things of the flesh and starts taking orders from the body, when she should be taking orders from the spirit. That is why St. Paul says that the spirit is against the flesh. Because both of them claim our soul, our human self: *"I say then, Walk in the Spirit, and ye shall not fulfill the lust of the flesh. For the flesh lusteth against the Spirit, and the Spirit against the flesh: and these are contrary the one to the other: so that ye cannot do the things that ye would"* (Galatians 5:16-17).

Our psychological self often considers the spiritual world to be nonsense or irrational, because it doesn't belong to the sphere of its understanding and is truly far away from him: *"But the psychological (psychic-ψυχικός) man receiveth not the things of the Spirit of God: for they are foolishness unto him: neither can he know them, because they are spiritually discerned"* (1 Corinthians 2:14).

Therefore when the psychological man turns to the things of the flesh he becomes, as we said, even opposed to the spirit and the Spirit: *"The carnal mind is enmity against God"* (Romans 8:7). In general the psychological man, our human self, cannot reach to the heights of the Spirit, to the heights of God: *"Which things also we speak, not in the words which man's wisdom teacheth, but which the Holy Ghost teacheth; comparing spiritual things with spiritual"* (1 Corinthians 2:13).

That is why it is said that man cannot reach God (see Babel's tower, Genesis 11:1-9), but only God can be revealed to man; that is He can offer him through his spirit the knowledge of Himself: *"Even so the things of God knoweth no man, but the Spirit of God"* (1 Corinthians 2:11).

We could say that the work of man, in a somewhat poetical sense but at the same time very literally, is to keep his heart pure, because only a pure heart is able to open to the spirit, and then to the Spirit...to God: *"Blessed are the pure in heart: for they shall see God"* (Matthew 5:8).

This work, however, even though it sounds simple and easy, remains truly difficult and far from us. Perhaps all of us believe unconsciously that we have pure hearts; that our soul is clean, but unfortunately, this is not the truth.

"A pure soul is God after God."

(Evagrius of Pontus, *Maxims 2*, Maxim 23, p. 231)

The truth is that our soul, our human self has been dirtied from her prodigality, which means from her wandering into the carnal world, and she has forgotten the house of her Father, the house of Love (Luke 15:11-32). We have lost our contact with the Divine part inside us and therefore with God Himself. So it is obvious that we don't stand anymore to these heights or depths of ourselves, of our spirit where we can be called Children of the Most High: *"But ye have received the Spirit of adoption, whereby we cry, Abba, Father"* (Romans 8:15).

We have turned our soul, the man inside us, to the surface, to the things of the flesh, and this is what leads us. So the imperative question follows: *"Where is it leading us?"* *"If ye live after the flesh, ye shall die: but if ye through the Spirit do mortify the deeds of the body, ye shall live"* (Romans 8:13).

So our aim is to return our attention to the depths of ourselves, to our spirit, and in that way be worthy of having God's spirit dwell in us: *"But ye are not in the flesh, but in the Spirit, if so be that the Spirit of God dwell in you"* (Romans 8:9).

At this point we could also detect the sense of sin. Man sins when, as a soul destined to live according to her spirit and in that way be united with the Spirit and follow the law of Spirit, the Will of God, he instead turns outside, towards his surface and becomes a slave to his flesh which should merely be in the service of his deeper self, of his spirit, in order for the things of the spirit to be manifested to the material world, *"Thy kingdom come. Thy will be done in earth, as it is in heaven"* (Matthew 6:10). That is the reason we were created: *"Know ye not that ye are the temple of God, and that the Spirit of God dwelleth in you?"* (1 Corinthians 3:16). But when the soul, our human self, turns to the surface and, without realizing it, is captured there, getting lost and forgetting her depths, she can no longer hear within her the voice of God, His Will.

So she starts following her own will, and surely her works, not being marked by Divine prudence and Divine discernment, inevitably degenerate in quality. Even if she starts with the best intentions, she then becomes a prey to her uncontrolled desires.

> "Our spirit lost its proper authority to rule over the soul and body, and conversely fell under the yoke of slavery to them; authority must be restored to the spirit. When the authority of the spirit was disrupted, the needs of the soul and body dispersed in different directions, and within our desires there came about confusion."
>
> (St. Theophan the Recluse, *The Spiritual Life*, p. 93)

These desires soon end up demanding their satisfaction without caring for their possible consequences, and in that way assume an egoistic character and turn into our known passions. Passions which eventually turn against even our own self, our own soul, which then becomes a prey to the lower, illogical element inside us, to our animal self, as it were. And then: *"The works of the flesh are manifest, which are these; adultery, fornication, uncleanness, lasciviousness, idolatry, witchcraft, hatred, variance, emulations, wrath, strife, seditions, heresies, envyings, murders, drunkenness, revellings, and such like"* (Galatians 5:19-21).

All these terms could be expressed with just one word: egoism. The works of the flesh are egoistic because its perception is egocentric.

In reality, our destination is completely different. We have been created as men, and we are called to become men-God, that is, "Sons of God." Or, in other words, we are called to return to this height of our self from where we have fallen. Otherwise, our reasonable tendency, in the event we don't ascend, is to *descend* and fall to the level of our animal self.

> "The flesh with its desire is opposed to the spirit, and the spirit opposed to the flesh, and those who live in the spirit will not carry out the desire of the flesh."
>
> (St. Mark the Ascetic, *226 Texts*, 32, p. 128, Vol. 1, Philokalia)

If we correspond to our destination, then our path is shaped differently, and the works of this path also belong to a different reality: *"But the fruit of the Spirit is love, joy, peace, longsuffering, gentleness, goodness, faith, meekness, temperance"* (Galatians 5:22-23).

Still, when we discover that we have this *possibility* of existing in these heights of the spirit and the Spirit, we consider it a *given* ability and in that way we fall to the sin of conceit and pride, and end up being cut off from the Spirit outside, not realizing that this will also have the result of being cut off from the spirit inside and *"surely die"* (Genesis 2:17). And then, of course, we lose all our possible value and the only thing left is turning to our lower parts. We continue, however, to imagine that we are still ruled by our higher parts. So we claim ideals that belong to our heights or our depths, but without being able to experience them in our everyday life.

"A person in whom there is no motion and action of spirit does not stand on the level of human dignity."

(St. Theophan the Recluse, *The Spiritual Life*, p. 49)

That is why we are called to know our self, to come out of the ignorance in which we live and remember our inheritance:

"The distinguishing feature of man is within it [the spirit]. The human soul makes us a little above the animals, while the spirit makes us a little below the angels."

(St. Theophan the Recluse, *The Spiritual Life*, pp. 48-49)

Even though in the beginning an intense inner struggle is necessary to return to our natural state and be re-orientated to our real spiritual destination, gradually we will experience the benefit of this real choice of ours.

The Inner Restoration of Christianity

The Meaning of Life

The Meaning of Life is the union of the spirit with the Spirit.

In other words, there is no meaning in a life which is not led by the spirit and the Spirit. There is no meaning in a life which is not spiritual. But since there are gradations in everything, we could say more accurately that the more directed by the Spirit, God, our life is, the more Meaning it has. So we can live a life with either more or less Meaning, according to our relation with the spirit inside us and *through that,* with God's Spirit.

"According to natural purpose, man must live in the spirit, subordinate everything to the spirit, be penetrated by the spirit in all that is of the soul, and even more so in all that is physical – and beyond these, in the outward things, too, that is, family and social life."

(St. Theophan the Recluse, *The Spiritual Life*, p. 61)

We often refer to the psychosomatic hypostasis of man, but we have forgotten his psychospiritual dimension. We acknowledge that the body affects the soul and equivalently the soul affects the body, but we ignore the effect of the soul to the spirit and of the spirit to the soul.

We are disconnected from our spirit. We turn all of our attention outside ourselves and in that way we don't pay attention to our spirit, we don't hear its calls and we are constantly getting further away from it.

"We see that we are not always free, because we are always chasing after needs to satisfy them; at the same time, dozens of other people are doing exactly the same thing. The minds and spirits of these people are inevitably famished, if not completely deadened, stopped up, and immersed in sensuality."

(St. Theophan the Recluse, *The Spiritual Life*, p. 33)

St. Theophan the Recluse is referring to three gradations of life: the carnal, the psychological and the spiritual by naming them accordingly, bodily (or carnal), mental (or intellectual) and spiritual:

> "Human life is complex and multi-faced.
> It has physical, mental and spiritual aspects."

(St. Theophan the Recluse, *The Spiritual Life*, p. 22)

So our life can be in different levels. Therefore, we have plenty of different possibilities in our ways of life.

> "His life [man's] is either spiritual, with spiritual views, habits and feelings; or it is carnal, with carnal thoughts, deeds and feelings. (I am not taking into consideration the states in between – the intellectual-spiritual, or the intellectual-physical, because I don't want too many categories.) This does not mean that when a man is spiritual that the intellectual and physical have no place in him, but only that the spiritual predominates, subordinating to itself and penetrating the intellectual and the physical parts. Equally, it does not mean that when a man is intellectual that his spiritual and physical parts no longer exist; rather, when the intellectual predominates, it rules everything and gives its tone to everything and envelops the spiritual with the cover

of intellect. Neither does it mean that when a man is carnal that his spiritual and intellectual parts no longer exist; rather, that everything about him becomes carnal, both the spiritual and the intellectual parts become carnal, subordinated to the flesh and trampled by it and held in its bondage."

(St. Theophan the Recluse, *The Spiritual Life*, pp. 57-58)

But the spiritual dimension of life is the one that justifies man and provides his existence and creation with meaning and essence.

"The standard of the holy, virtuous and righteous life is inscribed in the conscience. The soul, through binding with the spirit, and having received information about such a life, is drawn by its invisible beauty and majesty, and decides to introduce this life into its (the soul's) own life and domain of deeds, transforming even this according to the requirements of such a life. And everyone is sympathetic toward such yearnings, although not everyone wholly gives himself over to them; but there is not a single human being who has not at some time or other devoted his labors and substance to deeds in such a spirit."

(St. Theophan the Recluse, *The Spiritual Life*, pp. 54-55)

The aim of Christianity is not to reject life but to enrich it, *"I am come that they might have life, and that they might have it more abundantly"* (John 10:10). The aim of Christianity is the transfiguration of "life" to Life; its aim is for us to be in a state of Wholeness instead of being constantly possessed by a sense of dissatisfaction.

"Man has three (or five, including the intermediate) levels of life, the spiritual, intellectual and corporeal; that each one of them has its aggregate of needs, those natural and peculiar to man; that these needs are not all of equal worth, but instead, some are higher, and others lower; and that the balanced satisfaction of them gives man peace. Spiritual needs are above all, and when they are satisfied, then even though the others are not satisfied, peace exists; but when the spiritual needs are not satisfied, then, even though all other needs are richly satisfied, there is no peace. That is why the satisfaction of them is called *the one thing needful*.

When the spiritual needs are met, they teach a person to harmonize those needs with the satisfaction of the other needs, so that neither the needs of the intellect nor the needs of the body interfere with the spiritual life, but, instead, aid it. Then, established within a person is complete harmony of all motions and revelations of his life. There is a harmony of thoughts, feelings, desires, undertakings, relationships, pleasures. And this is Paradise!"

(St. Theophan the Recluse, *The Spiritual Life*, p. 82)

So when it is said not to walk "according to the flesh," that is, according to matter, that doesn't mean to reject the things of the matter, but that they should have their proper place in our life, their proper place inside us.

"No matter how spiritual someone is, he cannot help but give the intellectual and carnal their rightful place; he maintains just a little of them, in subordination to the spirit."

(St. Theophan the Recluse, *The Spiritual Life*, p. 60)

The lower cannot lead the higher. The spirit should lead the flesh and the soul; and not the flesh, or even the soul, lead the spirit. That is why we are given the commandment to seek first the Kingdom of God, that is, to seek first the things of the Spirit and walk guided by the spirit; and the things of the soul and the flesh shall follow and be added, because it's a fact that our soul also has her needs and she has to be fed as well as our body. But our biggest need is the *spiritual* food, *"Therefore I say unto you, Take no thought for your life, what ye shall eat, or what ye shall drink; nor yet for your body, what ye shall put on. [...] For your heavenly Father knoweth that ye have need of all these things. But seek ye first the kingdom of God, and his righteousness; and all these things shall be added unto you"* (Matthew 6:25, 32-33).

So very practically if upon waking up in the morning, our soul starts filling with the biotic and everyday cares (thoughts), with the things of the world, of "life" (and not the things of Life) – namely, from our job, obligations, anxieties, worries, problems and petty joys – and only at the end of the day (and this rarely) do we remember for awhile the things of the spirit and the Spirit, that means that the world, "life," is sucking us, is enslaving us and we are lost in it. So we are deprived of the connection and communication with Life, with the Spirit, with God, *"For to be carnally minded is death; but to be spiritually minded is life and peace"* (Romans 8:6).

We need as a guide, as our foundation, the spirit which is our Real Self and the Spirit which is God. Otherwise we are captured in the tentacles of "life" feeling constantly unsatisfied, running from one responsibility to another, from one "pleasure" to another, without ever reaching anywhere.

We come and go all the time from "happiness" to "unhappiness" until we reach the end of our lives saying, "That was all?" and hoping perhaps that our children will have a better fate. And that is why we try to leave them carnal (material) inheritances so they can have "better luck" without realizing that this kind of wealth didn't offer us any real joy. So no matter how much we increase it, it will offer no real joy to our children.

> *"Lay not up for yourselves treasures upon earth, where moth and rust doth corrupt, and where thieves break through and steal: But lay up for yourselves treasures in heaven, where neither moth nor rust doth corrupt, and where thieves do not break through nor steal: For where your treasure is, there will your heart be also"* (Matthew 6:19-21).

Jesus is not teaching the rejection of life but the Abundance of Life and in that sense we can say that He teaches the rejection of "life." So Christianity denies "life" and praises Life. That is why it teaches the remembrance of death.

When man comes face to face with the fact of death (either in reality or in his imagination) he instantly appreciates his life. He is sorry for the "life" he lived and he longs for the Life he didn't live. So it's not strange that he often turns at this last moment to the spiritual things, that is, to his spirit, because deep inside him the Spirit, God, informs him that it is only there he can find *meaning*.

> "Nothing created is capable of satisfying the spirit. The spirit comes from God, it seeks God, it wants to taste Him and, abiding in the living communion and bond with Him, it rests in Him. When it attains this, it is at peace, and, until, it has attained it, it cannot have peace. No matter how many creature comforts and blessings a person has, he has very little. Everyone, as you have already noticed, is always seeking. They seek and find something, but after they have found it, they cast it aside and start seeking all over again, so that they may once again cast away what they find. So it goes on endlessly. This means that they are seeking the

wrong thing in the wrong place, and not what they should be seeking, and not where they should be seeking it. Isn't this tangible proof that there is a force in us drawing us away from the earth and earthly sorrows towards Heaven?"

(St. Theophan the Recluse, *The Spiritual Life*, p. 48)

The Inner Restoration of Christianity

Remembrance of Death

"Some think mistakenly that remembrance of death poisons life. It does not poison life, but instead teaches us to be careful and to abstain from everything that poisons life. If we were to remember death a little more, there would be less confusion in our lives, both personal and collective."

(St. Theophan the Recluse, *The Spiritual Life*, p. 135)

But what does it mean to live a real Life?

We can live a short, essentially insignificant, egoistic life deriving some satisfactions, feeling a little joy and the equivalent sorrow, enjoying some things while suffering from others. We can also "achieve great things" and be admired by the people of our times and perhaps of later ages. In a few words, we can gain the whole world but what would be the profit for our soul? *"For what is a man profited, if he shall gain the whole world, and lose his own soul?"* (Matthew 16:26).

Our passage from this life, be that as it may, whatever we do, whatever we obtain, will be like dust in the wind: short with an unavoidable end... death. An end which we won't be able to avoid whoever we might be.

So that's what life is? A "life" of joy and sorrow, fame or insignificance, wealthy or poor, with or without posterity, where everything passes by? Where we just take care of ourselves, one way or another, knowingly or not? Or of our children as an extension of ourselves? And could there be some other perhaps more essential life?

"You once wrote me that you read a book titled, 'What the Spiritual Life Is.' It is mentioned there that there are three gradations of life: spiritual, psychological and carnal. These last two are characterized by egoism. The first one demands self-sacrifice both for its beginning and for the completion of every work.

"Why is it that in the psychological and carnal life are not any specific sacrifices? For in these two the desire and the objects of pleasure are obvious, sensible and tangible. Therefore, as we get used to this sensible reality from our childhood, we don't seek the spiritual life which prerequisites self-denial because we haven't tasted its heavenly pleasure; we haven't enjoyed its grace and joy, its peace and sweetness. This means that we know from experience the satisfaction of the objects of the world and this life but we don't know the satisfaction of the life in Spirit."

(St. Theophan the Recluse, *Guidance in the Spiritual Life*, pp. 159-160)

Why do we call egoistic the "life" (carnal or psychological) where we take care only for the things of ourselves, while we say instead that Life (the spiritual life) presupposes self-denial, when at the same time it is promised that from the Spiritual Life we will derive the highest satisfaction? How can our highest satisfaction be reconciled with self-denial?

Man wasn't created to suffer.

"God created man to be happy namely in Him, through living interaction with Him. For this, He breathed into his face the breath of His life, that is, the spirit, as has been mentioned already. The essential attributes of the spirit are consciousness and freedom, while the essential movements of it are confession of God the Creator, Providence and Requiter; with a feeling of complete dependence upon Him."

(St. Theophan the Recluse, *The Spiritual Life*, p. 88)

But when our soul (our human self) directs itself outside, through the senses, into the material world, she begins to get cut off from the spirit (our Divine self) and in that way she forgets her real origin and her real destination to a degree that we need *special education* in order to *remember* the Truth within us.

"I am not giving you a detailed explanation of all these manifestations of the spirit, I am just directing your thoughts toward the spirit's presence in us, and ask you to think it over a little more to convince yourself fully that there is a spirit within us."

(St. Theophan the Recluse, *The Spiritual Life*, p. 48)

The distortion we undergo when we direct our soul's attention, our heart's attention outwardly, is the turbulence and the fragmentation of our whole psychospiritual and psychosomatic structure. It means that our spirit, our Real Self, stands in mid-air, unable to connect with the Spirit, with God, and also unable to prevail over the soul and the body which push it around randomly, not caring about the consequences.

"The spirit had authority over the soul and body, because it was in living communion with God, and from Him it received divine power. When the living communion with God was disrupted, the flow of Divine power was also disrupted. The spirit, left by itself, was not able to rule the soul and body, but was drawn to and itself captured by them. The intellect ruled over man, and through the intellect, corporeality, and man became intellectual and carnal. Although the spirit was the same, it was without authority."

(St. Theophan the Recluse, *The Spiritual Life*, p. 91)

This is, as we could say, the decline (fall) of man because in his essence Man has been created for a different destination:

"Man is always free. Freedom is given to him along with consciousness of self, and together they constitute the essence of the spirit and the standard of humanity. Extinguish freedom and consciousness of self, and you extinguish the spirit, and man is no longer man."

(St. Theophan the Recluse, *The Spiritual Life*, p. 58)

The spirit has self-consciousness, it remembers itself, what it is, and also remembers and knows its Creator.

So what is the use of the remembrance of death?

Our soul forgets herself in her outward wandering and therefore loses her self-knowledge; but she still feels the need to *define herself as an entity so she assumes a bunch of false identities.* In order to feel a rudimentary safety, she creates a bunch of small "I's," false-definitions and false-selves, then puts them all together, names them "I" and conceives them as "herself."

Our soul has the need to know who she is, but being unable to remember, she identifies with anything that exists outside her: with her body, name, activities, attributes and traits; and she defends these identities with great fury in case she feels them threatened. The last place she will turn to is the spirit within her, to her Real Self.

And that is how the inflation of this pseudo-"I" begins: "I am this or the other," "I own this," "I managed that," "I want this," "I will do that." "I" "I" "I"... But if we are asked, "Yes but who are *You*?" the truth is that we have no answer...because we just don't remember, we don't know who we are.

All egoism starts when we turn towards our lower, outer parts of ourselves which feel constantly threatened; they need to possess, they need confirmation, to be recognized, etc. They feel absolutely insecure and they are right to feel that way because *they don't have any real existence*. They belong to the surface. Whereas they claim the characterization of "personality" or even of "individuality," in reality they belong to a very superficial, acquired part of ourselves (that could be called "false personality") which doesn't have any particular weight and is really ephemeral.

"When the spiritual reigns supreme in someone, then although this is his exclusive character and attitude, he does not err. This is because, in the first place, spirituality is the norm of human life, and so as a result, being spiritual, he is a real person, whereas the intellectual or carnal man is not a real person."

(St. Theophan the Recluse, *The Spiritual Life*, p. 60)

So man is a Man when he has consciousness of his Real I, of his Being, of his I Am, which along with his inherent inner freedom constitute his *spirit*.

When we are in these spiritual heights or depths of ourselves, we find out that we are no longer under this tyrannical sense of egoism which is related to our soul's vain effort to self-define and exist through her carnal and psychological characteristics. In these heights or depths we experience, as a spirit, the sense of I Am, the sense of *being*, completely differently and in immediate *relation* to its Giver.

"The spirit which is ever present within us as a significant force, itself contemplating God as Creator and Providence, also draws the soul into that invisible and boundless realm."

(St. Theophan the Recluse, *The Spiritual Life*, p. 53)

We experience our Self as a *person* who can come through his spirit and the Spirit, into communion (and be united) with every other *person*; because Real Love is possible only through this spiritual dimension.

Since our spirit can be connected personally with the Spirit of God, and since God is Love (1 John 4:8, 4:16), it can be connected and united by bonds of Love with every other human spirit even if its lower parts are hostile toward our spirit.

Our spirits are united in the Love of God.

Here, in this spiritual dimension, man discovers his Self; he realizes his existence and he can say, "I love therefore I am" in contrast to his intellectual (psychological) dimension which declares, "I think therefore I am." In his spiritual dimension, in the dimension of Love, man doesn't seek anymore the things of himself (see 1

Corinthians 13:5) and thus he can taste Paradise. Whereas when he is in the lower dimensions of his existence, he acts egoistically (he puts forth his pseudo-defined "individual I"), he seeks and he claims the things of himself, but in that way he harms his soul since he is being cut off from all kinds of possible unity; he is self-imprisoned and self-limited; he tastes only separation, isolation, loneliness, and in other words, *hell*. He gains the whole world but loses his soul.

Now we can understand the call for self-denial. We are called to deny our false, egoistic self in order to gain our Real Spiritual Self, *"For whosoever will save his soul shall lose it: and whosoever will lose his soul for my sake shall find it"* (Matthew 16:25). Yet, this happens not to benefit egoistically from this renunciation, but because it is our duty: *"So likewise ye, when ye shall have done all those things which are commanded you, say, We are unprofitable servants: we have done that which was our duty to do"* (Luke 17:10); as well as our destination, *"And he that taketh not his cross, and followeth after me, is not worthy of me"* (Matthew 10:38). Nevertheless, the result of our self-denial will paradoxically be the Divine Beauty.

> "Remember your spiritual experiences. Don't you recognize that they are incomparably higher than the psychological and carnal ones; that they are as far from them as heaven is from earth? So thanks to their experienced excellence, even a very small taste of them is able to put aside every other experience by drawing your heart and disposition."
>
> (St. Theophan the Recluse, *Guidance in the Spiritual Life*, p. 160)

Then our yoke will be lightened, and greater things will begin taking their place:

"Once this reunion [with God] is accomplished, everything else will start moving by itself. Instantly the spirit will gather strength, subordinate the soul and body to itself, put in order the needs and desires and expel the passions."

(St. Theophan the Recluse, *The Spiritual Life*, p. 94)

But let's remember our question:

What is the use of the remembrance of death?

"Our mind is so darkened by the fall that unless we force ourselves to remember death we can completely forget about it. When we forget about death, then we begin to live on earth as if we were immortals, and we sacrifice all our activity to the world."

(St. Ignatius Brianchaninov, *The Arena: An Offering to Contemporary Monasticism*, p. 90)

The remembrance of death can protect us from the captivity of our attention and therefore of our soul to outer things. It reminds the soul of the transience of everything that belongs to the intellectual and bodily life, and so it forces her to turn inward. That means to turn her attention within her, to her own heart and there to seek her identity.

The remembrance of death can help us *remember who we are* since it makes us confront the inevitable fact of the termination of almost all the things that constitute our life and generally our identity. So it helps us to remember ourselves and also to sustain this remembrance in our everyday life so we are not continually lost in whatever happens, or in our various desires or needs.

The remembrance of death can help us exist in a constant *present* where the aim is not, of course, to live dangerously or recklessly, but the complete opposite: extremely carefully!

> "You cannot pass a day devoutly unless you think of it as your last."
>
> (St. John Climacus, *The Ladder of Divine Ascent*, p. 135)

Our attention should be directed towards the day, "*Take therefore no thought for the morrow: for the morrow shall take thought for the things of itself. Sufficient unto the day is the evil thereof*" (Matthew 6:34), in the sense that we have a daily task which takes no postponement, "*And he said to them all, If any man will come after me, let him deny himself, and take up his cross daily, and follow me*" (Luke 9:23), because no one knows when his last hour will be, though it is inevitable for everyone.

> "David who was quick in running begged and implored God, asking to know the remaining time of his life and whether it would be enough to reach his aim. Because he says: "*Lord, make me to know mine end, and the measure of my days, what it is; that I may know how frail I am*" (Psalms 39:4).
>
> (Nilus of Sinai, *Peristeria – To Monk Agathios*)

Postponement is a psychological disease of the intellectual and carnal man who acts like he is immortal; so he gets "used" to life and takes it for granted, turning it into a "life" that results in a downgrade of *quality,* and therefore losing the ability of transfiguring it into Life. Whereas if he remembered the inevitable fact of his death, he wouldn't be able, for example, to remain angry very long with someone, especially with his beloved ones, *"Let not the sun go down upon your wrath"* (Ephesians 4:26].

If we realized the fact of our death, then each day, even each hour would assume a different significance and therefore quality. We wouldn't allow *even one hour* to find us angry with our neighbor, because we would know that everything which surrounds us, and we ourselves as well, will someday be gone; so we wouldn't take them for granted, we would appreciate what is really worthy, and we wouldn't be bothered with what is really vain.

And what is vain? Egoism, obviously along with its pursuits, aims and dreams.

> *"Surely every man walketh in a vain shew:*
> *surely they are disquieted in vain:*
> *he heapeth up riches,*
> *and knoweth not who shall gather them"* (Psalms 39:6).

And if we learn to recognize the transient and the vain, we will also learn to recognize the permanent and the essential: *"And now, Lord, what wait I for? My hope is in thee"* (Psalms 39:7).

The remembrance of death can teach us the *remembrance of eternity*. It can bring us face to face with the question: What can we perceive in our life in terms of eternity?

> "Incorruptible and imperishable actions are the following: tears of repentance, acts of charity, compassion, prayer, humility, faith, hope, love and whatever else is done in a spirit of devotion. Even while we are still alive such actions help to build us up into a holy temple of God, while when we die they accompany us and remain incorruptibly with us forever."

(Nikitas Stithatos, *On Spiritual Knowledge, Love and the Perfection of Living*, 79, One Hundred Texts, p. 165, Vol. 4, Philokalia)

If this gift of discernment were given to us – that is, to discern the everlasting elements of life from the ephemeral ones – then our "life" would be transformed into Life. We would be able to see life as a miracle and the miracles in life. Therefore our life would be a Life of gratitude.

So what is the everlasting element of life?

Whatever is related to the real sense of Love.

This kind of discernment between the everlasting and the transient would give us the capability of making every hour of our life worthy, and perhaps every minute, but surely every day of our life. So we would learn inescapably the value of the lost day.

"Struggle, be vigilant, be watchful, don't spend your life's time in vain, the time you were given for the cultivation of the soul and the acquisition of the everlasting goods. Make sure that not even one day will go by idly regarding the spiritual works."

(St. Dimitri of Rostov, *Spiritual Alphabet*, p. 77)

This is man's aim: the return to God; and this is the only way for him to Love Truly. There is no other way, until then we will just "love" and hate...

So let's pray for God to bestow upon us the remembrance of death in order not to desire anything vain, but only Him, only the Spirit, only Love. And may we live each day as if it is our first and last in the Love of God, living thus a truly whole and *multi-dimensional* life.

Life is a learning, a school in which we are trained to know who we are so we can discover our depths or, in other words, our heights in order to meet God there. Life is a gift which is given for us to make it worthy by travelling inside in order to return wiser this time to our Father's house, to our lost spiritual Paradise. Life is a test, a struggle where we are constantly called to deepen all the more in the essence of Life, in Love.

There is "life" which is death and Life which is Love. So we can ask ourselves: How much of our life is taken over by "life" and how much by Life? And we can be certain that the remembrance of death will release us from "life" and will always turn our attention to Life.

The remembrance of death benefits us in remembering Life.

The remembrance of death leads us to the remembrance of Love.

The remembrance of death helps us to remember our Real Self.

God

"Seek Him until you find Him and acquire Him.

But where will you seek Him?

Seek in all the places of the earth;

search for Him in the ends of the world;

search for Him in riches, in glory, in bodily beauty,

in enjoyments and pleasures...

Nowhere will you find Him.

Because He keeps you entirely in His hands and

you don't know it.

He is inside you entirely and you don't feel this either."

(St. Dimitri of Rostov, *Spiritual Alphabet*, p. 27)

"Is there God or not?"

This question has troubled men for centuries. There are three possible answers to it: yes, no, and I don't know. Usually the ones who give an affirmative or a negative answer want to convince others about the truth of their answer. The ones who answer "I don't know" are usually the less fervent exponents of their position.

Nevertheless, it is accepted by most men that the issue regarding the existence or non-existence of God cannot be proven, so it remains a matter of faith. Neither the atheists nor the theists can prove their allegations, not to mention the agnostics. So the whole issue ends up in a personal matter of faith: "I believe there is God," "I don't believe there is God" and "I don't know if there is God."

This situation however reveals a common and very frequent misunderstanding. The attitude of the agnostics shows us the way in which we should approach the whole issue and we could characterize it as very honest because in their position they admit their ignorance. What can we determine from this attitude?

That the whole issue of God is, in effect, a matter of knowledge and ignorance, not of faith and unfaithfulness in the sense that we usually understand these terms:

> "What I feel very strongly about it,
> is that I believe because I know that God exists."

(Anthony Bloom, *God and Man, The Atheist and the Archbishop*, p. 7)

So the aim is not to believe or not believe that there is a God through a subjective world view and perception of things. Many thinkers have maintained the existence of God through intellectual reasoning and their arguments seem really firm, but there have been an equal number of thinkers who maintain the non-existence of God and their arguments are often as strong. Some people study the outer world and end up with a certainty at least regarding the existence of a higher intelligence which creates, preserves and controls life in every form. Others conducting the same studies end up with exactly the opposite results.

We could develop here a whole comparison to see which arguments are stronger, which thinkers maintained the existence of God and which didn't, and who among them are most praised by humanity. And in the end we might come up with the conclusion that the brightest men in history believe in the existence of God or the complete opposite.

Yet, this kind of conclusion wouldn't be of any deeper value to us. We would still maintain our own beliefs and we would still be "tormented" by the same questions until *we ourselves* verify our beliefs and our questions have been answered *within us*. This is because our relation with the Divine is a personal inner affair and not an outer provable reality.

A modern scientific field called "neurotheology" proves that the brain is thus created in order to experience religious experiences, but it still cannot be proven whether the brain creates God or God created the brain that way for us to be able to feel Him.

Coming to a picture that we are given in the New Testament which says *"God is Spirit"* (John 4:24), we understand that these words entail a specific reality. If God is Spirit then He can be known and discovered (or revealed) only through the corresponding organ (faculty) of man; that means only through his spirit.

> "Divine Grace cannot actualize the illumination of spiritual knowledge unless there is a natural faculty capable of receiving the illumination. But that faculty itself cannot actualize the illumination without the grace which God bestows."

(St. Maximos the Confessor, *Various Texts*, 12, Fourth Century, p. 238, Vol. 2, Philokalia)

We cannot know God through our body or through the soul (through the intellectual or the psychological man) but only through the spirit. If our spirit makes known to us the existence of God through its relation with Him, then our soul, even our body, can partake in this knowledge through the medium of faith.

If we are not connected with our spirit, if we are not *spiritual* men, no matter whether we believe in God or not, our belief or disbelief consists basically of an intellectual conclusion which is not so valuable. This is because we examine a subject which belongs to the kingdom of spirit with an organ (faculty) which isn't fit for this search. The intellect of man cannot penetrate so deeply, namely, into the spiritual kingdom; it might be able to deduce some "truths" or "realities" by examining and investigating the facts which are at its disposal, but its conclusions (either real or false) would remain at the surface, since *by nature* it cannot penetrate this kingdom.

The human intellect is able, in effect, to be a receiver of the revelations of the Divine spirit within man and that is its use. Yet, we distort its function in trying to make known to our spirit the conclusions of our intellect!

So when we say to our spirit that there is no God because that's what our intellect tells us, our spirit just laughs with or cries for us. When, on the other hand, we inform it through an intellectual approach that God exists, our spirit tries to make known to us the essence and value of this intellectual conclusion in order that it not remain a fruitless belief, but rather, become a fruitful faith. When we inform it that we are ignorant whether God exists, our spirit is just patient with us.

The existence of God can be proven in only one way, and that is an inner one. Even if the existence of God were, or will be in the future, an outer objective proof (though many thinkers could claim it already is, that being the Creation itself), we would still need an inner personal verification of this proof; otherwise the existence of God would be a sterile, meaningless fact for us that would serve or not serve our worldview and life itself.

"To me the problem of God is this. He is not something I need to have a world outlook. I don't need God to fill gaps in my world outlook. I have discovered that He exists and I can't help it, exactly in the same way as I have discovered facts in science. He is a fact for me, and that's why He has significance and plays a role, in a way, exactly in the same sense in which having discovered that a person exists, life becomes different from the moment before you had become aware of the person."

(Anthony Bloom, *God and Man, The Atheist and the Archbishop*, p. 13)

That is why even those who acquire a certainty regarding the existence, let's say, of a higher intelligence which is responsible for all this marvel of life, as long as they remain turned outwards, as long as their attention is turned to the outer created world, they don't come to any particular conclusions concerning the nature of this intelligence. They don't know, nor can they conclude whether it is good or bad, or both, what are its aims, or what its actions ("energies") serve. Their studies don't lead them to something deeper beyond the fact of its impersonal existence.

Yet when this search is internal, its results are always decisive for our life, and transform our entire inner being, and in that way our outer life as well. As long as we don't perceive this kind of result, both in our inner and outer life, which proceed from our conception regarding the reality of God, we can be certain that our knowledge is, in effect, just an intellectual belief and not a heartfelt experience.

In this difference are owed all the "theological" conflicts, because usually what the intellect "knows" or "believes" it wants to impose onto others as well, while the heart is more silent and doesn't care to impose her truths, knowing that these kinds of realities are not proven verbally, but experienced internally.

Our heart constitutes our inner gate for the kingdom of spirit and therefore for the discovery (or revelation) of God's existence. So if we discover God inside us, within our heart, how is it possible to prove His existence in anyone else? The only thing we can do for someone is to turn his attention to the place where we ourselves ascertained the existence of God, that is, within himself.

Any reasonable proof which we might offer to a man who doesn't feel the truth of God in his heart, will leave him, in effect, unmoved; it might shake him intellectually for awhile, and in that way his beliefs may be questioned, but it won't affect him any deeper.

For example, if we present the perfection of the created world, the fact that every detail is studied and taken care of in the order of things in such a way that its least alteration could overbalance the world as we know it; if we refer to the greatness of the Universe which is beyond any intellectual conception of man; if we call upon the incredible beauty of Creation; still, even though these reasonable arguments can be pretty strong and might look persuasive for God's existence, for the existence of a higher power and intelligence which creates and conserves this grandeur, easily the opposite arguments can be found which talk about the "imperfections" of Creation; the human scientific research which understands deeper and deeper the universe's functions; or they could refer to the miracles of nature which don't need God, and so forth. So the discussion and arguments could go on forever with no result.

"So is there God or not?" asks the intellectual-psychological or carnal man, and these are the possible answers he can give: "I believe there is;" "I believe there is not;" "I don't know."

The spiritual man doesn't ask this kind of question because he *knows* God. He wonders *what the will of God is,* but not if there is a God, because he knows Him, he has tasted Him. And he possesses this knowledge through his spirit which informs him about the existence of God through his living relation with Him.

> "No one would be able to teach you to know God and to worship Him if this were not in the human spirit on account of some unassailable law."
>
> (St. Theophan the Recluse, *The Spiritual Life*, p. 290)

There are different "objective" personal proofs for the existence of God. One kind of proof has to do with the sense of the existence of a "new person" in our lives who we have discovered or has been revealed to us, who we can no longer avoid or ignore.

And from this sense derives the realization that God never forgets us even when we forget Him. If we felt that God existed only when we remembered Him, we could think at some moment that God is a product of our fanciful imagination.

> "God is everywhere. Whether we are thinking about Him or not, He is there all the same wherever we are, and He sees everything."
>
> (St. Theophan the Recluse, *The Spiritual Life*, p. 263)

At some moment, though, we realize beyond any doubt that God existed before we discovered and knew Him and that He never stops surrounding, guiding and Loving us, even when we forget Him or when we think we remember Him, yet in effect we behave – talk, feel, think, act – like He is not there.

And here comes a second kind of personal "objective" proof which is that God asserts the fact of His existence through His actions (energies) in our lives. But here, we don't refer to the known sense of "nothing is accidental" or "this wasn't just a coincidence," that is, to isolate occurrences which leave us with a feeling of meaning, or even of guidance and help, but are soon followed by other facts completely incomprehensible, random and foolish to us, and that leave us with a sense that all is chaotic, vain, perhaps unfair, and surely meaningless.

We refer to a *practical* action of a Higher Power which we see working not only in our lives, but also in the lives of other people! Sometimes this Power is called "Divine Providence," but for the spiritual men who are *personally* related to Her, Her action in their lives acquires much more the character of a very familiar person than of an impersonal power. So this action of God in our lives can constitute one of the strongest inner "objective" proofs for His existence.

Nevertheless, we could easily wonder: "If all this is true, how come many people don't feel the existence of God inside them and not only that, they feel instead very intensely His non-existence?" The answer to this is contained paradoxically in the question itself and is extremely simple: *"The fool hath said in his heart, There is no God"* (Psalms 14:1). Or we could express this answer with the lyrics of a song, "Who feels it, knows it." So in relation to God we could also say that whoever feels Him, knows Him and whoever knows Him, feels Him.

"A man knows God and is known by Him in so far as he makes every effort not to be separated from God."

(St. Antony the Great, *On the Character of Men and on the Virtuous Life*, Text 164, p. 354, Vol. 1, Philokalia)

The Inner Restoration of Christianity

Unfortunately our hearts are tainted and closed; so we cannot hear the Spirit knocking on our heart's door. Therefore, we not only don't feel God within us, but in feeling His absence, we question even His existence.

Atheism

> "This world which forgot God,
> is not but a valley of sin and a labyrinth of death."
>
> (St. Dimitri of Rostov, *Spiritual Alphabet*, pp. 50-51)

We live in a godless society; we live a godless life.

If we search to find God in the modern human expressions: works of art, shows, movies, songs; or if we seek to find Him in our daily life, conversations, thoughts, actions; even in modern "spiritual" practices, in different kinds of energetic healings, in "spiritual" systems; we will find out that God is, in effect, absent.

For example, the notion of God's will is nowhere to be found; God's help and action, the relation with God and the highest purpose for man: the union with Him; all these realities just don't concern us.

We are tormented daily by thousands of problems, we are struggling in relation to innumerable things, we fight to accomplish so many aims but we almost never say that we suffer because we are separated from God. Very rarely will someone be found struggling to know God and be related to Him. And very few of us set union with God as our aim in life.

We give little thought to God, and apart from our concept that "we are Christians," therefore God exists as well, God is completely missing from our life. He just doesn't exist. And that's because we have forgotten Him, we have pushed Him out of the limelight. So the idea of seeking first the Kingdom of God and the rest will follow, has been completely inverted within us. We give thought to everything else, and *then* for the things of God — and that, in the best case.

Our life in general is completely *anthropocentric*, our dreams and pursuits are all human, and all our actions, for the most part, revolve continually around ourselves.

We have even psychologically distorted the Bible teaching that God created man and gave him dominion over all things upon the earth (Genesis 1:26-28), and instead of perceiving our role as a responsibility, we consider it a right. And this psychological distortion gradually leads us to the concept that God created the world exclusively for our sakes. This distortion, in its final stages, causes us to forget that we, too, are a creation, and we perceive ourselves — because of our given role — as creators, ending up thinking we don't need a Creator, and claiming thus its Heights (Genesis 3:4-5).

So since God is no longer needed, we throw Him in a dark corner of our mind — as it is not possible to forget Him entirely — and we put man in His place. In that way we become anthropocentric in our thoughts, actions and of course our words.

Some words of our human speech are truly characteristic of our state. Words like self-awareness, self-realization, self-confidence, self-knowledge, self-reliance, without having some negative meaning by themselves, in our days are unconsciously over-emphasized. They become an end in themselves, instead of consisting of *means* for the achievement of a God-centric state which could be expressed with words that are either rarely used or don't exist at all. Words like God-awareness, God-realization, God-confidence, God-knowledge and God-reliance don't exist in our consciousness, and in fact sound very strange. Yet they symbolize what our ultimate aim should be in all of our human endeavors — an aim which could also be expressed with the word *Theosis*.

All these words which use the prefix "self-" (indicating of course *our self*...) have basically a "lower" meaning and don't constitute the aim of life; on the contrary, they constitute means for the aim which could be expressed with words using "God-" as a prefix. But man makes an end of the means: he sets self-knowledge as the highest aim, puts it in the place of God-knowledge, and in that way he unconsciously puts man in the place of God. And later he believes that it is possible for man to have created God, and not God the man!

This playing with words simply points out how we men reach to the point of becoming anthropocentric (or egocentric) by placing our self as the highest principle and thinking that we can manage without God. We feel then that we can count on *our own* strength and in that way our "independence" and "self-reliance" become the highest objectives. In the same way, our self-knowledge is extolled without understanding that the self-knowledge, which doesn't aim at God-knowledge, is conceit and arrogance. We believe that we can be man-taught or even self-taught in every domain of human life, but the idea of being God-taught seems to us extremely weird.

If all these observations are more or less true, the conclusion is obvious and pretty unpleasant for all those of us who like to say we believe in God. The most important aspect of Godlessness (atheism) doesn't refer to the people who claim to be atheists, because they are correct in declaring their disbelief in God, since they haven't known Him. The most serious aspect of atheism is related with the theists, with those of us who claim that we have a God, that we believe in God, but as a matter of fact, we live without Him. And since *we don't have God in our lives* and *we don't live with Him*, we are in effect *Godless* (a-theists).

So it's becoming obvious that atheism reigns in general, but mostly inside of us. And this phenomenon has specific reasons. We could say that the concepts of atheists and agnostics represent aspects of human nature which are inherent in everybody. And in that way we could explain the fact that while we'd like to consider ourselves as theist people, very often we function through these atheist and agnostic aspects.

The carnal mind which exists in man could be characterized, in effect, as atheist simply because it is dominated by the laws of matter, or nature, and confesses these laws as its ultimate principle. Therefore it is not strange that atheists acknowledge – often without realizing it – Nature as their god.

The intellectual-psychological mind in man is, in essence, agnostic. It is the human mind which investigates. It is the human aspect of man which, if it doesn't find what it is looking for, declares itself to be the result of its search and therefore the highest principle. This mind creates all the human ideals which believe they can manage without God, but usually more or less fall apart when they don't have the aid of God-reliance, because anthropocentrism is not very far from egocentrism when it doesn't aim ultimately in God-centrism.

The spiritual mind in man is theistic. The spiritual Divine aspect of man is the one which is related to God and informs the other ones about His reality; this aspect is not led by ideas and arguments, but by a clear experience.

So it is obvious that as long as we are not related to our spirit, our notions about God, His existence or His non-existence, His attributes and His nature are nothing more than intellectual conceptions which can easily be refuted, even by ourselves, since they don't have any essential affect on our lives. As long as we are not related to our spirit, our ideas about God are just sterile theories.

Yet our spirit continually calls us internally to live according to its precepts, and whether we realize it or not, it is only the internal precepts of our spirit that create all true human values and provide us with the ability and strength to *live* according to them.

Now, if a man declares himself atheist (intellectually), but without knowing it, is related much more to his spirit than someone who declares himself theist (intellectually), but is completely lost in his carnal or psychological mind, not having any contact with his spirit, then it is self-evident that the first man is much closer (whether he admits it or not) to God than the second one.

"Laski: I certainly think that belief in God and the religions that arose from belief in God did give a shaping and a pattern to life for which I can see no conceivable substitute and to that extent I would certainly grant to you that my life is poorer than that of a believer. My justification for it, and I say it as humbly as I can, is that it's founded on the truth as I see it. [...]

Bloom: I feel terribly happy about what you said because I think what really matters first of all is integrity and truth and I'm certain that if God exists, which I believe He does, He's happier about truth of unbelief than falsified belief."

(Anthony Bloom, *God and Man, The Atheist and the Archbishop*, p. 29)

Thus can the chasm be explained that we observe between our theories and our actions which so characterize us, the theist people, the faithful ones. As long as we are dominated by our carnal and psychological sides we will never be able to stand up to the heights or the depths of our spiritual side through which we can allow the manifestation of the Existence (Being) of God into our lives.

As long as we are not placing the spiritual life – that is the life of our spirit – as our main purpose in life, we will still display this chasm between our ideas and our actions.

> "In this remembrance [of God] it is necessary to fortify oneself in every way until it does not leave the mind. God is everywhere and always with us, by us, and in us. However, we are not always with Him, for we do not remember Him and, because we do not remember, we allow ourselves to do many things that we would not allow ourselves to do if we remembered God."
>
> (St. Theophan the Recluse, *The Spiritual Life*, p. 175)

As long as we forget God, as long as we are cut off from the life of the spirit and therefore the Spirit, we will act contradictory and inadequately. We will live on the surface of life without being able to perceive that the essence of things is Light, Love, God. As long as we don't grasp that the meaning of life is union with God, we will continue to live according to the precepts of our carnal or psychological mind in their better or worse version. We will be more atheists than theists, regardless of what we profess and whatever picture we have created for ourselves in order to rest assured.

But what is God?

And what does it mean to live with God? Or without Him?

Due to our ignorance about God we form many subjective ideas in relation to Him, and this ignorance is also responsible for all the corresponding conflicts around His Person, "God is this," "God is that." And here we are faced with the fact that, "Indeed, how can we be certain of what God is?"

It's been said, for example, that God is love (1 John 4:16), but how do we know this? Or that God is Spirit (John 4:24), but what does this mean to us? It's also been said that God is Father, that He is in the heavens and that He is perfect (Matthew 5:48), but what is the meaning of all this in our life? What is their effect and use?

There may be some people who have had a personal experience of God, but that is not enough for us; we must acquire the equivalent experience for ourselves.

Until St. Paul acquired his own personal experience of God, he had naturally formed his own *view* about Him and acted according to that view. But the acquisition of the real *knowledge* of God had the result of his *transformation*. Saul, who persecuted Christianity, transformed to the Apostle Paul who preached Christianity (Acts 9-13:9).

Whoever meets God in his heart, assures us that God is Love and that his own existence is beginning to be transformed. Whoever meets God in his mind, often disagrees about His attributes, and his being remains more or less the same. It might be improved in some respects, but it may worsen, especially toward others.

So we need a personal experience and knowledge in relation to God, which is possible only through our spirit. And as previously mentioned, the door for accessing our spirit is in our heart. Only through a pure and bright heart can we find access to our spirit which informs us all the time that *God is our perfect, heavenly Father who Loves us, who Is Love.*

It's not enough, however, to be informed of this Truth in some outer way; it must constitute a personal realization. Otherwise, it won't have any effect on our life and would be just another idea which could even make us worse until we ascertain the painful contradiction between our ideas and our actions: *"Beloved, let us love one another: for love is of God; and every one that loveth is born of God, and knoweth God. He that loveth not knoweth not God; for God is love"* (1 John 4:7-8).

The relation with God, when it's real and living, transforms and initiates us into a completely different dimension of life. In this dimension the concepts of Love, Silence, Prayer, Wholeness, Joy and Life acquire a completely different meaning and become states of being, not fruitless theoretical ideas which offer nothing, either to us or to our neighbor.

> "What I feel, to put it in two very short statements about God and religion, is that to me God is not someone I need to fill gaps. It's someone I have got to accept because from the experience of life I have, He does exist; I can't avoid the fact. And the second thing is that all the morals that develop from His existence are part, not of a duty to Him or a duty to people – I don't like the word duty – but an act of happiness and gratitude for God and for people, and that links with worship – a worshipful attitude to God, a worshipful attitude to people, a worshipful attitude to life; I think the sense of worship and joy and of a challenge which will make me grow into full stature are really what matter in practical life."
>
> (Anthony Bloom, *God and Man, The Atheist and the Archbishop*, p. 18)

So for this relationship with God to come into being and bring as well the expectation for the union with Him, we should at least remember God. We should stop forgetting Him, ignoring Him, pushing Him aside; we need to recognize Him and know Him, to take Him into account in our lives.

Let's not cherish illusions that we can live a spiritual life without God, because the life of the spirit is dependent on its relation with the Spirit, with God. Without God, our spirit is *starving*. We might be excelling in material or psychological life without any need of God, but as far as the spiritual life is concerned, we will be asleep or even dead; because as we've already seen, there cannot be any spiritual life without God.

"You were surprised; why did I keep talking about the same thing?

Remembrance of God is the life of the spirit."

(St. Theophan the Recluse, *The Spiritual Life*, p. 212)

The Inner Restoration of Christianity

Remembrance of God

> "This [the remembrance of God] is the very essence of spiritual life."
>
> (St. Theophan the Recluse, *The Spiritual Life*, p. 202)

Our only real problem is losing the remembrance of God. However difficult our situation is, if we can retain the remembrance of God, everything acquires a different character. And this is because His real remembrance introduces us into a different dimension of things; it makes us see everything under a more real light and through a deeper perspective; it provides us with exceptional strength and energy, because God's remembrance gives the ability to be related to Him. And through this relation all our inner and outer potential can be manifested; we can grow in essence and transcend all the inner and outer impediments. Yet the *real* remembrance of God is feasible only through our spirit. Or, in other words, our spirit can never forget God because it is connected with Him in a relation of Love.

> "Love ignites love. Once you have felt the Lord's love for you, you cannot remain indifferent toward Him; the heart itself is drawn toward Him with gratitude and love. Keep the heart under the influence of your conviction about the Lord's love for you, and the heartfelt warmth will soon grow into a flame of love for the Lord. When this comes about, then you will not need any reminders about remembrance of God, or any instructions on how to do it. Love will not allow you to

forget your beloved Lord for a single moment. This is the ultimate goal. Resolve, if you will, to embrace it in your mind with conviction. Then you will direct all the labors that are suitable for strengthening thought about God in your mind and heart toward it."

(St. Theophan the Recluse, *The Spiritual Life*, p. 204)

The remembrance of God helps us control ourselves and be vigilant in regard to whether we are truly alive, awake and connected with real Life within us, or whether we are asleep, walking like zombies and lost in our thoughts, passions and fantasies.

"There will be disruptions, sometimes in the form of idle and unnecessary thoughts, or at other times in the form of emotions and inappropriate desires, you will immediately notice this error and drive out these uninvited guests, rushing each time to renew the oneness of mind concerning the One Lord."

(St. Theophan the Recluse, *The Spiritual Life*, pp. 179-180)

Now we can understand better how much we have deviated, when we realize that we hardly ever remember God in our daily routine, and so He is almost completely absent from our lives. At the same time, we would feel offended if someone told us that we are not spiritual persons at all. We want to be spiritual without minding what this term might imply and whether we fulfill its requirements. We are not concerned about the fact that the foundation of this term consists precisely in the spirit and the Spirit which we ignore altogether. And in the meantime we wonder why our life is not peaceful; why it is not distinguished by love and meekness; why we feel empty and bored, irritable and unsatisfied; why we are full of tension and stress; why we don't derive any deep satisfaction from life, but only ephemeral pleasures.

"There is disorder within; this you know from experience. You must destroy it; this is what you want, and you have decided to do this. Begin by directly removing the cause of all this disorder. The cause of the disorder is that our spirit has lost its original foundation. Its foundation is in God. The spirit gets back to it again through *remembrance of God.*"

(St. Theophan the Recluse, *The Spiritual Life*, p. 179)

The oblivion of the *real spirituality,* as well as of God Himself, doesn't have only these unpleasant manifestations. One other manifestation, for example, is when we sit relaxing, feeling nice, but still...it is like waiting for something, there is an unfulfilled desire, and lo!... an irrelevant thought makes its appearance, an imagination, an anticipation...something remains unsatisfied...we have it all, we are good, but something is missing...we dismiss all the daydreaming and the thoughts, and peacefulness returns...it's beautiful, but there is no completion...and suddenly we realize: "Forgive me my God, I had forgotten You, You are also here!" And then the anticipation disappears, there is wholeness for as long as this state of remembering God lasts.

"Think more about God and things of God. Fix in your mind the remembrance that God is everywhere, both outside you and within, and never be separated from this remembrance as you go about; work, sit, sleep and be awake with it."

(St. Theophan the Recluse, *The Spiritual Life*, p. 279)

But why is the remembrance of God so difficult? Why is it that many of us have never even heard about it? Why should we need to be taught, or struggle to learn it? Why is it not self-evident? It is because our relationship with God is problematic. And this is due to the fact that our carnal and psychological aspects dominate us, as much as we like to imagine ourselves as theist people.

So God remains an abstract idea for us and not a specific (spiritual) Hypostasis with whom we can develop a personal relationship of Love. We can easily understand how possible it is to not forget a person you love, and how he can be in your remembrance, day and night, but we have difficulty to understand what this has to do with God, even when we accept His existence. We can understand everything about human loves, and naturally we long to experience them, but the concept of the Divine love remains an inexplicable mystery or a strange theory.

"When something is out under the sun's rays for a long time, it gets very warm; the same thing will happen for you. By keeping yourself under the rays of the remembrance of God and your feelings toward Him, you will be warmed more and more with an unearthly warmth, and then you will become completely fiery, and not just fiery, but ablaze. The following will be fulfilled for you: *I am come to send fire on the earth* of human hearts, and I could not wish for more other than that it inflame everyone as soon as possible (Luke 12:49)."

(St. Theophan the Recluse, *The Spiritual Life*, p. 210)

This is the Divine love! So let's practice the remembrance of God until it flows unhindered from our spirit, overwhelming our soul. Let's struggle to know Him in order to love Him and be united with Him so we can fulfill the aim of our existence. Let's learn to remember Him in the same way we remember all of our beloved ones; until we feel that we cannot forget Him even if we wanted to; so Love will accompany us in every step of our inner and outer life.

"It's true that in order to retain the remembrance of God, labor and struggle are needed. Undertake it determinedly! At the beginning of this struggle you won't be able to remember the Lord more than ten times per day. Towards its end, however, you won't be able to forget Him more than ten times per day."

(St. Theophan the Recluse, *Guidance in the Spiritual Life*, p. 97)

Let's begin remembering God again.

"Remembrance of God is necessary. It is necessary to bring this to the point where the thought of God becomes intimately linked with, and becomes one with the mind and heart and with our consciousness."

(St. Theophan the Recluse, *The Spiritual Life*, p. 202)

The Inner Restoration of Christianity

The Love of God

"And we have known and believed the love that God hath to us. God is love" (1 John 4:16).

"God is love." Yes, but how can we be certain about that? Simply because someone else informs us that "God is love," can we uncritically accept this assertion and count on that?

As much as we'd like things to be so simplistic, in reality they're not. Even if we accept, if we "believe" that "God is love" because that is what we've been taught since childhood, this belief won't have any application. Are we calmer, having been taught this assertion? Do we feel safer? Do we have more trust in our life? No, not at all. And to what is this due? It is due to the fact that the living knowledge of the above assertion hasn't preceded the faith in it. We ourselves have to know, to experience the Love of God before we are able to believe in it. The outer assurance is not enough, because when difficulty – and also easiness – appears, the assertion that "God is love" won't play any part at all, whereas the *experience* of God's Love completely transforms our lives: our thoughts, words and actions, all of our Being.

When we experience the Love of God, then our whole life acquires a different *Meaning*. Through the taste of Love we find out, for example, that concepts of good and bad acquire a relevant value. We find out that "good" and "bad" are transformed in the hands of God by *means* which have Love as their aim.

But how can man experience God's Love? And which personal proof can be so valid that it can counteract all the inner and outer "voices of the world" which rage, striving to convince us, not only that God is not love, but that He doesn't even exist? The simplest answer to this question is that each one of us is receiving an *internal call* to the communion of God's Love. The difficulty lies in the fact that few of us listen to it within us, and even fewer respond to it.

So the most common path leading to this experience of God's Love is traced out as follows: To the degree that we have been *disappointed* in ourselves and also in the ordinary outer reality, is the same degree to which we become *receptive* to this inner call. As long as we live assured and satisfied in our outer and superficial parts, it's impossible to respond to this deep and subtle inner invitation.

If this disappointment is prolonged and turned mostly to ourselves; if we are let down by this false outer and egocentric "self" which claims us and promises all the paradises, but keeps betraying us, leading us into every kind of hell; then it's very probable that the disappointment of our surface will make us turn to something deeper inside us. If this happens, then our main concerns will naturally be how to proceed further and remain in these deeper levels within. How will we be able, in effect, to become what we are, by not being what we've become.

If we turn our attention within, soon we will hear this inner call and we will taste the *One* calling. Then we will know and experience for ourselves that the One calling *is Love* and because of His Love He wants to set us free from this oppressive egoistic self in order to lead us to our free Real Self so we can sup with Him and taste His Love. *"Behold, I stand at the door, and knock: if any man hear my voice, and open the door, I will come in to him, and will sup with him, and he with me"* (Revelations 3:20).

In that way, we will be able to say through experience, without wavering and doubt, *"We have known and believed the love that God hath to us. God is love"* (1 John 4:16).

All our hardship and pain is "due" to the Love of God which wants to release us from our tyrant within who promises us everything, but in the end offers us nothing. God, on the other hand, appears to deprive us of a lot, but only temporarily and superficially, because later, or rather shortly, He gives us everything: the things He guards for us, the ones we've forgotten. This is the greatness of His Love: he deprives us of our "soul" in order to gain our Soul.

God doesn't tell us not to love ourselves. If we don't love our own self, we won't be able to love anybody else. It is precisely out of this true and deep love for our *Real* Self that our inner warfare and our hatred of the false self arise.

God simply tells us that putting ourselves first is not the way to true wealth and fulfillment or to reach the fullness that we are longing for inwardly and is our inalienable birth-right, because in doing so, we are enslaved by our inner devil. We end up being poorer without realizing it since we are alienated and cut off from God, from the Source of Love; while His message, His call is, *"I am come that they might have life, and that they might have it more abundantly"* (John 10:10). God promises us everything:

> *"Ask, and it shall be given you; seek, and ye shall find; knock, and it shall be opened unto you: For every one that asketh receiveth; and he that seeketh findeth; and to him that knocketh it shall be opened. Or what man is there of you, whom if his son ask bread, will he give him a stone? Or if he ask a fish, will he give him a serpent? If ye then, being evil, know how to give good gifts unto your children, how much more shall your Father which is in heaven give good things to them that ask him?"* (Matthew 7:7-11).

But as a real pedagogue who puts the interest of his children above their liking or disliking of him, he doesn't leave us prey to ourselves even though He grants us the freedom to choose, *"Father, give me the portion of goods that falleth to me"* (Luke 15:12). Still, he urges us to ask for His own Will, *"Thy will be done" (Matthew 6:10)* since He surely knows as our Creator what's best for us, *"For your heavenly Father knoweth that ye have need of all these things"* (Matthew 6:32). God doesn't want to bereave us of anything. On the contrary, He preserves our Paradise for us until we cease to choose our hell, like the prodigal son:

> *"And when he came to himself, he said, How many hired servants of my father's have bread enough and to spare, and I perish with hunger! I will arise and go to my father, and will say unto him, Father, I have sinned against heaven, and before thee, and am no more worthy to be called thy son: make me as one of thy hired servants. And he arose, and came to his father"* (Luke 15:17-20).

He waits patiently for us without ever accusing us of ingratitude; He runs, instead, to welcome us before we even have time to return to Him, and without any blaming, He offers us even more than before:

> *"But when he was yet a great way off, his father saw him, and had compassion, and ran, and fell on his neck, and kissed him. And the son said unto him, Father, I have sinned against heaven, and in thy sight, and am no more worthy to be called thy son. But the father said to his servants, Bring forth the best robe, and put it on him; and put a ring on his hand, and shoes on his feet: And bring hither the fatted calf, and kill it; and let us eat, and be merry: For this my son was dead, and is alive again; he was lost, and is found. And they began to be merry"* (Luke 15:20-24).

This is God's Will for us: Love. But as some lyrics say: "In the abundance of water, the fool is thirsty." In the same way, in the abundance of Love, we remain thirsty as fools. And it's true that many of us have a lot of reasons to think and even feel that God's Love is not abundant, and that on the contrary, She is very limited. Our real problem, however, is that we keep turning our attention outside, this time to God Himself, judging Him, instead of turning our attention within, valuating our own inner reality.

Very often, for example, we say we feel sad, yet don't realize that the problem is our closed heart, which results in not being able to hear God's call within; we don't feel the Love inside us, despite our allegations that we love and that we are sad precisely because of our love! If, instead, we felt at that moment, "Forgive me my God, my heart is closed and I can't feel You, I don't hear You, forgive me," then our sadness would immediately vanish because our heart would open with God's aid and it would acquire more space in order to accept His *abundant* Love. So how receptive are we *really* to God's Love?

Could the reason for not being able to perceive Her, be our self-limiting egoism?

The truth is that in order to love we must be without egoism; but in order to *be loved* we must also be without egoism, otherwise we question Love, we cannot perceive and appreciate Her and that is why we keep asking for more (when in fact She is being given abundantly). So in order to not become greedy and spoiled, voracious and uncontrolled, God "hides" His Love from us until we are truly ready to receive and appreciate Her; and *that is* the proof of His abundant Love for us!

Our heart's soil must become receptive enough to accept the seeds of His Love. Our attention should stop turning outwards; it should aim to the internal requirements for God's Love to be cultivated in our soul. Then all our anxieties, fears, distresses, pains, problems and dead-ends will cease to stand between us and Love, and will no longer cause us to "feel" that God's Love must be very limited... if She even exists!

Whatever fights us wanting to throw us down in order to capture us, if we experience the Love of God as we often experience the love of our beloved ones, we will be able to see with the eyes of our soul that everything has a relevant value, and we won't be dazzled by the glamour of anything. In short, if we have Love in our hearts, we won't fear anyone or anything.

In the state of Love, in this luminous and open state, there is broadness and receptivity; there are no muddled thoughts, plots, hatred and enmity, accusations or worries. There is Light which embraces everything, good and bad, beautiful and ugly; there is sobriety, pureness; there are no cares or stresses, future or past, there is space, peacefulness, stillness; and *deep Breathing*, real prayer, and God. There is gratitude and freedom from everything. So our real problem is simple: We don't have enough Love in our hearts and that is why we should pray to receive Her:

"Lord, have mercy on us. There aren't any enemies; there is only one enemy and it is internal: our "self," our egoism. Lord, forgive us. Give us the strength to be freed from our oppressor. Lord, guide us. Lead us to our depths so we can find You there and taste Your Love."

"He who lives in love, lives in God. Where is love, there is also God."

(St. Paisius Velichkovsky, *Field Flowers*, p. 35)

The Inner Restoration of Christianity

The Love of Man

"After a careful study of your disposition, which life has encouraged you to undertake, you have at last come to see that you have never loved; nor do you know or understand anything about love."

(Starets Macarius of Optino, *Russian Letters of Direction*, Letter 243)

Through His Love for us, God teaches us Love for our neighbor and for the whole Creation around us.

"Ye have heard that it hath been said, Thou shalt love thy neighbor, and hate thine enemy. But I say unto you, Love your enemies, bless them that curse you, do good to them that hate you, and pray for them which despitefully use you, and persecute you; that ye may be the children of your Father which is in heaven: for he maketh his sun to rise on the evil and on the good, and sendeth rain on the just and on the unjust" (Matthew 5:43-45).

Let's not cherish illusions. In order to truly love we must be in a state of Love, which means to be united with God, with the Source of Love. Otherwise our "love" quickly turns to anxiety, worry, impatience, even to dislike and hatred. We cannot really love as long as we remain cut off from God, from Love.

"Since man was estranged from God, he was also estranged from himself and separated from other people."

(Metropolitan of Nafpaktos Hierotheos,
A Night in the Desert of the Holy Mountain, p. 132)

That is why our love is egoistic. What does egoistic mean? It means that it is *our* love; it's not the *Love of God* and therefore its supply is not from the inexhaustible Source of Love. Consequently, *our* love constitutes a very small streamlet which constantly dries. So inevitably, through the sense of *our* love we end up saying "*I* have done this for you, what have *you* done for me?" or "*I* sacrificed that for you, *you* must sacrifice this for me."

We compare and *measure* our loves and this is very reasonable since our love is derived from our limited supply, and it's very important to know whether we received as much love as we gave. Otherwise we consider ourselves having lost and been deprived in our relationships!

This explains why our love turns to hate, our liking to disliking, and our attraction to aversion. When our personal supplies of love are ending, when we give what we had to give, when we "love" as much as we could, then we are exhausted, we get tired and we begin to "hate."

All the tensions, insecurities and rivalries in our relationships are based on a subjective valuation which constantly calculates, "How much do I love you?" and "How much do you love me?"

True Love, however, is a completely different (and rare) state of being. This is not to say that in the state of Love we shouldn't determine the quality of relationships we seek and our expectations from them. But we have, in essence, basic expectations of ourselves first and foremost.

And this expectation we have of ourselves is to not usurp the Love of God which springs from within us, thereby demoting Her to *our* love, because by this action we limit Her to a subjective give and take.

In the state of Love we experience an ever new and refreshing wholeness which allows us to give without waiting to receive in return, and without feeling exhausted, since in reality we get back what we give two-fold and three-fold, but not from the one we gave to. No, we get back from the One we took from; that is, the Source of Love which we have found inside us.

This is the only way to have Love for all humanity according to the example of Jesus Christ, otherwise we have at our disposal only as much love as our personal "supplies" allow us. So our love is limited usually to our family, friends and animals, and whatever else satisfies us.

But this proves once again the subjective, limited and quantitative character of our love in contrast to the impartial, unlimited and certainly qualitative character of God's Love, who loves all people the same no matter whether they are good or bad.

"For he maketh his sun to rise on the evil and on the good, and sendeth rain on the just and on the unjust" (Matt. 5:45).

We have difficulty understanding this idea even if we've known it since childhood. How is it possible to love everyone the same? How is it possible to love our enemies? We might accept in theory that God, as God, loves everyone, but still in practice it's not something understandable. The concept of God's Love is distorted in us without us realizing it, and we often feel that God doesn't love us enough, or we feel that because of our virtuous acts God will love us more than other, less virtuous people.

That means we cannot surpass the quantitative measure of God's Love. And perhaps we don't mind so much if God loves us even less than others; but exactly the same? *Exactly* the same? No! This we cannot grasp. And if they tell us that we must struggle to gain God's

Love, that could be a motive to us; if they told us that no matter what we do, God loves us the same... this would be really disappointing!

All this confusion is due, of course, to our lack of understanding. It is due to the fact that we confuse our distorted perception of "love" with the real Love of God.

> "If someone thinks that he has love while his love is not equal towards everyone – that is, if he discriminates between persons and differentiates the poor from the rich, the ill from the healthy, the sinner from the righteous, the enemy from the friend, the stranger from the familiar – then he hasn't perfect love but partial. True and perfect love embraces all the same, both friends and enemies."
>
> (St. Paisius Velichkovsky, *Field Flowers*, p. 101)

What we must struggle for is just to open ourselves to God's Love, to the Light of God which shines without exception upon all of us. The only difference is that saints become full recipients and transmitters of this Light, while sinners are just closed to it, deflecting it out of their hearts. If we are open to God's Love, then we don't love qualitatively and limitedly, but we *become* Love and Her attributes, some of which are universality, unlimited space and true strength, are alive and working within us.

> "Perfect love does not split up the single human nature, common to all, according to the diverse characteristics of individuals; but, fixing attention always on this single nature, it loves all men equally. It loves the good as friends and the bad as enemies, helping them, exercising forbearance, patiently accepting whatever they do, not taking the evil into account at all but even suffering on their behalf if the opportunity offers, so that, if possible, they too become

friends. If it cannot achieve this, it does not change its own attitude; it continues to show the fruits of love to all men alike."

(St. Maximos the Confessor, *Four Hundred Texts on Love*, 71, First Century, p. 60, Vol. 2, Philokalia)

All this is very good we say to ourselves, but in *practice*, how do you love your enemy? Very often we are not in the position to love our friends, our beloved ones and our family, how will we be able to love a stranger or even more, our enemy?

"When children learn to read books, they first learn the letters, then spelling, and later on they learn to read. Christians should proceed in the same way in Christian doctrine. First of all they should learn to return good for good, which is gratitude; then not to return evil to evil, insult for insult, offense for offense, and not to take revenge either in word or in deed on the offender; and then after this, even to love their enemies and to do good to those that hate them, and to return good for evil.

This is the ladder by which Christians ascend towards perfection, that is toward love of enemies."

(St. Tikhon of Zadonsk, *Journey to Heaven*, p. 148)

When our heart is opened we can contain and forgive plenty of things; because when our heart is expanded there is space for God. And God is not limited, resentful and vindictive; He is limitless and truly all-mighty; so accordingly, this allows us to have more space within, to hold and heal many things. In a few words, to Forgive and to Love according to the example of Jesus Christ, *"Father, forgive them; for they know not what they do"* (Luke 23:34).

So we begin grasping that the whole issue of Love is a matter of choice: *"For if ye love them which love you, what reward have ye? Do not even the publicans the same?"* (Matthew 5:46).

We are responsible for the side we choose to be on. Do we side with pettiness, weakness, selfishness and self-interest, or even with human justice which doesn't hesitate to kill in the name of the law? Or do we side with Divine justice, that is, with Forgiveness and Love, with wholeness, greatness and magnanimity?

We are responsible for what we let affect us.

If we have Love in our hearts, nothing can touch us. In this point, our mind hastens to inform us about all the terrible dangers which we might have to face by our imaginary enemies, and in that way it attempts to question the commandment, "Love your enemies" as an utopian idea or even as a foolish assertion.

We hear the commandment "Love your enemies" and we imagine that someone is robbing us with a knife or that he wants to kill us, or that he threatens our beloved ones. We imagine all kinds of horrible and evil people which we probably won't ever meet and we wonder whether we can love our imaginary enemies. We argue about whether this commandment is feasible or unfeasible, and we either reject it or we accept it, and love, in our imagination, our imaginary enemies; we might even accept it with our own terms, "Yes I will love the one who will rob me but not the one who will kill my friend." In reality, there is a much more obvious meaning in this commandment which is completely different.

My friend who says something inappropriate to me, or who doesn't say something good about me when I need to hear it, is becoming my enemy; my neighbor who doesn't greet me is becoming my enemy; my companion who doesn't care enough about me or who cares more than I want (!) is becoming my enemy. A disease or an accident is an enemy of my body. The bad mood of someone close to me is an enemy of my joy. An adversity is an enemy of my good-willed plans.

So everything and anything can become my enemy when it opposes me and doesn't act as I would like, the moment I would like, despite whether this opposition is harmful to me or not, and despite whether my want is right or wrong. Therefore *every day* and *every moment*, countless enemies are appearing *in reality,* which we must *really* love.

Christ poses the question: What will we profit if we love only the ones who love us, or in other words, what will we profit if we are well, if we are happy, *if we have love*, only when things are going well and are favorable to us?

Especially in our human relations – a truly difficult field of learning and growing – it's really true: what will we gain if we love only the ones who tell us what we want to hear and happen to do exactly what we expect them to do, and are not opposing us in any way? How many are there who will act in any moment as we want them to act and will be as we want them to be? They are minimal.

So we can easily understand what we will gain if we love not only the ones who love us (who act in the way we want), but also our enemies (who don't act as we want); we will gain dozens of harmonious relationships.

We will gain our participation in a communion of Love with God and our neighbor. Then the parable of the Good Samaritan will reveal its meaning, the one that Jesus Christ relates to us when He is asked who our neighbor is. And without responding directly, he makes them understand that everyone is our neighbor, even if we are separated from him by any seeming or real hostility.

But let's examine in what way we love the ones who love us, before we attempt to love the ones who don't love us or are hostile to us. We ask, for example, one we love to bring us a glass of water and he refuses to serve us because he is bored, and tells us to get it ourselves. Do we love him at that moment as we would love him if he brought it to us? Or as we would love him if he refilled it for us?

Does *real Love* define our relationships of love or the constant actions and reactions, "You treat me good, I treat you good," "You treat me bad, I treat you bad?" Can we neutralize our reactions when we feel annoyed in any way and respond to negativity with positivity, to anger with meekness, to hostility with Love?

"Keep yourself scrupulously, in order that, if you are afflicted by any troublesome business whatever, and pain or anger occurs in you, you may be quiet and say nothing at all besides what is seemly, until your heart is first made calm by unceasing prayer, and then you may thus entreat your brother. If you ever must reprimand your brother, and you see him in anger or confusion, say nothing to him, in order that he may not be stirred up worse with anger; but if you see both yourself and that brother in great composure and mildness, then at that time speak, not as one who reprimands, but as one who is mindful with all humility and mildness that you not speak a word of your mouth in anger."

(Abba Ammonas, *Useful Servanthood*, p. 162)

There are many ways we can act in every case but *One* is the *Way of Love*. It would indeed be very interesting for us if we would seek in every occasion what the way of real Love may be.

We must be as steady as rocks before whatever accusations, discouragements or injustices come our way, because when our beloved ones come to ask our forgiveness, if we have even the slightest contact with our Conscience, we will be ashamed for speaking ill of them in the open, and most of all, internally. We will feel very petty for forgetting, at the slightest opportunity, what these people mean to us and in what ways they supported us in the past, and that we were quick to judge and think badly of them in the moment of their weakness.

"We human beings do not know how to be loved or how to be honored. We have lost our sense of balance. For if someone endures his brother even a little, when the latter is angry or afflicted, then when that brother comes to his senses and recognizes how the other has endured him, he would give his own life for that person."

(Abba Zosimas, *The Reflections of Abba Zosimas*, p. 22)

Our aim should be to benefit the ones we love and not hurt them, though we often hurt them in the name of "our love." If we see, for example, that someone is lost in the dark tunnel of his negativity, weakness and false self, how will we act?

Will we push him into deeper darkness with our attitude towards him, driving him to even worse reactions, the whole time feeling we are right while we claim to love him and want his best? Or will we continue in the Love within us, shining the Light of God to him which flows from our hearts?

"The fact that we are present in a situation alters it profoundly because God is then present with us through our faith. Wherever we are, at home with our family, with friends when a quarrel is about to begin, at work or even simply in the underground, the street, the train, we can recollect ourselves and say, "Lord I believe in you, come and be among us." And by this act of faith, in a contemplative prayer which does not ask to see, we can intercede with God who has promised his presence when we ask for it. Sometimes we have no words, sometimes we do not know how to act wisely, but we can always ask God to come and be present. And we shall see how often the atmosphere changes, quarrels stop, peace comes."

(Anthony Bloom, *Courage to Pray*, p. 56)

If we remain in the Light within us, we will find out that by our unshakable attitude and our staying in the Light, it increases! According to Heraclitus "Everything changes, and no thing abides," it either goes forward or backwards, either up or down. If we are facing a challenge which tends to carry us away from the state of Love, but we hold on, the result will simply be that we will be rendered more steadily in Love. Here we can verify the simple truth of the saying, "What doesn't kill you, makes you stronger." Whatever is trying to lessen the Light in us, if it doesn't succeed, which is completely up to us, the result will be an increase of Light.

Our initiation into this art of therapy – that is, the art of *transforming the negativity to positivity*, the hatred to Love – will lead to the transformation of every little thing from its distorted, negative elements, to the restoration of its initial purity.

And then we will grasp a deeper urge to "Pray for our enemies and bless them that curse us" since we will realize that any hostile situation can become, if we choose, an opportunity for *progress* and *inner strengthening*. It can be a blessing to us if we are able to seize this chance. So our only reasonable reaction would be, in our turn, to bless our enemy, whomever that might be, and even more, to sympathize with him for his negative state and pray for him in order for the *therapy* to become feasible.

> "Strive to acquire humility. And charity – the real charity, which never limits itself to gifts no matter how generous, but, consuming the heart with infinite compassion for all creatures, generates a pure flame of goodwill and the firm decision to help every single one of the great host of unfortunates."

(Starets Macarius of Optino, *Russian Letters of Direction*, Letter 233)

But what applies in the imaginary case should our enemies threaten our lives or the lives of our beloved ones?

What is important is that we do not daydream, but realize the hostility that dominates our daily routine and, in the end, governs our whole lives. With this realization we can perceive the benefit of a life marked by Forgiveness and Love. How much more fulfilling and rich such a life would be!

Still, our mind might keep wondering:

But how should we deal with the enemies who are more dangerous than the ones in our everyday lives, and to what extent, then, does the command to "Love our enemies" apply?

We should first ask and observe where these fears and questions are coming from, as well as what we feel deeper within us that is being threatened by these imaginary enemies.

Typically, the things we are most afraid of are related, basically, to our bodily existence, which comprises our supreme good. This is why we keep saying, "Above all, health," without realizing that a healthy body with a dead soul is infinitely worse than a sick body with a healthy soul.

But as long as we keep living with our carnal minds, our god will be the health of the body and generally the things of the body.

> *"Fear not them which kill the body,*
> *but are not able to kill the soul"* (Matthew 10:28).

Nevertheless, for most of us who haven't even advanced to the level of loving our loved ones when they're manifesting their love to us – let alone when they're acting hostile – it's pure arrogance and conceit to think that we could love an actual violent enemy. Still, the path to perfection has already been mapped out for us by Jesus Christ and indeed includes these inconceivable heights: to love, after having forgiven, even our persecutors and torturers, as well as anything that might trouble and pain us.

But for we who are still considering whether we want to truly begin this inner journey; whether we want to tread this *initially* rough path of perfection, this path of metamorphosis; it should be wise to focus our attention on our present abilities and begin by loving those who love us, in order to get to the point of loving those who don't love us, or who may even be hostile to us.

> "Let us sincerely love our neighbors, and let us be true, and not false, Christians. For, as the Lord teaches, by this is a true Christian known; *By this shall all men know that ye are My disciples, if ye have love one to another* (Jn. 13:35)."

(St. Tikhon of Zadonsk, *Journey to Heaven*, pp. 159-160)

Forgiveness

"Forgive us our debts, as we forgive our debtors."
(Matthew 6:12)

In reality, our debts don't belong to us; they belong to the false, superficial egoistic self, to our inner devil. That is why we are asking for them to be released (according to the Greek text of the New Testament) and to not be charged to *us*. However, in order to ask to be released from our debts we must also repent of them.

Repent (metanoia) means to "change mind," which could be interpreted as a *movement* to *another* part of ourselves. We leave our outer egocentric mind, which has committed all kinds of errors, and enter into our deeper, spiritual mind which remains unstained and pure.

In reality, *we ourselves* don't have any intention to sin, deviate, or hurt anyone or anything. We want to be virtuous, alive, awake, creative, conscious, useful, bright, beautiful and full of Love, but in practice we find that this state of being demands struggle. A struggle to be released from those sides of our ourselves which rule us and cause us to do all kinds of things we don't want to do: *"For that which I do I allow not: for what I would, that do I not; but what I hate, that do I. [...] Now then it is no more I that do it, but sin that dwelleth in me. [...] For to will is present with me; but how to perform that which is good I find not. For the good that I would I do not: but the evil which I would not, that I do. Now if I do that I would not, it is no more I that do it, but sin that dwelleth in me. [...] For I delight in the law of God after the inward man: but I see another law in my members, warring against the law of my mind, and bringing me into captivity to the law of sin which is in my members. O wretched man that I am! who shall deliver me from the body of this death?"* (Romans 7:15-24).

A direct result of this inner conflict is that *we ourselves will suffer first*, if, of course, the voice of our deeper Divine self, our Conscience, is still alive in us, which doesn't stop informing us about our deviation. She is always there, truthful to her duty, and whispers to us (or yells at us if we have a good relationship with her): "We're not going well," "We must change course because we're leading to the precipice."

So it's obvious that these sides of ourselves which lead us to a constant slough, are as hideous to us as they are to our neighbors and everything else around us, all which bear the consequences of their actions.

When they become apparent to us and we discover that they constitute a living entity in us, inevitably we will want to be freed of these beasts and be forgiven – released from the debts we have been charged with by this inner devil.

All of this, of course, has come about with our approval, since if we are honest with ourselves we must admit that we had hoped to gain something by our action; this tyrant was promising us paradise. We were promised either comfort or safety or happiness by our personal Pharaoh, which was the reason we accepted our slavery. There comes a time, however, when we can no longer tolerate it, and we long for our freedom – the real Promised Land which is promised to us by God inside us.

It's not possible, though, to seek this freedom only for ourselves. When we realize our enslavement to our inner tyrant, and know that we've been charged with his crimes and ask for our release from these debts in order to be free, it's self-evident that we can no longer keep charging our neighbor with the crimes of his own tyrant, thus continuing to bind him. For our part, we must free him from our accusations, we have to acquit him (Matthew 18:21-35).

But if he doesn't repent, if he doesn't agree that he has done anything to be forgiven of, to be released from, what happens then?

In that case he has the "right" to keep himself captive despite the chance he has been given to be released from the offenses of his inner devil. We ought to withdraw his charges, acknowledging that he himself is not truly responsible for his wrong actions, but his inner devil is. Still, if he himself is not willing to regret and repent, he will just remain a victim of his surface. For this reason it's worthwhile to sympathize with him even more by also releasing his future errors.

This doesn't mean that any of us are entitled to irresponsibility, nor can this be an excuse for doing whatever we want. But if we realize that our neighbor is weak and that this is the reason he remains enslaved to his lower parts – in this way condemning himself and suffering every kind of inner hell – let's not burden him any further by charging him with his weakness, even if it's "voluntary," even if it looks "convenient" or even if he "defends" it. Weakness might often appear convenient and self-seeking, and it might also present itself as "strength," but it doesn't cease to be weakness and faint-heartedness, and it will always lead us to our worst enslavement.

If all this is not enough to forgive the weakness of our neighbor, let's have one last thought: we could easily be found in our neighbor's shoes, and when we have fallen down we would hope for a helping hand and not a pointing finger.

So if we learn to forgive, then we will also learn to ask for forgiveness, and vice versa.

"Break down the idol of pride which is in your heart, and bow down with humility before your neighbor whom you have offended. And when you bow down in body, also bow down in heart. When you beg forgiveness with your lips, also beg with your heart."

(St. Tikhon of Zadonsk, *Journey to Heaven*, p. 141)

The truth is that we don't know how and why we should ask forgiveness. We are skillful in the art of self-justification, but we are completely ignorant when it comes to the art of asking forgiveness. Asking forgiveness is something rare in our lives, and even constitutes a form of life which is threatened by extinction.

Even though we are constantly in the midst of conflicts and tensions in our lives and in our relationships, we rarely hear ourselves asking forgiveness; we just utter some hurried "sorry" from time to time, and this is usually for insignificant matters. Yet we chatter all the time, both internally and in the open, justifying ourselves, explaining (always in the event) the "logic" of our every thought, word and action.

If we are sincere with ourselves, we have to admit that we avoid asking real forgiveness "like the devil avoids incense"… because it's true that every sincere and heartfelt forgiveness that we ask, is a deadly blow for our inner devil, our egoism. And this is because when we ask forgiveness, its existence is being spotted, which is the worst thing for it. Our inner devil is fed by darkness; the light burns it all over, exactly in the same way it happens in the vampire stories.

Our inner devil, our own personal vampire, literally drinks our blood; it's fed by our being, and always remains in the dark, because it cannot stand exposure to the Light. That's why it keeps hiding through long speeches of self-justification.

So true forgiveness (not the hurried "sorry" which again, covers it up) is the Light which exposes and burns it.

Indeed it will be something very revealing to us when we find out – after being taught the art of asking forgiveness – that there is much more delight and relief in "self-accusation" than in self-justification.

There is a tremendous sense of release when we find the fault in ourselves, even if the initial reason for the tension and the conflict *is not* to be found in us. In these moments of "self-accusation" we are released from the unbearable burdens and the heavy chains of our pride, self-righteousness and vanity; and then we are lighter and more able than ever to fly to the heavenly heights of Beauty, Forgiveness and Love. Otherwise, we continue wallowing in the mud and the mire of our endless chatty thoughts of self-justification, "Yes, but it wasn't my fault," "She started it," "You know what he has done to me…."

It is a tiring babble with no end, which dooms us, crawling in the pettiness of controversies which always lead to a deadlock. On the other hand, if we simply recognize our own share of responsibility and ask forgiveness for that, "Yes, you are right, it's my fault. I just didn't have enough love in my heart and so *reacted* in this way…" then we will open up to a completely different state of Being with one of its traits consisting of real *Strength*.

We often worry that if we ask forgiveness the people around us will interpret it as a sign of weakness. But where does the strength lie? In trying to hide behind our finger pretending to be irreproachable while everyone else clearly perceives our inadequacies? Or in having the courage to expose ourselves to the light, confessing our sins and faults, and asking forgiveness for them? And we can be certain that the real Strength of the latter attitude will soon be perceived by the people around us, and they will most likely respond accordingly. We can also be sure that the former attitude, the one of weakness, will have its corresponding, infectious effects too.

When we are taught the highest forms of this art, we find out that it is not so important whether we acted or just *re*acted negatively and without love; in both cases we are equally responsible. And then we discover that no matter how long we resisted our admission that we didn't have enough love in our hearts, this acknowledgment sets us free from the narrow prison of our egoistic self and so we feel an unprecedented and inconceivable joy.

In the same way we find out that in the higher forms of the art of forgiveness, we learn to forgive on the spot, and not only in the event that we are asked. We discover a newly found Strength inside us which prevents us from reacting all the time to whatever "threatens" us. By forgiving instantly we remain composed in the beauty, in the heights or the depths of our Self, of Love, and then we realize that *not* forgiving is nothing other than pettiness and weakness.

We often feel a distorted sense of power by declaring, "I will never forgive you this" until we realize that this constitutes the manifestation of our utmost weakness and small-heartedness, "How could he say that to me," "How could she treat me like this." Then, we understand that the enemy of forgiving is self-pity. And so we discover that as long as we put ourselves first, we will be unable to forgive anything or anyone.

At this point we might again wonder about the extent of forgiving and its possible range. But before imagining ourselves as incredible large souls who can forgive all and everything, or on the contrary, before revolting against the idea that we should forgive really harmful men or situations, let's turn our attention first to the ones we love who often suffer a harsh fate because of our "love:"

"Then came Peter to him, and said, Lord, how oft shall my brother sin against me, and I forgive him? Till seven times? Jesus saith unto him, I say not unto thee, Until seven times: but, Until seventy times seven" (Matthew 18:21-22).

Nevertheless, it's beneficial to examine also the higher achievements of the art of forgiveness, the heights of this path of perfection which have been defined for us by the inner and outer journey of Jesus Christ and which often (or rarely) don't consist of some kind of utopia for man, but his very tangible reality:

"Do you know the prayer that was reported in the *Sud Deutsche Zeitung* of the man who died in a concentration camp: 'Peace to all men of evil will. Let vengeance cease and punishment and retribution. The crimes have gone beyond measure, our minds can no longer take them in. There are too many martyrs... Lord do not weigh their sufferings on your scales of justice, and let them not be written in their act of accusation and demand redress. Pay them otherwise. Credit the torturers, the informers and traitors with their courage and strength of spirit, their dignity and endurance, their smile, their love, their broken hearts which did not give in even in the face of death, even in times of greatest weakness... take all this into account Lord for the remission of the sins of their enemies, as the price of the triumph of justice. Take good and not evil into account. And let us remain in our enemies' thoughts not as their victims, not a nightmare, but as those who helped them overcome their crimes. This is all we ask for them.' "

(Anthony Bloom, *Courage to Pray*, pp. 59-60)

The idea of forgiveness might seem unrealistic when it has to do with various inhuman criminal acts, but for those of us who have been in contact with the Voice of God on the inside, with their Conscience, it is *much worse to harm than to be harmed*. When we come in contact with Love inside us, we know that those who harm suffer much more than those who are harmed, because the victimizers are cut off from Love within, and therefore suffer greatly; this is the reason they inflict so much pain upon others, and on everything around them.

> "There is the example of a man who came back from Buchenwald and, when asked about himself, said that his sufferings were nothing compared to his broken-heartedness about those poor German youths who could be so cruel, and that thinking about the state of their souls, he could find no peace. His concern was not for himself, and he had spent four years there, nor for the innumerable people who had suffered and died around him; but for the condition of the tormentors. Those who suffered were on the side of Christ, those who were cruel were not."
>
> (Metropolitan Anthony of Sourozh, *Living Prayer*, p. 17)

On this point, however, we should mark the difference between forgiving or releasing, and repressing. Perhaps out of our strong desire to forgive (perhaps in order to be forgiven as well), or out of an inflated idea about ourselves being extremely large-hearted, we might be driven to repress things that really hurt or wronged us, and then think that we released our debtor's transgression, while in reality, we have just swept them under the carpet and often remain in a state of self-pity, "Me the poor one" and "If you knew what I've been through."

When we haven't been taught or do not understand the art of forgiveness in its essence and meaning, and we conceive it only in an outer way as an imperative way of living or a necessary virtue in order to retain our self-righteous picture, then it's very easy to bury and repress instead of releasing.

But the things we have buried begin to accumulate and rot inside us, and sooner or later their stench will surface and deluge us. This can easily be verified when we see emerging from within us, with great vehemence, things we thought we had forgiven and transcended; while in effect, we had only repressed them, possibly even due to a fear of *facing* them and dealing with them emotionally. That is why true forgiveness, true release, is so difficult.

> "The sign of sincere love is to forgive wrongs done to us. It was with such love that the Lord loved the world. We cannot with all our heart forgive someone who does us wrong unless we possess real knowledge. For this knowledge shows us that we deserve all we experience."

(St. Mark the Ascetic, *226 Texts*, 48-49, p. 129, Vol. 1, Philokalia)

In this point we can easily conclude that the aforementioned are valid in both directions. When we are liable for something, it's not enough to ask forgiveness (however difficult that is), but we should show, in a practical way, our repentance and our willingness to make amends for our error. It's not enough saying, "I asked forgiveness, now he can do whatever he likes...." We should *whole-heartedly* back up our apology with real and *practical* repentance.

These are simple and self-evident things which, in their application, are still far from us. That is why many people consider forgiveness an excuse for unaccountability.

True forgiveness, whether we ask it or offer it, is based on a deep understanding that leads us to the healing of wounds, as well as to allowing ourselves to be open and vulnerable again.

We must be very careful here because as long as our egoistic self is still active inside us, whatever constitutes it will remain "alive" as well; that is, all his memories, accounts, debts, all the negative elements by which it's fed.

That is why the releasing of debts, in whichever direction it aims, whether we forgive or ask forgiveness, is directed against this inner devil and eliminates his strength by depriving him of his food. Both of these *interconnected* practices lead the superficial false self to starvation.

Jesus Christ taught the art of forgiveness and in particular through His personal drama He elevated it to one of the basic conditions for our soul to be able to fly in the heavenly heights. On the cross, one of the thieves who symbolizes our lower nature asks forgiveness, *"Lord, remember me when thou comest into thy kingdom"* (Luke 23:40-42) and Christ, who symbolizes our higher nature, forgives, *"Forgive them; for they know not what they do"* (Luke 23:34).

Whatever we refuse to forgive and whatever we haven't asked forgiveness for, keeps us chained to the ground, and we sometimes drag them along for many years. On the other hand, what we forgive and ask forgiveness for, are removed from us, we are released from them, and they don't impede our soul's elevation. The lighter and freer our soul is, the higher she can fly. And our soul is lightened and released with Love and Forgiveness.

That is why Christ, only after he forgave, said, *"It is finished"* (John 19:30). Only in that way was His Spirit able to reconcile *"My God, my God, why hast thou forsaken me?"* (Matthew 27:46) with His Father's Spirit, *"Father, into thy hands I commend my spirit"* (Luke 23:46).

It is not possible to be in the Light, in the Kingdom of Heaven, while we retain in our hearts even the least bitterness towards any man. We can't pray in that condition, that is, we can't be in a communion of Love with Love. God includes everything in His greatness which He wants to bestow upon us, but in order to be able to receive this gift, we must spare the same space; we have to be *large-hearted*. If our heart remains narrow, or if she is tainted by enmities and grudges, she cannot accept the pure dazzling Light of God's Love. That is why it is demanded of us to be reconciled with our neighbor before we attempt to enter into the communion of Love with our prayer.

> *"Therefore if thou bring thy gift to the altar, and there rememberest that thy brother hath ought against thee; leave there thy gift before the altar, and go thy way; first be reconciled to thy brother, and then come and offer thy gift. Agree with thine adversary quickly, whiles thou art in the way with him; lest at any time the adversary deliver thee to the judge, and the judge deliver thee to the officer, and thou be cast into prison. Verily I say unto thee, Thou shalt by no means come out thence, till thou hast paid the uttermost farthing"* (Matthew 5:23-26).

Otherwise our desire to be with God can only be deficient and limited:

> *"If a man say, I love God, and hateth his brother, he is a liar: for he that loveth not his brother whom he hath seen, how can he love God whom he hath not seen? And this commandment have we from him, That he who loveth God love his brother also"* (1 John 4:20-21).

In that way we will progress so we can climb to the gradation of perfection from where we will be able to forgive our enemies, love them and pray for them.

"Our love of God finds expression in our love of men. And even when men hate us we should thank them for it, because they are then the tools of our correction."

(Starets Macarius of Optino, *Russian Letters of Direction*, Letter 105)

Prayer

> "No one can teach you the real and pure prayer except the Lord. Prayer hasn't any other teacher except God Himself, *"He that teacheth man knowledge"* (Psalms 94:10). Therefore follow that disciple's lead who asked with simplicity from Christ: "Lord, teach us to pray" (Luke 11:1)."
>
> (St. Dimitri of Rostov, *Spiritual Alphabet*, p. 87)

Prayer is the noblest virtue and the paramount practice of spiritual life. Prayer constitutes both the means and the end. It is an exercise and a state. So due to the fact that prayer is such a high form of art, it is not wise to rest only upon our strengths for its understanding, but it is prudent to seek advice from those who have studied it long before us.

> "Everything said by them on this subject comprises a science of prayer, which is the science of sciences. [...] I would also add that there is nothing more important than prayer."
>
> (St. Theophan the Recluse, *The Spiritual Life*, p. 72)

That is why we will resort to testimonies of men who have lived their whole lives in prayer and in effect through prayer, in order to grasp various aspects of it as a practice, but basically as a state. Let's begin with the importance of prayer:

"Prayer [from the heart] is the life of the spirit. Here the spirit dwells in God and unites with Him."

(St. Theophan the Recluse, *The Spiritual Life*, p. 72)

"Without prayer the soul is doomed to die from spiritual suffocation, like the body when it is deprived of oxygen."

(St. Dimitri of Rostov, *Spiritual Alphabet*, p. 84)

"Bread is food for the body and holiness is food for the soul; spiritual prayer is food for the intellect [nous]."

(Evagrios the Solitary, *On Prayer, 153 Texts*, 101, p. 67, Vol. 1, Philokalia)

But what is prayer?

"Prayer is essentially standing face to face with God."

(Metropolitan Anthony of Sourozh, *Living Prayer*, p. 57)

"The essence of prayer is the lifting of the mind and heart to God."

(St. Theophan the Recluse, *The Spiritual Life*, p. 195)

"To pray is to *stand before God*, to enter into an immediate and personal relationship with him; it is to know at every level of our being, from the instinctive to the intellectual, from the sub- to the supra-conscious, that we are in God and he is in us."

(Bishop Kallistos Ware, *The Power of the Name*, p. 1)

So in essence, prayer is a *live relationship*:

"It is very important to remember that prayer is an encounter and a relationship, a relationship which is deep, and this relationship cannot be forced either on us or on God. The fact that God can make Himself present or can leave us with the sense of His absence is part of this live relationship."

(Metropolitan Anthony of Sourozh, *School for Prayer*, p. 24)

"Prayer begins at the moment when, instead of thinking of a remote God, 'He,' 'The Almighty,' and so forth, one can think in terms of 'Thou.'"

(Metropolitan Anthony of Sourozh, *School for Prayer*, p. 111)

"I am quite certain that if someday 'O Thou my Joy!' or any other cry of this kind bursts out of you, it will be the moment when you will have discovered a relationship between Him and you which is your own, which is not a relationship that you share with many other people."

(Metropolitan Anthony of Sourozh, *School for Prayer*, p. 118)

But where does this meeting, this contact, happen? Where does this relationship take place?

"If we cannot find a contact with God under our own skin, as it were, in this very small world which I am in, then the chances are very slight that even if I meet Him face to face, I will recognize Him. St. John Chrysostom said 'Find the door of your heart, you will discover it is the door of the kingdom of God.' So it is inward that we must turn, and not outward – but inward in a very special way. I am not saying that we must become introspective. I don't mean that we must go inward in the way one does in psychoanalysis or psychology. It is not a journey into my *own* inwardness, it is a journey *through* my own self, in order to emerge from the deepest level of self into the place where He is, the point at which God and I meet."

(Metropolitan Anthony of Sourozh, *School for Prayer*, p. 49).

"To find God we must dig in search of this inner chamber, of this place where the whole kingdom of God is present at the very core of us, where God and we can meet. The best tool, the one which will go through all obstacles, is prayer. The problem is one of praying attentively, simply and truthfully."

(Metropolitan Anthony of Sourozh, *Living Prayer*, p. 108)

There are, however, certain conditions in order for this meeting to be feasible:

"Thousands of prayers come from men's tongues while their mind is wandering over vain, worthless or even filthy things. How can God listen and answer these people?"

(St. Paisius Velichkovsky, *Field Flowers*, p. 89)

"Never pray in haste. Pray with keen participation of the mind and heart in the meanings of prayer."

(St. Theophan the Recluse, *Selection of Letters*, p. 24)

"Prayer without attention is not prayer."

(St. Theophan the Recluse, *Guidance in the Spiritual Life*, p. 50)

"The rapt attention which keeps prayer completely free from distraction and from irrelevant thoughts and images is a gift of God's grace. We evince a sincere desire to receive the gift of grace – the soul-saving gift of attention – by forcing ourselves to pray with attention whenever we pray. Artificial attention, as we may call our own unaided attention unassisted by grace, consists in enclosing our mind in the words of the prayer, according to the advice of St. John of the Ladder. If the mind, on account of its newness to the work of prayer, gets out of its enclosure in the words, it must be led back into them again. The mind in its fallen state is naturally unstable and inclined to wander everywhere. But God can give it stability and will do so in His own time in return for perseverance and patience in the practice of prayer (Ladder 28:17)."

(St. Ignatius Brianchaninov, *The Arena: An Offering to Contemporary Monasticism*, p. 70)

So how do we acquire this attention or, rather, how will we be worthy of the God-given attention?

"(Brother Lawrence): One way to recollect the mind easily in the time of prayer, and preserve it more in tranquility, is to not let it wander too far at other times; you should keep it strictly in the presence of God; and being accustomed to think of him often, you will find it easy to keep your mind calm at the time of prayer, or at least to recall it from its wanderings."

(Metropolitan Anthony of Sourozh, *Living Prayer*, p. 61)

"You will recall that I wrote you previously about the necessity for strengthening oneself through the attention of the mind in the heart, and there incessantly rising up and calling to the Lord. [This is the same thing we are talking about now; that is, one must appeal to the Lord with prayer when passionate thoughts, feelings or desires arise.] One must appeal to the Lord, going down with the attention of the mind into the heart and calling out to Him from there. If we were to carry out the following little rule unfailingly, that is, after strengthening ourselves through the mind in the heart and then standing before the Lord with fear, reverence and faith, then not only would passionate desires and feelings never arise within us, but neither would idle thoughts. It is our misfortune, however, that we mentally fall away from the Lord out of the heart and wander with our thoughts into a far country. It is at this time that the passionate thoughts invade, and before you know it, the passionate feelings have already commenced, and likewise the desires have begun to stir. You are in for a struggle! And who is to blame? If you did not allow the thoughts to wander, there would be no battle."

(St. Theophan the Recluse, *The Spiritual Life*, p. 234)

We have been subjected to a distortion, and what was natural to us, has ended up being a result of intense struggle and effort.

"Prayer, on the other hand, invigorates and purifies the mind for the struggle, since it is naturally constituted for prayer."

(Evagrius of Pontus, *Praktikos*, Chapter 49, p. 106)

"Prayer is the energy which accords with the dignity of the intellect (nous); it is the intellect's true and highest activity."

(Evagrios the Solitary, *On Prayer, 153 Texts*, 84, p. 65, Vol. 1, Philokalia)

So in order to pray as we should, that is, to be related to God, there are certain further necessary conditions:

"Bear in mind that prayer alone, unaccompanied by moral improvement, is useless. St. Macarius of Egypt says of such prayer that it is unreal; that it is, as it were, a mask of the real prayer."

(Starets Macarius of Optino, *Russian Letters of Direction*, Letter 105)

"Prayer is not simply an effort which we can make the moment we intend to pray; prayer must be rooted in our life and if our life contradicts our prayers, or if our prayers have nothing to do with our life, they will never be alive nor real."

(Metropolitan Anthony of Sourozh, *Living Prayer*, p. 123)

"Prayer is an adventure which brings not a thrill but new responsibilities: as long as we are ignorant, nothing is asked of us, but as soon as we know anything, we are answerable for the use we make of that knowledge. It may be a gift, but we are responsible for any particle of truth we have acquired; as it becomes our own, we cannot leave it dormant but have to take it into account in our behavior, and in this sense we are to answer for any truth we have understood."

(Metropolitan Anthony of Sourozh, *Living Prayer*, pp. 11-12)

Prayer is a way of life, or demands a specific way of life so it can grow and bring fruits:

"If you long to pray, do nothing that is opposed to prayer, so that God may draw near and be with you."

(Evagrios the Solitary, *On Prayer, 153 Texts*, 66, p. 63, Vol. 1, Philokalia)

"If you desire to pray as you ought, do not grieve anyone; otherwise you 'run in vain.'"

(Evagrios the Solitary, *On Prayer, 153 Texts*, 20, p. 59, Vol. 1, Philokalia)

"Having prayed as you should, expect the demon to attack you; so stand on guard, ready to protect the fruits of your prayer. For from the start this has been your appointed task: to cultivate and to protect. Therefore, having cultivated, do not leave the fruits unprotected; otherwise you will gain nothing from your prayer."

(Evagrios the Solitary, *On Prayer, 153 Texts*, 49, p. 61, Vol. 1, Philokalia)

"If you endure something painful out of love for wisdom, you will find the fruit of this during prayer."

(Evagrios the Solitary, *On Prayer, 153 Texts*, 19, p. 59, Vol. 1, Philokalia)

"When your intellect (nous) in its great longing for God gradually withdraws from the flesh and turns away from all thoughts that have their source in your sense-perception, memory or soul-body temperament, and when it becomes full of reverence and joy, then you may conclude that you are close to the frontiers of prayer."

(Evagrios the Solitary, *On Prayer, 153 Texts*, 62, p. 62, Vol. 1, Philokalia)

"If you long for prayer, renounce all to gain all."

(Evagrios the Solitary, *On Prayer, 153 Texts*, 37, p. 60, Vol. 1, Philokalia)

If our praying grows roots in our way of life, then it will be really *alive*; which, in other words, means that it will take place in the *present*:

"This is the kind of thing we must learn about prayer, to establish ourselves in the present."

(Metropolitan Anthony of Sourozh, *School for Prayer*, p. 92)

"To contemplate means, first of all, to be present where one is – to be *here* and *now*. But usually we find ourselves unable to restrain our mind from wandering at random over time and space. We recall the past, we anticipate the future, we plan what to do next; people and places come before us in unending succession. We lack the power to gather ourselves into the one place where we should be – *here*, in the presence of God; we are unable to live fully in the only moment of time that truly exists – *now*, the immediate present."

(Bishop Kallistos Ware, *The Power of the Name*, p. 14)

"Learn to master time, and you will be able, whatever you do, whatever the stress, in the storm, in tragedy, or simply in the confusion in which we continuously live – to be still, immobile in the present, face to face with the Lord, in silence or in words."

(Metropolitan Anthony of Sourozh, *School for Prayer*, p. 103)

Yet the most essential condition and requirement for praying is for *We* ourselves to pray. This might seem self-evident, but it's not. What point can praying have if the one who prays inside us is our false, superficial and egoistic self which might even derive pride from this practice of the highest humility.

> "Whenever our prayer subtly conceals that sharp icicle, our pride, it acts as a poison and can only lead us further away from God."
>
> (Starets Macarius of Optino, *Russian Letters of Direction*, Letter 145)

What is the point of our praying when it doesn't come from our depths, from our Real Self; when *We* are not the ones who pray?

> "Not to speak of all the occasions when we should be aware that He cannot come to us because we are not there to receive Him."
>
> (Metropolitan Anthony of Sourozh, *School for Prayer*, p. 28)

> "There are other ways, too, in which God is 'absent.' As long as we ourselves are real, as long as we are truly ourselves, God can be present and can do something with us. But the moment we try to be what we are not, there is nothing left to say or have; we become a fictitious personality, an unreal presence, and this unreal presence cannot be approached by God."
>
> (Metropolitan Anthony of Sourozh, *School for Prayer*, p. 30)

"The basic one [condition] being that the person praying should be real. In social life we have a variety of facets to our personalities. The same person appears as one in one setting and quite different in another, authoritative in any situation in which he commands, quite submissive at home, and again quite different among friends. Every self is complex, but none of these false personalities or those which are partly false and partly true, are our real selves to such an extent as to be able to stand in our name in the presence of God. This weakens our prayer, it creates dividedness of mind, heart and will. As Polonius says in *Hamlet*: 'To thine own self be true, and it must follow as the night the day, Thou canst not then be false to any man.'

"To find the real self from among and beyond those various false persons, comes at a great cost and cannot be accomplished easily. We are so unaccustomed to being ourselves in any deep and true sense, that we find it almost impossible to know where to begin the search. We all know that there are moments when we are nearer to being our true selves; those moments should be singled out and carefully analyzed in order to make an approximate discovery of what we truly are."

(Metropolitan Anthony of Sourozh, *Living Prayer*, pp. 95-96)

"A person who has become real and true can stand before God and offer prayer with absolute attention, unity of intellect, heart and will, in a body that responds completely to the promptings of the soul. But until we have attained such perfection we can still stand in the presence of God, aware that we are partly real and partly unreal, and bring to him all that we can, but in repentance, confessing that we are still so unreal and so incapable of unity. At no moment of our life, whether we are still completely divided or in process of unification, are we deprived of the possibility of standing before God. But instead of standing in the complete unity that gives drive and power to our prayer, we can stand in our weakness, recognizing it and ready to bear its consequences."

(Metropolitan Anthony of Sourozh, *Living Prayer*, p. 101)

"The more we clean, the more things disappear, and it seems to us that we have created a mess where there was at least a certain amount of beauty; perhaps not much, but some beauty. And then we begin to discover the real beauty which the great master has put into his painting; we see the misery, then the mess in between, but at the same time we have a preview of the authentic beauty. And we discover that what we are is a poor person who needs God; but not God to fill the gap – God to be met. So let us set out to do this and let us also every evening of this week, pray a very simple prayer: 'Help me, O God, to put off all pretences and to find my true self.'"

(Metropolitan Anthony of Sourozh, *Living Prayer*, p. 115)

"How can you expect to be heard by God, when you do not hear yourself? How do you expect God to remember you when you pray, if you do not remember yourself?"

(*The Art of Prayer – An Orthodox Anthology*, p. 48)

For prayer to be *real* prayer and not intellectual chattering or emotional fantasies, there is a demand for a certain deepening and a special subtleness. In order for prayer to be alive, the participation of our whole Being is necessary.

The texts of the Fathers refer to the mental (noetic) prayer and the prayer of the heart. We should be careful, though, not to misinterpret the term "mental (noetic) prayer" with some kind of sterile intellectual approach, because it constitutes, in effect, another term for the concept of "spiritual prayer." The same is true for the term "prayer of the heart" which doesn't refer to some kind of sentimentalism, but to our deep and heartfelt participation in prayer.

In a few words, real prayer emerges from the depths of our whole Being, when the mind and the heart have become One according to their deeper spiritual sense.

"This mental (noetic) prayer is a light enlightening the soul of man and inflaming his heart with the fire of love for God. It is a chain uniting God to man, and man to God."

(*On the Necessity of Constant Prayer for all Christians in General*, From The Life of St. Gregory Palamas, by St. Nikodemos of the Holy Mountain)

"There is no gap between the time we make our prayer and when it is heard; the only necessity is that it come from our heart. It is our telegraphic line to Heaven. The very same prayers, which are not from our heart, but which come only from our head and tongue, do not produce a ray which rises to heaven, and they are not audible there. Those are not even prayers, but only prayer-like modes."

(St. Theophan the Recluse, *The Spiritual Life*, p. 71)

"When you pray with feeling, where is your attention if not in the heart? Acquire feeling, and you will acquire attention as well. The head is a crowded rag market: it is not possible to pray to God there."

(*The Art of Prayer – An Orthodox Anthology*, p. 184)

Even though prayer demands intense struggle and hard work in order to be feasible, at the same time it constitutes a weapon to this effort! Without prayer, no victory is possible in this inner unseen warfare.

"Prayer acts murderously on our old man, the unregenerate self or nature. As long as it is alive in us, it opposes prayer like death."

(St. Ignatius Brianchaninov, *The Arena: An Offering to Contemporary Monasticism*, p. 71)

"The purpose of prayer can be summarized in the phrase, 'Become what you are.' Become, consciously and actively, what you already are potentially and secretly, by virtue of your creation according to the divine image and your re-creation at Baptism. Become what you are: more exactly, return to yourself; discover him who is yours already, listen to him who never ceases to speak within you; possess him who even now possesses you."

(Bishop Kallistos Ware, *The Power of the Name*, p. 3)

But prayer, as with every exact science, also has its dangers, as well as its deviations which are related to its aim and purpose.

"Spiritual prayer is not done with psycho technique (psychological) methods. It is the noetic (mental) presence of the soul in front of the Lord and her surrender to His hands with faith, hope and childish simplicity. This is the way we should pray. And if we pray like this, we must be satisfied with the experiences which God sends. We should not seek anything else. The spiritual work is not to be found in ecstasies. Its best expression as "a broken spirit; a broken and a contrite heart." (Psalms 51:17)

(St. Theophan the Recluse, *Guidance in the Spiritual Life*, p. 66)

"But let us be careful not to seek mystical experience when we should be seeking repentance and conversion. That is the beginning of our cry to God. 'Lord make me what I should be, change me whatever the cost.' And when we have said these dangerous words, we should be prepared for God to hear them. And these words of God are dangerous because God's love is remorseless. God wants our salvation with the determination due to its importance. And God, as the Shepherd of Hermas says, 'does not leave us till he has broken our heart and bones.' "

(Anthony Bloom, *Courage to Pray*, p. 17)

"In our struggle for prayer the emotions are almost irrelevant; what we must bring to God is a complete, firm determination to be faithful to him and strive that God should live in us. We must remember that the fruits of prayer are not this or that emotional state, but a deep change in the whole of our personality. What we aim at is to be made able to stand before God and to concentrate on His presence."

(Metropolitan Anthony of Sourozh, *Living Prayer*, p. 62)

"The day when God is absent, when he is silent – that is the beginning of prayer. Not when we have a lot to say, but when we say to God 'I can't live without you.' "

(Metropolitan Anthony of Sourozh, *School for Prayer*, p. 19)

"The true God is the only object of our seeking, the only partner in authentic prayer."

(Anthony Bloom, *Courage to Pray*, p. 22)

Prayer means, of course, guidance as well. Prayer teaches, feeds and helps us grow, because the main responsibility for it is God Himself and not us, even though the opposite appears to happen:

"True inner prayer is to stop talking and to listen to the wordless voice of God within our heart; it is to cease doing things on our own, and to enter into the action of God."

(Bishop Kallistos Ware, *The Power of the Name*, p. 2)

Also the relationship with God which is growing in prayer, is subtle and specific:

"When you are praying, do not shape within yourself any image of the Deity, and do not let your intellect (nous) be stamped with the impress of any form; but approach the Immaterial in an immaterial manner, and then you will understand."

(Evagrios the Solitary, *On Prayer*, *153 Texts*, 67, p. 63, Vol. 1, Philokalia)

"Never try to see a form or shape during prayer. Do not long to have a sensory image of angels or powers or Christ, for this would be madness: it would be to take a wolf as your shepherd and to worship your enemies, the demons. Self-esteem is the start of illusions in the intellect (nous). Under its impulse, the intellect attempts to enclose the Deity in shapes and forms. I shall say again what I have said elsewhere: blessed is the intellect (nous) that is completely free from forms during prayer."

(Evagrios the Solitary, *On Prayer, 153 Texts*, 114-117, p. 68, Vol. 1, Philokalia)

So praying consists of a relationship of Love. And as in all relationships of love it should have duration. In relation to our family, friends and companions, we don't claim that today I love you while tomorrow I don't. We could say that we are in a constant relationship of Love with them despite whether we are close to them or if we are "separated" by circumstances.

In that way we can understand the concept of unceasing prayer. Unceasing prayer is a real and stable relationship of Love with Love, with God. If we can be constantly united internally, through our relations of love with our close ones whom we "meet" initially outside us, how much more reasonable it is to be constantly united internally through a relation of Love with God, whom we meet basically inside us!

Unceasing prayer is not something bizarre, utopian or unachievable, or even hard-accomplished for the simple man, but is a natural consequence of our relationship with God.

"To pray unceasingly – what does this mean?

It means to be in a constant state of prayer with the mind in the heart; that is, to be steadily united with God both in thinking and feeling."

(St. Theophan the Recluse, *Guidance in the Spiritual Life*, p. 46)

"St. Basil the Great solved the question of how the Apostles could pray without ceasing, in this way: in everything they did, he replied, they thought of God and lived in constant devotion to Him. This spiritual state was their unceasing prayer."

(*The Art of Prayer – An Orthodox Anthology*, p. 83)

"This total commitment to God, when it is stabilized within you, will be obvious in each act and will direct the whole of your life. Due perhaps to various cares and works, your thoughts may be carried away from the Lord from time to time, but will gradually get used to doing everything without losing His remembrance.

"So take diligent care to turn your mind and heart towards God, and keep these two close to Him. Then you will be in a state of prayer even without words of prayer."

(St. Theophan the Recluse, *Guidance in the Spiritual Life*, p. 47)

Unceasing prayer works again both as a means and as an end in itself.

"He who does not train himself to frequent prayer will never receive unceasing prayer. Unceasing prayer is a gift of God."

(St. Ignatius Brianchaninov, *he Arena: An Offering to Contemporary Monasticism*, p. 83)

"Experimental physics proves that all objects are heated by friction. The same happens with the soul: she is heated by the constant "friction" of prayer. And when the soul is heated, the thoughts become calm and prayer becomes pure. Still, everything comes from the grace of God. God's grace will eventually grant us the real prayer. That is why we should pray... in order to receive prayer!"

(St. Theophan the Recluse, *Guidance in the Spiritual Life*, p. 53)

"Do not wait for a specific time to pray and do not ask a special place for this, because God isn't to be found in any specific time or place. You can discover Him in your own intellect [nous] as well as in every spot of His domination."

(St. Paisius Velichkovsky, *Field Flowers*, p. 79)

"Let no one think, my Christian Brethren, that only persons in holy orders, or monks, are obliged to pray unceasingly and at all times, and not laymen. No, no! It is the duty of all us Christians to remain always in prayer."

(*On the Necessity of Constant Prayer for all Christians in General*, From The Life of St. Gregory Palamas, by St. Nikodemos of the Holy Mountain)

Prayer has stages and gradations. The deeper we go into it, the deeper we are related to God and so the more we discover its essence and value.

"To beginners the law of prayer is burdensome, like a despotic master; but to the more advanced it is like an erotic force, impelling those smitten by it as a hungry man is impelled towards a rich banquet."

(Evagrios the Solitary, *On Prayer, 153 Texts*, 153, p. 71, Vol. 1, Philokalia)

"As soon as the mind begins dwelling continually with God during prayer, it does not want to leave Him afterward, for this is attended by such sweetness that once it has been tasted, it does not want to taste anything else."

(St. Theophan the Recluse, *The Spiritual Life*, p. 197)

"If when praying no other joy can attract you,
then truly you have found prayer.."

(Evagrios the Solitary, *On Prayer, 153 Texts*, 153, p. 71, Vol. 1, Philokalia)

So we can now perceive that prayer is our participation in a communion of Love. After we are restored, in an initial sense at least, and have staged our relationship with God through and in prayer, we will then discover the necessity of including all people in this communion of Love.

"It is right to pray not only for your own purification,
but also for that of all your fellow men, and so to imitate the angels."

(Evagrios the Solitary, *On Prayer*, *153 Texts*, 40, p. 60, Vol. 1, Philokalia)

This communion of Love is universal; it's neither partial nor exclusive. God's Love includes all and everything, since *"He maketh his sun to rise on the evil and on the good, and sendeth rain on the just and on the unjust"* (Matthew 5:43-45).

Now we can understand the requirement of praying for our enemies. If we want to enter in this communion of Love, we cannot enter with half a heart in the sense that one half of our heart loves while the other half hates... we have to enter whole-heartedly and that means with a wholeness of Love.

When we pray for our enemies we invite them into a communion of Love, and through the therapeutic warmth of Love, the ice of enmity begins melting. Only in that way is it possible to experience the therapeutic action of forgiveness which can heal every wound.

One of the basic conditions of praying is forgiveness. Why? Because prayer is a relationship of Love which includes both God and our neighbor, as well as everything that exists in Creation around us.

If we are in adversity with our neighbor, we are obviously out of the state of Love. So our only possible *prayer* at that time, the only possible *relation* of Love is, *"Forgive us our debts, as we forgive our debtors"* (Matthew 6:12), which means, "Forgive me, my God, for my enmity towards my neighbor, and give me the strength to forgive him."

If this approach to Love is sincere, the necessary forgiveness will come and this will make the continuance of prayer possible, that is, the further contact with God.

We usually don't know that prayer is something that needs to be studied; that we should be taught how to pray. But praying is a real Divine science which needs as much labor and study as any known human science, in order to be educated in it.

Nevertheless, as with every other art, our true love for it, as well as the practice itself, will teach us what we cannot be taught theoretically by anyone until we ourselves experience these teachings.

"From experience in the spiritual life, it can fairly be concluded that he who has zeal to pray needs no teaching how to perfect himself in prayer. Patiently continued, the effort of prayer itself will lead us to prayer's very summit."

(*The Art of Prayer – An Orthodox Anthology*, p. 90)

Concluding, we could also examine shortly what we should ask in our prayers since there is a constant interaction in praying, as in any other relationship. What we can offer to God, to Love, is relatively easy to understand; what else beyond love, thanksgiving and praise? What we should ask, for some reason, confuses us...

"In your prayer seek only righteousness and the kingdom of God, that is, virtue and spiritual knowledge; and everything else 'will be given to you.' "

(Evagrios the Solitary, *On Prayer, 153 Texts*, 39, p. 60, Vol. 1, Philokalia)

One of the main benefits of praying is that we allow God to teach us and we give ourselves a chance of listening to God inside us. In order to listen to Him however, we must learn the art of silence. We must learn to be silent internally so we can *hear*. We are afraid of silence, simply because we don't trust God enough; we don't feel Him enough inside of us so we try to fill His "absence" with our words.

"Real silence is something extremely intense,
it has density and it is really alive."

(Metropolitan Anthony of Sourozh, *School for Prayer*, p. 103)

When we deepen in this inner silence which offers us the opportunity of hearing God within us, we find out that *in essence we are not the ones who pray,* but *God is praying in us* and *He is teaching us, through prayer, His Will.*

"*Prayer is God* – it is not something that I initiate but something in which I share; it is not primarily something that *I* do but something that *God* is doing in me."

(Bishop Kallistos Ware, *The Power of the Name*, p. 2)

Yet, for this interaction, this relationship, to happen, our desire must spring from a true *need*. Only then prayer is *flowing* inside us.

And our need should be a need for the Love and the Light of God. We don't realize that the *request of every prayer* should eventually be *God Himself* and that *the solution to every problem* is God, Love.

What else could we ask in our lives except Love?

Therefore if we are in a state of Prayer (and consequently of Love) everything is all right and we don't need to fear anyone or anything.

So the essence of praying could be summed up in the following: Thanksgiving to Love for Her unlimited and everlasting Love; forgiveness from Love for our rich egoism and our poor love; guidance from Love so we can walk with Her help, towards Her, for Her sake.

So prayer is a *relation* of Gratitude, Forgiveness and Guidance which aims *essentially* at a Union with Love.

"Prayer gives thanks for blessings received and asks for failures to be forgiven and for power to strengthen us for the future; for without God's help the soul can indeed do nothing. None the less, to persuade the will to have the strongest possible desire for union with and enjoyment of Him, for whom it longs, and to direct itself totally towards Him, is the major part of the achievement of our aim."

(St. Theodoros the Great Ascetic, *Theoretikon*, p. 46, Vol. 2, Philokalia)

The Inner Restoration of Christianity

The Will of God

"Do not pray for the fulfillment of your wishes, for they may not accord with the will of God. But pray as you have been taught, saying: 'Thy will be done in me' (Luke 22:42). Always entreat Him in this way – that His will be done. For He desires what is good and profitable for you, whereas you do not always ask for this.

"Often when I have prayed I have asked for what I thought was good, and persisted in my petition, stupidly importuning the will of God, and not leaving it to Him to arrange things as He knows is best for me. But when I have obtained what I asked for, I have been very sorry that I did not ask for the will of God to be done; because the thing turned out not to be as I had thought."

(Evagrios the Solitary, *On Prayer, 153 Texts*, 31-32, p. 60, Vol. 1, Philokalia)

God's Will for us is Love.

Biological parents want the best for their children according to their love for them; correspondingly the Source of Love, Love Herself, wants exactly the same for Her children (Matthew 7:7-11).

But what is our attitude towards Her? It is similar to the one we have for our physical parents. Even though they often sacrifice for our well-being, we question them; and indeed they are not all-knowing and they are not aware of our supreme good, yet we don't only question their indications, but also their intentions, as well as their love. In the same and often worse way, we question God and

His Love. And that's how we are refusing His Will, either knowingly or not, preferring to follow our will; besides, who other than us knows what is best for us? The only one we can really trust is our own self. But is this true?

In this point we need to remember our distinction between our two main selves, the old man and the new which is emerging; our false and Real Self.

"We should indeed be cut in two by a wise decision of our own free will; we should be our own worst enemy."

(St. Hesychios the Priest, *On Watchfulness and Holiness*, Section 164, p. 191, Vol. 1, Philokalia)

The truth is that we have two wills (or more...); one is egoistic, limited, unstable and short-sighted, and the other one is the will of our Real Self which is broader, selfless, loving, deeper and sincere, and is *identical* in essence with the Will of God.

And this is because the will of our Real Self is *one and only*; it is, *"Thy will be done"* (Matthew 6:10). The will of our essence, of our Truth, is the *same* with the Will of God which we get to know deep in our hearts and consists of our natural desire, since we know deep within that its origin is Love. And even more, we recognize that it constitutes a part of ourselves, it is *Us*. While the will of our outer self is foreign to us and is nearly always, in effect, opposed to us and to all Creation, since being limited and selfish cannot help but produce some kind of disharmony.

The Will of God instead brings about harmony; it *is* Harmony. Even if it often includes a sense of difficulty, sacrifice, pain or transcendence, its ultimate aim is always Harmony. It might *seemingly* produce destruction, agony or hardship, but in reality these are only surgical tools in the hands of God. The Will of God is the ultimate perfection which can be found in every moment. It constitutes our noblest possibility and the most beautiful reality.

Our physical parents want our best possible in our physical settling down, and they often struggle all their lives in order to offer it to us *according to their strength*; the Creator of our whole being wants our best physical, psychological and spiritual setting up, and offers it to us *according to our strength*.

He offers us as much wonder as we can hold. Or we could say that he gives us as much wonder as we *really* want. And he gives us only as much marvel as we *whole-heartedly* want; otherwise we wouldn't appreciate it, and would reject it, and would then have to face the detrimental consequences.

So God's Will is to prepare and lead us deeper into the experience of Love. What else could a biological mother possibly offer to her children, other than deep love? So what else could Mother-Love, Creator-Love, offer to Her children-creations, other than Love?

Still, we usually spend a whole lifetime before we are able to perceive this simple, obvious and self-evident truth, though we have tasted it all of our lives!

Many times we think that the Will of God will consist of some kind of deprivation, some hardship and in the best case we say: "Ok, I will endure this as well." We cannot grasp that God's Will for us is just Paradise, and nothing else.

Now, if, in order to enter into our paradise, we need to go through our personal "hell," the price is small to pay. And this happens only when it's necessary; when there is simply no other way, either because we are not clean and will taint our paradise, or because we won't appreciate it, thus losing it. God doesn't let us be "sifted as wheat" (Luke 22:31) due to some whim.

In order for a surgeon to carry out a life-saving operation, he is forced to create a chaos: blood, tension, upheaval. But this is the view of the outer, untrained eyes, because he acts with full awareness and accuracy, estimating his every motion and anticipating a specific result.

In this way, the Doctor of the souls may be forced to create any kind of chaos in order to proceed to a soul-saving operation. And again, the untrained eyes often question the abilities of the Doctor, or even His existence!

Yet, He knows the soul's need and benefit, and in His eyes the *seeming* chaos is just a necessary, unpleasant perhaps, consequence of the *real* chaos that the soul He is trying to heal has created. As in a surgical operation, the real problem is not the upheaval that will be produced at the operation; it is the disease which needs to be cured.

We are facing the following paradox: Because of our egoism we end up with *less* than what we are really entitled to or worthy of. Through our constant preoccupation with ourselves, we are anxious, blinded, impatient and competitive, so we don't have the clarity to perceive what really fits us and is destined for us.

We struggle for things which just shine to us and we mistake them for gold. This happens because we are not prudent, peaceful or relaxed enough to be able to examine all the data concerning each case. We don't have the patience to be sure that what is shining is really gold and so we rush, we cannot wait, we are afraid of losing what shined to us, so we attach ourselves to it and no longer hear or see anything else. And usually, if not always, what is shining is not *our gold*, not what we are entitled to and worthy of. All this is due to the fact that we don't turn to Him, saying, "Thy Will be done." And as a matter of fact, we are worrying in vain, because what is destined for us cannot be so easily lost since it's in God's care.

They say, "Be careful what you wish for, because it might come true."

It's true that we can't know the energetic potential and the consequences of our desires. We can't know what their actualization might bring. We want, for example, to acquire more money, to make a career, to fall in love, to have a family, even to make spiritual progress and obtain spiritual gifts. Yet, the truth is that we don't really know what all this entails, and whether we are in the position to handle it. We don't know if it will truly benefit us, and neither do we know the right moment that anything should be given. The only thing we know is our desire, irrespective of whether it is right or wrong, timely or untimely, beneficial or harmful.

And here we are referring personally to ourselves, because God's Will is not something generalized and abstract. It is very specific and personal, related to every detail of our lives, as well as its totality. It might be expressed generally through the commandments of His Divine Word, but it is expressed also completely particularized through the voice of our Conscience which is God's Voice inside us.

"The voice of conscience is the voice of God."

(St. Dimitri of Rostov, *Spiritual Alphabet*, p. 21)

So His Will always has a specific direction, a specific purpose which constitutes the *Supreme Good,* both for us and everything else around us.

> "When God, using our conscience, calls us to righteousness and yet our self-will opposes Him, He respects our freedom and lets our own will be done; but then, alas, our minds grow dull, our will slack, and we commit iniquities without number."

(Starets Macarius of Optino, *Russian Letters of Direction*, Letter 51)

God's Will is related to everything.

It's not related only to our actions, "I must do what God wills to do." It's related also to our thoughts, emotions, ideas, words, movements, glance, humor, everything. So it's not unreasonable or extravagant to be willing to "Think what God wants me to think," "Feel what God wants me to feel" and "Act according to God's Will in relation to every little detail."

The Will of God, however, cannot be limited in some predetermined behaviors: "I will be like this" and "From now on I will behave like that." In that way there cannot be any room for the actualization of God's Will which might be *multi-dimensional*.

God's Will is *alive* and *flowing*; it is responding in every case in the most appropriate way. *It doesn't mean assuming a rigid attitude* which limits everything – the greatness of life – in order to confine it to its narrow space. The Will of God includes the whole range of life and is related to her in the best possible and most ample way.

Yet, we remain cut off from this possible Divine Harmony, entrapped in our limited self, and thus in our will. We keep saying: "At this point I want to do this…," "Nowadays I like that… or I am interested in the other…" and so forth. We believe we have the right to do whatever we want, as long as – according to our thinking and imagination – we don't hurt anyone. But we cannot grasp the extent of our interaction with people around us and the whole of Creation as well. In our limited view, the concept of not "hurting anyone" consists usually in not committing a crime in some obvious and heinous way. But the concept of harmony and disharmony, and the idea of a Divine Plan, as well as our participation in it, are pretty far from us, since our eyes can't see any farther than ourselves.

We have great difficulty in realizing that whatever we might do at the expense of ourselves will have immediate consequences in everything around us, either because we will infect our environment with our negativity, or because we will be inadequate and incapable of responding to the needs, both of other people, and of life itself.

For example, if one day we are "just" in a bad mood or "down" psychologically, we say naively, "What's the problem? Am I bothering anyone?" And so we constantly claim our right to negativity without realizing in the least what the consequences of our mood might be for our environment, since it consists of an actual energetic emanation.

In one way or another, our attitude and our life might hinder the smooth outcome of the Divine Plan which takes thought for all and everything, and which we not only ignore, but also refute Its existence. We might even laugh at the idea of such a Plan.

This is our egocentric attitude which creates, as much as we don't want to admit it, a profound disharmony in direct contrast with the God-centric attitude and view which creates an exceptional harmony. And that is why we are given the prayer, *"Thy kingdom come, Thy will be done in earth, as it is in heaven"* (Matthew 6:10).

When we conceive, even a little bit, this broader Divine view which aims at the Highest Harmony and the Perfection of Love, we cannot help but desire to sacrifice this egocentric, narrow view and therefore will in order to do everything for God.

In this point we could acquire a criterion to discern whether we act egocentrically or God-centrically. This criterion can be formed in relation to whether we do something for our sake or for the sake of God. So let's ask ourselves for whom do we do this or the other? Why am I saying this? Why do I want that?

Whether right or wrong, if we try doing what we do for *God's sake*, we will learn to distinguish what He wants and what he doesn't want. We will begin to know deep inside us what God's Will is in every case. But to reach that state, we must gradually long to do everything for Him and not for ourselves.

> Keep yourself scrupulously. Since you are always in the presence of God, do nothing besides his purpose, but if you wish to do something, whether to work at or to say the least thing, or to visit or meet someone, or to go to sleep or do any other business whatever, first test whether this is a rational and needful business or the will of God."

(Abba Ammonas, *Useful Servanthood*, p. 164)

God's will entails the right thinking, word, gesture, in every situation. And the term "right" is being used here in the sense of harmonic, tuned and necessary, not in the sense of a sterile "priggishness" which lays rigid and outer "moral" regulations that eventually imprison us in standardized and fake behaviors.

But how will we be able to really *feel* God's Will within us without approaching it mainly through intellectual searching, so our actions won't originate only from our intellect, but mostly from our heart, or even better, from our whole Being?

"Open your heart, perceive the will of God.
From Him seek help, in Him seek consolation."

(Starets Macarius of Optino, *Russian Letters of Direction*, Letter 64)

In order to reach this open, pure and receptive inner state, struggle and effort in discernment are needed (to receive the God-given discernment) which is turned, of course, against our false self and as a result to our egocentric will.

"The struggle for subordinating one's will and character is not easy. Without it however, we cannot be saved, even if we struggle hard in the rest; because our will and character are erected like a brass wall between us and God. As long as we are enslaved to our character and will, we cannot approach Him."

(St. Paisius Velichkovsky, *Field Flowers*, p. 123)

As long as we remain attached to our desires, ideas and "truths," and as long as our heart is full of egocentric fantasies, it's impossible to hear God's Voice inside us, and we cannot know His Will. Only our Real Self, our Divine *spiritual* self, can hear God's voice, and therefore know God's Will.

"The will of God is a divine mystery. *No one knows the thoughts of God*, says the Apostle, *except the Spirit of God* (1 Corinthians 2:11). Consequently, men can obtain knowledge of the will of God only through divine revelation. *Teach me to do Thy will*, prayed inspired David, *for Thou art my God. Thy good Spirit will guide me to the right land* (Psalm 142:10)."

(St. Ignatius Brianchaninov, *The Arena: An Offering to Contemporary Monasticism*, p. 54)

Only the spirit inside us can be taught by the Spirit outside us, which again we meet within us. So until we grow in spiritual life, until our heart is clean, we must continue struggling against the inner and outer enemies which want their will to be done. We'll have to be flexible, seeking in various ways what God's Will might be in every moment, and aiming essentially at learning to recognize it inside us.

"What should we do, however, when we face a complicated problem for which we cannot derive a direct and clear solution from the commandments of God?

"Sometimes we can solve it using our own experience. Other times we can benefit by the experience of others. Sometimes pious people with discernment will give us the solution. In other cases we will reach to the solution by ourselves through appropriate reasoning, combining various known commandments. And other times God will let us know secretly what to do, after we pray with fervor to Him. This last way would be the best, if our heart, released from the passions, could hear God's voice clearly."

(St. Theophan the Recluse, *Guidance in the Spiritual Life*, p. 100)

Before we learn to hear what God wants from within, perhaps we can start in the opposite way, learning to perceive what God *doesn't* want. This might be more easily perceived, because it's usually accompanied by some visible or covered, but *intense* reaction of our egocentric self when it feels that its desire *won't* be satisfied. So by the egocentric self informing us what *its* will is, it often informs us without knowing it, what God's Will is!

There are many cases, of course, where after we have silenced the voice of our false self, we just don't know what is best, what exactly we should do or not do. Again, in relation to what we *shouldn't* do, things are usually easier. God shows us what He doesn't want us to do by the appearance of a very subtle form of resistance. There emerges in us an imperceptible resistance, known only to us. And then we are given some time to not follow a certain direction in relation to which there is a gentle "no," "don't." Sometimes, of course, the resistance is very strong and the "no" is almost violent, like a slap in the face… when we risk falling off the cliff, for instance.

If, however, we learn to be more *relaxed*; if we don't try to press and control things, and impose our own desire, then we will be able to surrender more to God's guidance. And we can be certain that the facts themselves, as fruits of our choices, will begin informing us whether we walk by His Will or not.

If, sooner or later, our energies (actions) create disharmony, we should learn something from this. If they truly bring good fruits, *"For a good tree bringeth not forth corrupt fruit; neither doth a corrupt tree bring forth good fruit. For every tree is known by his own fruit"* (Luke 6:43-44), then we will begin perceiving around us (and in us) an essential and deep harmony. It's certain that if we begin hearing and participating in God's Will, we will discover a completely different quality of life (Acts 21:14).

In the beginning perhaps, we might even fear the idea that someone else will determine what we will do, even if this one may be God Himself. We really worry; He might make us do things we resent or He might want something extremely difficult, unpleasant or dangerous! We might say, "Thy Will be done" but we don't feel it whole-heartedly, and we might even be terrified by this thought.

That is why our desire for the Will of God should derive from a real and practical experience. We should begin gradually *trusting God* again! We should regain the trust we lost because of our going away from Him. And after we regain some part of it, we must struggle to retain it, because our false self, at the expense of who we built our trust upon, will try to knock it down in order to regain his control inside us.

> "You should continually and unceasingly call to mind all the blessings which God in His love has bestowed upon you in the past, and still bestows for the salvation of your soul. You must not let forgetfulness or evil or laziness make you grow unmindful of these many and great blessings, and so pass the rest of your life uselessly and ungratefully."
>
> (St. Mark the Ascetic, *Letter to Nicolas the Solitary*, p. 148, Vol. 1, Philokalia)

It's true that we tend to constantly forget, and with every small difficulty we question Love's Providence and sacrifice the living *taste* of the perfection of God's Will, as we fall back into anxiety, insecurity and hopelessness. This is the time, however, that we should force ourselves to remember, "To come to himself" (Luke 15:17), and in that way our inner reality will be transformed and a different relationship will be born, both with our false self and God's Providence.

> "If a man always thinks in this way and does not forget God's blessings, he encourages and urges himself on to the practice of every virtue and of every righteous work, always ready, always eager to do the will of God."
>
> (St. Mark the Ascetic, *Letter to Nicolas the Solitary*, p. 149, Vol. 1, Philokalia)

After we suffer enough from our will and desires, and after we taste the perfection of God's Will, we might be genuinely indignant enough with ourselves to declare within us: "That's enough! At some moment I have to be certain that You Are the utmost regulator of my life. Ok, I might keep asking or demanding like a spoiled child for my egoistic desires to be satisfied, but that's the limit! I must, at last, learn to respect You, hear You and trust You!"

And then praying will emerge naturally from inside us: "My God, free me from the 'freedom' of choices and grant me the freedom *from* choices... leave me only one choice... Your Will; since Your Will is the *same* with the Will of my Essence!"

There is a constant *miracle* surrounding us. To perceive it, an equivalent, subtle attention on our part is needed. If we tune into this ceaseless subtle miracle, everything is fine, everything is *alright* because we are tuned into God's Will. And when we are tuned into the Will of God, gratitude, joy and Love are begetting inside us. There is Harmony.

So let's say whole-heartedly and *without any fear*, "Thy Will be done," and let our fear be only this one thing: to not perceive, and then to repudiate His Will, thus hindering the coming of His Kingdom and the fulfillment of Good in both our life and the lives of our neighbors, as well as in the entirety of Life.

The Inner Restoration of Christianity

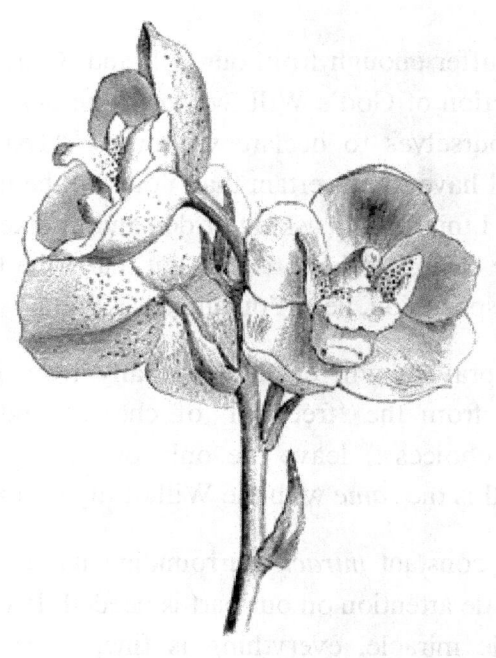

The Bitter Cup

"O my Father, if it be possible, let this cup pass from me: nevertheless not as I will, but as Thou wilt" (Matt. 26:39).

There is a certain stage in our spiritual ascent or deepening that could be illustrated with the term "bitter cup" which symbolizes a kind of threshold. After we climb some steps, we meet this point of transcendence which introduces us to a new reality. We could say that the trials we face are the steps in our spiritual ascent while the bitter cups are the thresholds.

This procedure, as well as its meaning, is presented in Jesus Christ's story when He faces the last threshold He needs to pass through in order to resume His mission. This threshold is His Passion and Crucifixion.

"Then cometh Jesus with them unto a place called Gethsemane, and saith unto the disciples, Sit ye here, while I go and pray yonder. And he took with him Peter and the two sons of Zebedee, and began to be sorrowful and very heavy. Then saith he unto them, My soul is exceeding sorrowful, even unto death: tarry ye here, and watch with me. And he went a little further, and fell on his face, and prayed, saying, O my Father, if it be possible, let this cup pass from me: nevertheless not as I will, but as thou wilt. And he cometh unto the disciples, and findeth them asleep, and saith unto Peter, What, could ye not watch with me one hour? Watch and pray, that ye enter not into temptation: the spirit indeed is willing, but the flesh is weak. He went away again the

second time, and prayed, saying, O my Father, if this cup may not pass away from me, except I drink it, thy will be done. And he came and found them asleep again: for their eyes were heavy. And he left them, and went away again, and prayed the third time, saying the same words" (Matthew 26:36-44).

We tend to picture Christ as an ideal "superman" but in that way we distort the meaning of His mission and exclude Him, knowingly or not, from our life's reality. We have difficulty in thinking Christ showing weakness, but the illustrations of the Gospel are very vivid.

"And he was withdrawn from them about a stone's cast, and kneeled down, and prayed, saying, Father, if thou be willing, remove this cup from me: nevertheless not my will, but thine, be done. And there appeared an angel unto him from heaven, strengthening him. And being in an agony he prayed more earnestly: and his sweat was as it were great drops of blood falling down to the ground" (Luke 22:41-44).

What is the use of Christ as a Teacher, Guide and Doctor, if He didn't taste and wasn't troubled by the disease of egoism? In Him this disease might have manifested in some "higher" form, without ever reaching the despicable bog which we feel in our souls, but He certainly experienced it when He lost courage in front of His entrusted work of salvation. He certainly thought of himself, and this is revealed from the known illustration in which He disapproves of Peter, telling him that he is an offense (temptation) unto Him.

> *"From that time forth began Jesus to show unto his disciples, how that he must go unto Jerusalem, and suffer many things of the elders and chief priests and scribes, and be killed, and be raised again the third day. Then Peter took him, and began to rebuke him, saying, Be it far from thee, Lord: this shall not be unto thee. But he turned, and said unto Peter, Get thee behind me, Satan: thou art an offense unto me: for thou savourest not the things that be of God, but those that be of men"* (Matthew 16:21-23).

If Jesus Christ hadn't already thought of this self-interested way out, He wouldn't have seen Peter's words as an offense (scandal); He wouldn't be scandalized by him. If He thought of Peter's words as absurd and unsubstantial, He would have disapproved of Peter for his little faith and wouldn't have accused him of tempting Him.

These illustrations are not random; they aim to teach us something. Even though Jesus Christ appears to be ready with the courage to carry out His self-sacrifice, *"And he began to teach them, that the Son of man must suffer many things [...] And he spake that saying openly [with boldness, The English Majority Text Version]"* (Mark 8:31-32), without thinking of himself, trusting in His Father's Will; at the same time his own personal limited will is hidden inside him, which is why he was scandalized by Peter, and considers him as a temptation.

> "Every affliction tests our will, showing whether it is inclined to good or evil. This is why an unforeseen affliction is called a test [temptation[1]], because it enables a man to test his hidden desires."

(St. Mark the Ascetic, *226 Texts*, 204, p. 143, Vol. 1, Philokalia)

---

[1] *"Peirasmos"* (temptation) in the Greek text which means "to have experience – *peira* – of something."

His personal will is revealed during His prayer at the Garden of Gethsemane where He prays three times, a highly symbolic number, for the passing of this cup from him. Nevertheless, He carries out His transcendence and sacrifices himself and his will for the fulfillment of God's Will.

In a few words, Jesus Christ had to experience the diseases, weaknesses and inadequacies of the human nature, even if this ruins our idealized image of Him. And this took place in order to transcend them and open this path of metamorphosis to us.

The bitter cup that Christ asked to be removed from him, but in the end accepted, saying, *"Nevertheless not as I will, but as thou wilt"* (Matthew 26:39), that is, *"Thy Will be done,"* in our experience might take any form. It might be anything we are called to face which is incredibly bitter *for us*, so we say, "Lord let this cup pass from me." Jesus, however, teaches us that we should say, *"Thy Will be done"* because *"God is Love"* (1 John 4:16), and never abandons us, even when appearances seem to assert with tremendous strength the exact opposite, *"My God, my God, why hast thou forsaken me?"* (Matthew 27:46).

And this bitter cup is not theory, at all; it is whipping and humiliation, thorns and pain, usually psychological, but often physical as well, and it might be connected with any situation of our daily life. So in order to endure it we must pray, "God give me strength to drink this bitter cup for your sake because You Are Love."

There are times we must make a personal transcendence during which our faith will be transferred from ourselves to God. There are situations where we need to experience a transfer from the faith in our will, to the faith in God's Will: "How long will I keep disbelieving in You? How long will I keep doubting You? How long will I keep saying, "I know better," and not fear losing my comfort, or having a hard time, or not obtaining the object of my desires? How long will I keep perceiving myself as my own supreme good?"

In these situations we feel like we are buried under a huge rock which is pulling us down into a dark abyss. *We feel a huge weight in our hearts.*

At these moments we usually seek for some grip to hold onto, but if we turn to false outer aids, as soon as we try to hold onto them they will disappear like a mirage; and then, without realizing why, we will sink even deeper.

"God helps us when there is no one else to help. God is there at the point of greatest tension, at the breaking point, at the centre of the storm. In a way, despair is at the centre of things – if only we are prepared to go through it. We must be prepared for a period when God is not there for us, and we must be aware of not trying to substitute a false God."

(Metropolitan Anthony of Sourozh, *School for Prayer*, pp. 18-19)

The false aids are driving us even lower. So what can we do?

What is the way-out of this seeming dead-end? What is the secret?

The secret is to realize that the rock which is crushing us has only as much strength as *we* acknowledge; it has as much weight as *we believe* it to have.

But how can we not believe in its weight when we feel it crushing us, pulling us down? Even if we say, "I know that the *heaviness of my soul* is illusory, this weight is not real" we still feel the same. Because the situation we feel from the rock hasn't changed, it's still there. *If* it disappeared, *yes* we wouldn't feel any weight, *if* this cup was passing from us, we wouldn't feel its bitterness. But *now* we *feel* it since it's *here* and we *must drink* it.

The way for the rock's pressure to be lessened (or even be annihilated) is *forgiveness*, which, in essence, consists in a *transcendence* of our limited self. When forgiveness makes its appearance, the situation lightens; it loses its glamour and strength.

Yet again, in this point there are some secrets. We're not really in a position to say, "I forgive anyone or anything related to this situation that makes my soul heavy," because by ourselves we don't have the necessary power of understanding, forgiving and transcending. That is why the only thing we can say is: "God *give me* strength so that evil, hate, lack of faith, despair, sorrow and agony shall not penetrate my heart. Forgive me for doubting Your Love. Give me strength to endure, to suffer, to transcend all that which drives me away from Your communion, Your prayer, Your kingdom. Hold me to You and forgive us all; whoever is involved for whatever he is doing; whatever is involved and for what it causes; and me, for forgetting You and for turning to false gods, for still taking care for the things of myself."

If what troubles us is shown under the Light of Forgiveness, it will lose much, if not all, of its power over us. And then we will repeat with more fervor and perhaps joy: "Thy Will be done."

Yet, in this point, a reasonable question might be posed: "And why should I drink this bitter cup? What is the reason for this?"

When Jesus reveals His bitter cup to His disciples, Peter says, 'Master do not drink it, stay here with us' and He replies with force, 'Go away temptation; besides it is profitable for you that I drink this cup:' *"Nevertheless I tell you the truth; It is expedient for you that I go away"* (John 16:7).

This shows that there is always a reason behind this request to drink a bitter cup; we don't drink it uselessly. But if we seek a way out, then the aim won't be accomplished; the plan that Love has perceived won't be completed. A plan which always aims at the *utmost benefit* for everyone involved, and that means to our own higher good as well. In the case of Jesus Christ this plan was related to the benefit of the whole of humanity.

So if we avoid our bitter cup, sooner or later, we will come face to face with it again, perhaps in some worse way. It is similar to when we avoid a medicine. Later we might need a larger dose, or a more drastic and unpleasant treatment.

And perhaps every time we can find many excuses for not drinking some bitter cup, "I am not ready yet," "I don't think it's really needed," "I think there is another way." Or we might try to sweeten it, claiming that, "I drank it, but I also did what I had to do, I said what I had to say...." For example, something unpleasant happens and while we know that we should assimilate and transcend it, and we really try to, at the same time, we seek some other way out: alcohol, drugs, or whatever else, "just to *get away* a little." Or we try to accept it large-heartedly, but as soon as we find an opportunity, we complain, we search for outer responsibilities; we *accuse* someone or something, even God Himself.

Very often, however, to not express anything in relation to what troubles us can become extremely bitter, and we feel we will be relieved if we get what burdens us off our chest. And indeed, according to the instructions of Jesus Christ, this is not bad in itself; we might need help on our way, and someone to relieve us a little from our burdens, from our cross: "*And as they came out, they found a man of Cyrene, Simon by name: him they compelled to bear his cross*" (Matthew 27:32).

Still, we are forced, if we want to enter and remain in the Kingdom of God, to carry our Cross ourselves until the end, and to crucify our egoism and our self-interested will upon it: *"And he bearing his cross went forth into a place called the place of a skull, which is called in the Hebrew Golgotha, where they crucified him"* (John 19:17-18). We must drink our bitter cup, otherwise, without knowing, we sweeten the beast of egoism which is fed by the sweetness while it *suffers* and *starves* by the *bitterness*.

So this is the reason for the bitter cup!

This is the use of both the small and the large bitter cups. They constitute a medicine.

And if Jesus Christ himself had to experience the human nature, he also had to experience its disease and treatment, its self-interest and its will, as well as its bitter cup. Jesus sacrificed himself and his personal human will and was crucified for our sake. In the same way we must crucify our egoistic self and sacrifice our will for His sake.

It's true that when some situation troubles us and breaks us apart, we have the right, according to the example of Jesus, to acknowledge it as a cruel and unfair situation.

"And when he had thus spoken, one of the officers which stood by struck Jesus with the palm of his hand, saying, Answerest thou the high priest so? Jesus answered him, If I have spoken evil, bear witness of the evil: but if well, why smitest thou me?" (John 18:22-23).

Jesus Christ teaches us to also offer the other cheek when they smite us (Luke 6:29), but in the case where they smite Him, not only does He not offer the other cheek, but He wants to know the reason for this injustice against Him; he claims His right.

Why? Does He contradict His own teaching? Or perhaps He exemplifies a healthy and whole attitude of life?

The Teaching of Jesus is not a victimized attitude; He doesn't teach us to be spineless victims, preys to whatever conditions arise. On the contrary, He shows us with His attitude that He courageously defends what is right, but at the same time He has the strength to forgive the wrong, even endure it, if there is some higher benefit to it. He can transcend the *law of retaliation* which is based on human justice, introducing the *law of forgiveness* which is based on Divine justice.

Nevertheless, he acknowledges the lawlessness, and He is not afraid at all to be quite severe in His attitude, *"And when he had made a scourge of small cords, he drove them all out of the temple"* (John 2:15), without, however, being removed from the Love inside Him which grants Him the strength to endure even His unjust death so long as it serves the higher good.

So at the crucial hour, He neither defends Himself against Pontius Pilate, nor tries to avoid His bitter cup, resulting in even gaining the admiration of Pilate, *"But Jesus yet answered nothing; so that Pilate marveled"* (Mark 15:5).

The greatness that we are taught by Christ is that we are not to pretend to be victims, but to have the courage to endure whatever might be against us, so long as we realize that there will be an underlying benefit by our acceptance.

So let's be grateful, because the trials we experience spring from the Love of God. They can be surpassed with the help of His Love and aim in *strengthening* Love inside us. And even more, let's ask God to give us the strength to endure our various bitter cups in order that we may be more able to taste our biggest Bitter Cup: the Crucifixion of our egoism.

The Inner Restoration of Christianity

Unseen Warfare

"There is within us, on the noetic plane, a warfare tougher than that on the plane of the senses."

(St. Philotheos of Sinai, *Forty Texts on Watchfulness*, Text 1, p. 16, Vol. 3, Philokalia)

So we have a war; unceasing; and no one should give way to the *seeming* greatness of the enemy. No one should bend from his hand-over-hand strikes. Be courageous, because this enemy has been defeated many times in the past.

Let's be constantly vigilant because the warfare doesn't ever stop; it is carried on even in the midst of the night; it doesn't know about holidays or the need to rest. So let's be watchful, let's not be complacent; even in our rest periods, let's leave enough guards on watch. Because the enemy is constantly at the entrance gate and will not give up his claims unless he is defeated, vanished from the face of the earth, *humbled* to the last.

And no one should be fooled into thinking that we are referring to an enemy outside of us. Woe to the one who won't perceive, or who forgets that the enemy is inside; that the one we are fighting against is our "self," our egoism.

"The first victory over oneself – the condition and basis of all other inner victories, which alone makes them possible – lies in breaking our own will and in surrender to God."

(*The Art of Prayer – An Orthodox Anthology*, p. 218)

This inner warfare is conducted, in essence, on two fronts. One is connected to what is *contrary to nature* (unnatural), where we try to restore the natural state of things. The other front is connected to what is *according to nature* (natural) where we try to transcend it and be led to what is *beyond (above) nature* (supernatural); we try for the transcendence.

"The term *nature* is equivalent to the incorruptible *before the fall nature* of man who has been reborn in Christ. *Contrary to nature* is the diseased man who is led by the blameworthy passions. *Beyond (above) nature* is the *according to nature* man who receives the uncreated energies of the Holy Spirit and in that way transcends the natural standards and becomes 'super human human.' "

(*Introductory Comments* to St Maximos the Confessor, in Vol. 2 of Philokalia, p. 46, publ. by To Perivoli tis Panaghias, Greece)

This is our holy or spiritual war. It is a holy war against our egoistic carnal self who enslaves us in what is contrary to nature; and against our psychological human (self-interested) self who limits us to the *subjective*, on one hand natural, but on the other quite selfish, order of things.

Man is created and born with the ability of living as an *animal*, as a *man* or as a *God-man*, that is, as a *Son or Daughter of God*, "*For as many as are led by the Spirit of God, they are the sons of God*" (Romans 8:14). The real destination of man is this third ability to live as a Child of God because only then can he actively participate in the Divine Plan for which he was created, "*And God said, Let us make man in our image, after our likeness: and let them have dominion over the fish of the sea, and over the fowl of the air, and over the cattle, and over all the earth, and over every creeping thing that creepeth upon the earth. So God created man in his own image, in the image of God created he him; male and female created he them"* (Genesis 1:26-27). Only the spiritual man can fulfill the Divine Will, *"Thy kingdom come. Thy will be done in earth, as it is in heaven"* (Matthew 6:10).

In the second case where he lives as a *man*, he can only passively participate in the Divine Plan, sometimes promoting it and sometimes impeding it. He cannot really know the Divine Plan since he defends and claims his own subjective will.

In the first case where he lives as an animal (or more accurately as a *sub*-human) he just obstructs the action of Divine Providence, creating disharmony, chaos and all the evil we see everywhere around us, because the Will of God is certainly not all this conflict, tribulation and negativity which prevails in the world. This is not the Kingdom of God we pray for, *"Thy Kingdom come"* (Matthew 6:10).

Whatever we see around us is due exclusively to the will of carnal, egoistic men, and to the will of psychologically subjective, self-interested men.

As psychological men (that is *human* humans) despite our good intentions, we remain in large part disconnected with the plans of Divine Providence, of Divine Harmony, because we are not in contact with the necessary internal intuition through which we can be participants of the Divine Will. As long as we are disconnected from our spirit, we mainly create disharmony, even when we have, as already mentioned, the best intentions. We are *enslaved* to ourselves, our ideas, beliefs and subjectivity; we are in "our own world."

So our spiritual war is between our will (whether this comes from our carnal or psychological mind) and the Will of God (which is *identical* with the will of our spiritual mind).

It is waged between the contrary to nature man and the according to nature man; and then, between the according to nature man and the beyond (above) nature man. That means between the animal and the man inside us, and then between the man and the god inside us. But the human part doesn't abolish the animal one, just as the Divine part doesn't abolish the human one; each one simply takes its *proper place* and resumes its proper function. The inner warfare is conducted in order to regain our real Divine self and in that way be able to fulfill God's Will, that is, Love's Will. It is carried on for Love to triumph.

So our spiritual warfare has stages and gradations. In our present state it is directed initially against our contrary to nature existence, against our egoistic carnal mind.

"The kingdom of which we are speaking is a kingdom of love, and superficially, it would be seemingly so nice to enter it; yet it is not nice, because love has a tragic side; it means death to each of us, the complete dying out of our selfish, self-centered self, and not dying out as flower fades away, but dying a cruel death, the death of the crucifixion."

(Metropolitan Anthony of Sourozh, *Living Prayer*, p. 40)

Unfortunately we have fallen from the heights of human value and we must engage in an inner battle in order to restore the human inside us. We have distorted our natural state to the point where we "philosophize" whether man is inherently evil or not. We have difficulty in realizing the obvious truth that all human wickedness is a distortion of nature, a *contrary to nature* situation which claims the attributes of nature when it is perpetuated. When we return, however, to our natural state, we discover with amazement that good flows unhurriedly from within, and goodness is the most logical and self-evident thing.

We must become natural again, human, and goodness, not because we should, not because we will have to face the consequences of the law if we break it, if we sin, but because this is the way *we feel*; this is what our *inherent* human goodness determines.

If we conquer these inner depths, then our inner warfare can be conducted at a new, deeper and higher level. Then we try to transcend what is according to nature in order to reach beyond (above) nature, to the level of saint. For in the natural level, if someone harms us or our beloved ones, it's reasonable and fair for him to suffer the consequences of his actions. That means if someone smites us, the natural reaction is for us to smite him as well. But this is not the commandment of Jesus Christ.

After we are restored to our natural level, the inner battle is next conducted in order to become real Christians. In our days, the term "Christian" is so degenerated that even an atrocious murderer can claim he is a Christian, let alone us, the "simple" everyday people. In reality there are at least three basic levels regarding the property of a Christian:

The *desire* to be a Christian.

The *effort* to become a Christian.

And *being* a Christian.

The real Christian is only the saintly, spiritual man, because only he *can* apply the commandments of Christ, *"Not everyone that saith unto me, Lord, Lord, shall enter into the kingdom of heaven; but he that doeth the will of my Father which is in heaven"* (Matthew 7:21). We, in the best case, can *try* to apply them. So all of us either desire to be Christians or try to become Christians.

Our strong *desire* to be Christians and the corresponding inner battle can restore what is according to nature by killing and crucifying what is contrary to nature.

The intense *effort* to become Christians and the corresponding spiritual warfare can transcend what is according to nature by self-sacrificing and crucifying it, making us capable of tasting and experiencing what is beyond (above) nature. For the commandments of Christ transcend the natural law of the Old Testament.

> *"Ye have heard that it hath been said, An eye for an eye, and a tooth for a tooth: But I say unto you, That ye resist not evil: but whosoever shall smite thee on thy right cheek, turn to him the other also. And if any man will sue thee at the law, and take away thy coat, let him have thy cloak also. And whosoever shall compel thee to go a mile, go with him twain. Give to him that asketh thee, and from him that would borrow of thee turn not thou away.*
>
> *Ye have heard that it hath been said, Thou shalt love thy neighbor, and hate thine enemy. But I say unto you, Love your enemies, bless them that curse you, do good to them that hate you, and pray for them which despitefully use you, and persecute you; That ye may be the children of your Father which is in heaven: for he maketh his sun to rise on the evil and on the good, and sendeth rain on the just and on the unjust"* (Matthew 5:38-45).

The Inner Restoration of Christianity

The commandments of Christ don't abolish the natural law, *"Think not that I am come to destroy the law, or the prophets: I am not come to destroy, but to fulfill"* (Matthew 5:17), but fulfill it, that is, transcend it, introducing the super-natural, spiritual law of Forgiveness and Love, *"Then came Peter to him, and said, Lord, how oft shall my brother sin against me, and I forgive him? Till seven times? Jesus saith unto him, I say not unto thee, Until seven times: but, Until seventy times seven"* (Matthew 18:21-22).

The restoration of the natural order inside us is an imperative necessity, otherwise we condemn ourselves to an inner hell which certainly has its unpleasant consequences, both for us and everything else around us. Nevertheless, the call to tread on the narrow way of Christ (Matthew 7:14) is a matter of personal decision and volition.

"There is but one road to the kingdom of God – a cross, voluntary or involuntary."

(*The Art of Prayer – An Orthodox Anthology*, p. 231)

If, however, we truly want to engage in this inner warfare in order to experience the procedure of crucifixion, and tread on the path to the Kingdom of God as defined by Jesus Christ, then we are obliged to follow His lead, *"We must through much tribulation enter into the kingdom of God"* (Acts 14:22).

"A soul untried by sorrows is good for nothing."

(*The Art of Prayer – An Orthodox Anthology*, p. 231)

Initially, he who desires to undertake this inner warfare might be motivated by the desire to be freed from his oppressing self. In the midst of this struggle, however, he finds out that this motivation cannot lead him very far and this is because what is demanded of him seems unbearable and insufferable. Therefore, soon he desires to return to his former state, which might be a state of enslavement, but also has its "advantages:"

> *"Hast thou taken us away to die in the wilderness? Wherefore hast thou dealt thus with us, to carry us forth out of Egypt? [...] For it had been better for us to serve the Egyptians, than that we should die in the wilderness. [...] Would to God we had died by the hand of the Lord in the land of Egypt, when we sat by the flesh pots, and when we did eat bread to the full"* (Exodus 14:11-12, 16:3).

As long as the motivation for this inner journey is only our personal benefit, we reach inevitably to the point of wondering whether it's really worth the trouble. And then we realize that the only reason to carry on with this harsh battle is because by changing ourselves everything around us changes as well; our metamorphosis is beneficial to our whole environment. We discover our duty towards everything that exists, and the necessity to change in order that we not contribute in any way to the general disharmony and unhappiness around us.

Our initial, still self-interested motivation is reinforced by a second motivation, more altruistic, which provides us the necessary strength and energy to carry on this inner battle more successfully. This new motivation which is related to the *benefit of others,* constitutes a necessary reinforcement in order for this victory over ourselves to take place.

This broader perception regarding our growth makes its appearance when we realize that we are indissolubly connected with everything and that there cannot be any personal growth which excludes anything since the *only real growth* which is possible for us is the one which includes everything in a communion of Love. So we no longer keep fighting only for the sake of ourselves, but for the sake of everything.

Yet, in our course, we will again discover that this struggle is extremely exhausting and truly above our strengths. Whatever we do in the end, we seem lost like the rich man of the parable, *"But when the young man heard that saying, he went away sorrowful"* (Matthew 19:22).

These two motivations which were urging us are proving not to be enough to defeat this, at least seemingly, undefeatable inner adversary. So we feel that our entrance into the Kingdom of Heaven still remains uncertain, and then it's reasonable to get full of despair. At this point a further reinforcement becomes necessary which will, in essence, make this whole endeavor feasible. Otherwise, we really wonder, *"Who then can be saved?"* (Matthew 19:25).

Here we realize that as long as we carry ourselves with us, as long as we struggle based on our *own* strength, it is inevitable to remain *rich in ideas* about ourselves which are much nicer than the former ones. We now consider ourselves righteous.

We struggle against ourselves trying to apply all the commandments of God, but we have forgotten the essential condition of this struggle which is to deny ourselves, *"If any man will come after me, let him deny himself"* (Matthew 16:24).

But what does this mean?

It means that our initial motivation to struggle in order to be freed and saved, basically for the sake of ourselves, cannot lead us very far; simply because our self is still in the center of our efforts.

In the same way, our additional motivation to struggle for the sake of everything around us doesn't necessarily constitute a complete self-denial because essentially our environment is us, and we are our environment. Everything around us can be seen in a self-interested way as an extension of ourselves: *our* family, *our* friends, *our* companion, *our* land, *our* species, *our* planet, and so forth.

So we need a *third motivation* which will be able to complete the two former ones and place them in the right perspective. This motivation makes its appearance when we decide to struggle *for the sake of God;* when we realize that *nothing can be done without God* and also that everything is done for His sake, since He Himself is *self-sacrificing* for our sake.

Equipped with these *three motivations* which now acquire a reverse priority from the sequence in which they were born: armed with our duty towards God, the motivation for the benefit of everything around us, and the motivation for the salvation of our soul, we can be certain that our victory in this struggle, our victory over our "self," is absolutely feasible.

Having now the glory of God as a deeper motivation in this struggle, we will be open to the things that happen according to the truly effective Will of His Love, and not according to our own short-sighted will. In that way, we will be able to constantly turn towards Him for reinforcement, knowing that if we count only on ourselves we will be hopelessly lost.

> "So a man must be helped in the spiritual life and in the work of salvation by a supernatural and all-powerful force.

The Inner Restoration of Christianity

He must be victorious over his own self; but how can this be without the power of God present, which is able to do all things?"

(St. Tikhon of Zadonsk, *Journey to Heaven*, p. 96)

Here we learn to place all our hopes in Him and so we obtain access to an unlimited Source of energy and strength which will metamorphose this yoke, *"Come unto me, all ye that labor and are heavy laden, and I will give you rest. Take my yoke upon you, and learn of me; for I am meek and lowly in heart: and ye shall find rest unto your souls. For my yoke is easy, and my burden is light"* (Matthew 11:28-30).

"He who places his hope in God, no longer takes care for the things of himself and finds psychological benefit in all he is doing, in everything."

(St. Paisius Velichkovsky, *Field Flowers*, p. 132)

The Inner Restoration of Christianity

Hope

"Struggle; struggle in every way; but your hope of salvation place it to the Lord, the only Savior, not to your struggle. This is very important.

"The more confidence in ourselves, strength and good works is increased, the more our dependence on the Lord is lessened. And then we deviate from the path of salvation."

(St. Theophan the Recluse, *Guidance in the Spiritual Life*, p. 103)

Hope in God opens us to God; and opening to God means being related with the Source of inexhaustible Strength and Energy. Our own energy supplies are not unlimited; our "own" strength to love and forgive is limited. So we are quickly exhausted in our inner journey, especially when we are engaged in inner battles, often with the result of feeling, "I am tired, I cannot take it any longer."

And beside the fact that our personal strength is limited, if we count on it alone during our holy struggle against our "self," soon we will be led to pride and vainglory. Even though this holy war will be against our self, since we will be counting on it, at the end of every battle we will meet ourselves again! In a few words, we will be entrapped in a vicious cycle.

"No support can be better than His. The greatest danger lies in the soul thinking that it can find this help within itself; then it will lose everything."

(*The Art of Prayer – An Orthodox Anthology*, p. 136)

God's help is not just a nice idea so we won't feel despair. It is an existent and real Power which provides us with the *energy* we need in order to endure all these terrible revelations about ourselves. It also provides us with the courage to suffer every kind of pain and frustration, and above all It feeds us with the energy of Love which can heal, invigorate, understand, be patient, and of course, *Love*.

> "Do not rely on your own ability, and God will come to your aid."

(Abba Ammonas, *Useful Servanthood*, p. 146)

Divine Grace is the one who will make every one of our efforts fruitful, and the one who will metamorphose us.

> "Only when this quickening power of grace comes will the inner work of the transformation of our life and character really begin. Without it, we cannot expect success; there will only be unsuccessful attempts. [...] Work, with confident expectation. Grace will come and set everything in order."

(*The Art of Prayer – An Orthodox Anthology*, p. 145)

That is what *"being born again"* (John 3:3) means, and only in that way is our spiritual metamorphosis *possible*. Otherwise, it is utopian and unfeasible, *"But Jesus beheld them, and said unto them, With men this is impossible"* (Matthew 19:26).

And here is revealed a truly hopeful message of the *Gospels*: that we have at our disposal a Source of feeding for which all is possible, *"But with God all things are possible"* (Matthew 19:26). And the *Good News* is that this Source is constantly calling us inside (Revelations 3:20), but It can only be approached if we cease believing in our limited strengths.

> "The help of God is always ready and always near, but is only given to those who seek and work, and only to those seekers who, after putting all their own powers to the test, then cry out with all their heart: Lord, help us. So long as you hold on to even a little hope of achieving something by your own powers, the Lord does not interfere."
>
> (*The Art of Prayer – An Orthodox Anthology*, p. 133)

If we rely on human beings or anything else outside of us for help and reinforcement, the result will be disappointment. If we aspire to God, we won't ever be disappointed, because we won't place our hopes in anything ephemeral, changeable and limited.

> "Keep yourself scrupulously, as one who is always in God's presence, in order that you may hope for nothing from anybody, except from him alone with faith."
>
> (Abba Ammonas, *Useful Servanthood*, p. 164)

Besides, only the Divine Action is in the position to restore our whole existence, our whole Being. Only the Divine Grace can heal our diseases, reinforce our weaknesses, compliment our inadequacies and fulfill our capabilities. Only the Divine Strength can clean, enlighten and restore us as Children of God.

If we don't acknowledge God as the supreme Power which provides us with the requisite strength, both in this inner struggle and our life in general, then anything will be able to take God's place inside us and will constitute for us an idol of God.

In that way we will believe and hope in the idols of our own making which we will recognize inevitably as our God, and will have the form either of ourselves or of every other thing, *"Thou shalt have no other gods before me. Thou shalt not make unto thee any graven image, or any likeness of anything that is in heaven above, or that is in the earth beneath, or that is in the water under the earth"* (Exodus 20:3-4).

And naturally, when we build these false gods, placing them in God's place, we end up *suffering in vain*, *"They that make a graven image are all of them vanity; and their delectable things shall not profit"* (Isaiah 44:9). Especially when, in this inner warfare, our idol takes the form of ourselves and we adore it, believing in it (with our *self*-confidence) and enumerating its rich achievements, *"All these things have I kept"* (Matthew 19:20), very often we will catch ourselves saying, "I am tired...."

On the contrary, when we place our hope in God and engage sincerely in this inner battle, even if we are "forced" to express our disappointment, disheartening and despair, let's not say, "I can't bear it any longer," let's say, "I cannot bear *me* any longer." Let's stop hoping in ourselves and let's learn to hope in God.

When we place all our hope in Love, we obtain access to an infinite Source of Energy through which we will never again feel "tired," "disappointed," or "desperate," no matter what happens. For this Source will always revive and strengthen us. So our Hope won't consist in fond hopes, but in a real Power which urges and supports us in our every God-pleasing enterprise.

The Inner Restoration of Christianity

And so we will find out that Real Hope in God isn't at all related to some kind of future postponement, "Tomorrow will be better," "Better days will come," but to an essential Strength which *prepares the future by making a worthy use of the present.*

In order, however, to place all our hopes in God, we must – after many trials and several bitter cups – begin experiencing the *state* of *humility.*

Humility

Humility essentially means only one thing: to attribute *all* our gifts, talents, virtues, strengths and abilities to God. And at the same time, it means to recognize our weakness without God's aid.

The parable of the rich man in the Gospels describes the necessary state of humility in which man must be, in order to be saved, that is, to enter in the Kingdom of God.

The rich man who converses with Jesus is not rich in material goods, but in "spiritual," which is very obvious since when he approaches Christ, he doesn't refer to any material possessions but only to psychological "possessions" (Matthew 19:16-22). When Jesus says, *"Verily I say unto you, That a rich man shall hardly enter into the kingdom of heaven. And again I say unto you, It is easier for a camel to go through the eye of a needle, than for a rich man to enter into the kingdom of God"* (Matthew 19:23-24), he doesn't refer in essence to *material* wealth, otherwise His disciples wouldn't be so amazed, *"When his disciples heard it, they were exceedingly amazed"* (Matthew 19:25), and they wouldn't hasten to ask, *"Who then can be saved?"* (Matthew 19:25). There are a lot of people who aren't rich in *material* goods and even more who are very poor, so the exceeding amazement of His disciples is not reasonable.

The wealth to which Christ is referring is the "spiritual" wealth, the ideas we have for ourselves which are derived mainly from our psychological gifts which make us feel righteous and great (even without realizing it) and fill us with pride. That is why Jesus says, *"Blessed are the poor in spirit: for theirs is the kingdom of heaven"* (Matthew 5:3). He doesn't say blessed are the poor in body, in matter, but in spirit.

What does this mean? It means that blessed are the ones who don't have any idea of themselves, the ones who don't "own" any spiritual wealth because they *attribute everything* to God; so they are, and remain, poor in spirit.

On the contrary, when we attribute our *gifts* to ourselves, *"All these things have I kept from my youth up"* (Matthew 19:20), then we are rich in "spiritual" possessions and in that way we don't have the necessary inner space for the coming of the Holy Spirit, *"When the young man heard that saying, he went away sorrowful: for he had great possessions"* (Matthew 19:22).

When we ask, *"What lack I yet?"* (Matthew 19:20), we exhibit again our pride because it's like saying, "I am perfect, I am righteous, but if there is anything else that I still have to do, *I* will do it, because everything so far, *I* have done as I should." And when we hear that we must deny ourselves sacrificing all "our achievements," *"If thou wilt be perfect, go and sell that thou hast, and give to the poor, and thou shalt have treasure in heaven: and come and follow me"* (Matthew 19:21), we walk away sorrowful because this is truly and literally *above our* strength.

Therefore it's reasonable for the disciples to be amazed, saying in effect, "But if the ones who have kept the commandments and are decent, righteous, honoring the ones they should, not hurting anyone, cannot enter into the Kingdom of Heaven, who can?"

The true answer, however, to this seemingly reasonable question is, *"With men this is impossible"* (Matthew 19:26). But why? Because for man to enter into the Kingdom of God, God Himself must raise him through His Divine Grace, and in His greatness, make him a participant of His Love. And in order for God to be able to raise him, he must first allow Him to by humbling himself, that is, by saying, "My God I am nothing by myself; only through You am I something, so accept me, come to me and do whatever You will with me." Only with this confession of humility can man really allow God to act in him.

If man raises himself thinking he can become god, then he doesn't allow God to act, he doesn't leave anything open inside him to accept the Divine Grace, so inevitably God, *"Makes sport of [resists] the men of pride"* (Proverbs 3:34, Bible in Basic English). Not because God is revengeful, but simply because we *make it impossible* for His help to penetrate us; when we "raise" ourselves to His Height, we're saying *practically,* that we *don't* need Him, *"Every one who is exalting himself shall be humbled, and he who is humbling himself shall be exalted"* (Luke 14:11).

If we are not humbled, that is, if we don't enter into the state of humility through which we feel and experience our own limited strength and at the same time the unlimited Strength and Love of God, we will never be able to accept His Divine Grace, simply because, knowingly or not, we refuse it, *"Yet to the humble He doth give grace"* (Proverbs 3:34, Young's Literal Translation).

No man, however, can claim that he is humble, because he attributes to himself a property which doesn't belong to him. He will become rich again when, as we've already seen, *"Blessed are the poor in spirit"* (Matthew 5:3). The only thing we can do is constantly realize that we are not, and cannot be, anything without God.

Without God we are just a small ant which puffs itself up with ideas about itself feeling like the master of the universe.

> "Fear no one. Just a little tap from God can knock down the most powerful person on earth – even the ants will be walking over him."

(Mersine Vigopoulou, *From I-ville to You-ville*, p. 93)

When we gradually experience this sense of nothingness apart from God's aid, we enter into a state of humility through which we begin deriving an unlimited force and a complete fearlessness, since we are related to the omnipotence of Love.

If, however, after having tasted the *gifts* of Spirit for some time, we begin attributing them to ourselves again, even by the simplistic conviction that we deserved them in some way, then we fall again to the sin of pride and thus we come out of the state of humility. Pride and humility are mutually exclusive, and as the latter lessens, the former increases, and the reverse is true as well.

> "When pride retreats from a man, humility begins to dwell in him, and the more pride is diminished, so much more does humility grow. The one gives way to the other as to its opposite. Darkness departs and light appears. Pride is darkness, but humility is light."
>
> (St. Tikhon of Zadonsk, *Journey to Heaven*, p. 75)

Humility, contrary to the beliefs of our time, doesn't indicate weakness, wretchedness or degradation, but absolute freedom and absolute power; while pride, which wears the façade of strength, boldness and dignity, in reality consists of disguised weakness, insecurity, sense of inferiority and essentially, fear.

In the state of humility we are empty of ourselves, and in that way we have room for the coming of Love, of God, who *only then* can offer us happiness, fulfill all our God-pleasing pursuits, and give us all His gifts in abundance.

In the state of humility we become, in effect, a fertile soil where Diving Grace can bring fruits; in other words, our Divine spiritual self can emerge so we can become true Sons and Daughters of God. Only thus can we enter into the Kingdom of God, when we are born from above, that is, from God, as His Children.

For, for man it is impossible to become god, *"And the serpent said [...] ye shall be as gods"* (Genesis 3:4-5). And when he attempts to, he just excludes himself from the Kingdom of God; he just throws himself out of his Paradise, *"The Lord God sent him forth from the garden of Eden"* (Genesis 3:23).

Still, many of us might not feel like gods, and don't believe that we can become gods. Perhaps we don't have a big idea of ourselves and we might even feel somewhat humble. But is this true? And is it related at all with the state of humility that we describe?

"It is impossible for a person who is still in the realm of carnal sophistry and who has not received the spiritual realization of fallen human nature not to give some value to his actions and not to consider himself of some worth, however humbly he may speak and however humble he may appear outwardly."

(St. Ignatius Brianchaninov, *The Arena: An Offering to Contemporary Monasticism*, p. 37)

Could there be, for example, some simple and humble person who neither believes in God, nor acknowledges any Supreme Power which created, sustains and controls everything? Certainly not. For by excluding the concept of God, this person raises himself, since he raises man, despite whether he may even base his claim on some nihilistic view that neither himself nor human beings have any particular value. All this doesn't have anything to do with the real state of humility.

So we must distinguish the notion of humility from all the tendencies of underestimation, nihilism or even reasonable modesty. And if we are honest deep inside us, we will acknowledge that even if we are characterized by this side of the coin which is called "underestimation," or more nicely, "modesty," we cannot avoid the other side of the same, in essence, egocentric coin which is characterized by some imperceptible and "innocent" conceit or prettified idea of ourselves (which might be derived exactly from this impression that, at least, we don't have a big idea of ourselves)!

> "Not one of us can boast of having acquired humility: our actions, the whole of our life, prove the contrary. And where there is a lack of humility, pride is always present. Where light is wanting, darkness reigns."
>
> (Starets Macarius of Optino, *Russian Letters of Direction*, Letter 123)

Real humility can be related only to the truly *spiritual* man. Otherwise we would be in a state of utmost peacefulness and serenity in which nothing could offend or disturb us and we wouldn't be constantly used up in offering our "right" advice.

> "Remember always that the whole of our human misery is the consequence of pride. Humility alone is the path to joy, the gate to the blessed nearness – the intimacy of God."
>
> (Starets Macarius of Optino, *Russian Letters of Direction*, Letter 73)

The personal story of St. Paul which is described in his Epistles, teaches us the necessary state of humility which man should experience in order to acquire a place in the Kingdom of God.

"The Lord sometimes leaves in us some defects of character in order that we should learn humility. For without them we would immediately soar above the clouds in our own estimation and would place our throne there. And herein lies perdition."

(*The Art of Prayer – An Orthodox Anthology*, p. 271)

This story is connected with the famous thorn of St Paul:

"It is not expedient for me doubtless to glory. I will come to visions and revelations of the Lord. I knew a man in Christ above fourteen years ago, (whether in the body, I cannot tell; or whether out of the body, I cannot tell: God knoweth;) such an one caught up to the third heaven. And I knew such a man, (whether in the body, or out of the body, I cannot tell: God knoweth;) How that he was caught up into paradise, and heard unspeakable words, which it is not lawful for a man to utter.

"Of such an one will I glory: yet of myself I will not glory, but in mine infirmities. For though I would desire to glory, I shall not be a fool; for I will say the truth: but now I forbear, lest any man should think of me above that which he seeth me to be, or that he heareth of me.

"And lest I should be exalted above measure through the abundance of the revelations, there was given to me a thorn in the flesh, the messenger of Satan to buffet me, lest I should

be exalted above measure. For this thing I besought the Lord thrice, that it might depart from me. And he said unto me, My grace is sufficient for thee: for my strength is made perfect in weakness. Most gladly therefore will I rather glory [boast] in my infirmities [weaknesses], that the power of Christ may rest upon me" (2 Corinthians 12:1-9).

We often think in relation to various truly spiritual men, "But how is it possible for him to have this weakness? How could he not be able to surpass this thing or the other?" And this weakness might be connected to something that even we might have transcended. The reason is that he couldn't transcend it simply because it wasn't in his power. For if God doesn't want it, nothing can be done.

This is what happened with St. Paul. God didn't fulfill his wish in order for him to be humbled. And what does it mean to "be humbled?" It means to acknowledge that without God *nothing* can be done, whoever you might be. If God doesn't want it, it's impossible for anything to happen, let alone to enter or remain in the Kingdom of God.

And since we don't know what this thorn of St. Paul's was, we tend to underrate his personal drama and agony. It sounds very theoretical to us; we take it superficially. We think, "Ok, he had one thorn, so what?" and we don't realize that this thorn in the flesh could be something humiliating that made St. Paul ashamed of himself (Galatians 4:14) and in that way forced him to glory [*boast*] in his infirmities [weaknesses]! For a spiritual man like him to have a thorn in the flesh, symbolizes very clearly the inability of man to do anything without God's help. Even if he attains the utmost spiritual heights and receives the highest divine revelations, he won't be able, *by himself* and if God doesn't want it, to transcend even the slightest weakness.

"You cannot do anything without God's help. Everything that you have belongs to God and from Him you receive it freely. So, *"What hast thou that thou hast not received? And if thou hast received, why dost thou glory, as if thou hadst not received it?"* (1 Corinthians 4:7).

(St. Dimitri of Rostov, *Spiritual Alphabet*, pp. 37-38)

The truth is that whatever we have is a gift. Everything has been given to us as *charisma*.

"The goods that they have [the proud] they ascribe to themselves, to their own efforts and labors, and not to God. O man! What can you have of your own self, who came naked out of your mother's womb? What can you have should God, the source of all good, not give it to you? What can our effort and labor accomplish without His help, Who alone is able to do all things, and without Whom everyone is as nothing, as a shadow without a body?"

(St. Tikhon of Zadonsk, *Journey to Heaven*, p. 74)

This spiritual point of view can also be connected with the notion of God's Will. When we are in the state of humility, attributing our existence and all of are our talents to God, then we are open to His aid and guidance and certainly to His Will.

In this state of humility we experience the abolishment of all our imaginary ideas about the control we can exercise to the totality of our lives; ideas that offer us an illusory sense of security and, of course, importance. We begin to realize that we don't have any real control upon our physical life and vital energy. Essentially, we can only do what God indicates to us internally, in order to have the best possible physical health.

Correspondingly, we don't have any control over our psychological life and psychic energy. We don't really determine our intelligence, kindness or goodness, because we are not the creators of these gifts (*charismas*). Again, the only thing we can do in relation to our psychological life is to do the Will of God in order to promote our best possible psychological health.

In this point, we can go even deeper, and acknowledge that all the aforementioned is equally true, if not more so, in regards to our spiritual life.

If we carry God's will into effect, we will have the best possible health, physically and psychologically, and in that way we will be able to open to the spiritual life. If we learn to attribute our physical and psychological virtues to God, it will be self-evident that the virtues and beauty of spiritual life will naturally be attributed exclusively to God also: Faith, Hope, Love, objective reason and conscience, gratitude, inner peace and stillness, and inner freedom.

> "The virtues you attained without the *nous*, only these belong to you, since your *nous* is a gift from God. The great things you manufactured without the use of your body's limbs, only these are due to you, since your body is a creation of God. The achievements you attained before you were born, only for those you ought to be praised, since the achievements after you were born, as well as your birth itself, were a gift from God.
>
> So what do you own to be proud of?"
>
> (St. Dimitri of Rostov, *Spiritual Alphabet*, p. 35)

This spiritual perception initiates us into the state of humility in which we have nothing left to be proud of except our weaknesses. In that way vanity, vainglory, self-complacency, egocentrism and pride are beginning to retreat as opposite views and attitudes of being. And if we want, we can really boast, according to the example of St. Paul, of our weakness and this will again result in our benefit, *"Most gladly therefore will I rather glory [boast] in my infirmities [weaknesses], that the power of Christ may rest upon me"* (2 Corinthians 12:1-9).

Let's not assume, however, that the transfer to this spiritual perception of things and our entrance into the state of humility will be easy and effortless, or that our *metanoia* will be unhurried and self-evident. For this specific demon of pride, which abhors humility, is a truly dangerous enemy.

> "The demon of pride brings the soul to the very worst sort of fall. It induces the soul to refuse to acknowledge that God is its helper and to think that it is, itself, the cause of its good actions."

> (Evagrius of Pontus, *Praktikos*, Chapter 14, p. 100)

If humility makes our soul's soil fertile in order to accept the Divine meanings and the seeds of the Spirit, pride, in exactly the opposite way, makes it sterile, condemning it to a spiritual starvation.

> "Nothing removes us farther from God than pride and egoism. Behind every fall, pride is hidden. And behind the spiritual goods which you gather laboriously, pride is again hidden in order to scatter them."

> (St. Dimitri of Rostov, *Spiritual Alphabet*, p. 35)

Pride is, in effect, exactly the opposite way of being, from the spiritual conception of things. It is the notion which puts man in the place of God, thus making the Divine Action impossible.

> "The passion of pride arises from two kinds of ignorance, and when these two kinds of ignorance unite, they form a single confused state of mind. For a man is proud only if he is ignorant both of divine help and of human weakness. Therefore pride is a lack of knowledge both in the divine and in the human spheres. For the denial of two true premises results in a single false affirmation."
>
> (St. Maximos the Confessor, *Various Texts*, 64, Third Century, p. 226, Vol. 2, Philokalia)

So our *metanoia* is not an easy case because it consists in being *transferred* from a state of ignorance. Ignoring both the Divine Help and our human inadequacy is something deeper than an intellectual perception, and is related to a real experience.

Until we experience with our whole Being the reality of our nothingness we will remain lost in an illusory perception of ourselves.

> "If you really knew yourself, you wouldn't be proud.
> The lack of self-knowledge, leads you to pride."
>
> (St. Dimitri of Rostov, *Spiritual Alphabet*, p. 33)

So let's not be in a hurry to claim that we have arrived to the state of humility or that its sacred place is not far from us, because the inner devil of pride is the first to maintain that he has conquered its heights or that he is not far away from it.

And as we already said, let's not think that the virtue of humility can be in any way a result of our efforts, because the most contradictory thing is to claim that we achieved humility. The state of humility is again, more than anything else, a Divine gift.

We should be very careful during our inner spiritual journey in relation to the concept of praises and recognition, because the personal praises and acknowledgment cause, even against our will, conceit.

> "We should avoid a lot of praise from everyone,
> because it makes people prideful."

(Mersine Vigopoulou, *From I-ville to You-ville*, p. 71)

People who honor us in any way just don't see deeply enough to perceive that only God is worthy of every honor.

> "The prophet said, "Thy eulogists are causing thee to err and the way of thy paths are swallowed up" (Isaiah 3:12, Young's Literal Translation). That means they cause conceit which hinders your progress in good."

(Nilus of Sinai, *Peristeria – To Monk Agathios*)

For example, if someone told us, "Well done, you are a remarkable organ of the Divine Grace and you function excellently as a channel of inspiration," or, "Good for you, Divine Grace uses you remarkably as a conductor of deep perception," it's pretty sure that we would be offended or, at least, amazed by his irrational comment. But if he told us, "You are very inspired" or "You have deep perception," his remark would seem very understandable and rational.

In that case, however, when we receive a compliment or a praise, if we don't respond (inwardly or outwardly) through a state of humility, that the inspiration and deep perception are gifts, we will inevitably be led to conceit and pride, because we will consider ourselves creator and master of things which we neither created nor own. We will attribute the *gifts* of God to ourselves. And this will be a result of a wrong perception, both by the person who delivers the praise, and from we who receive it.

"When one man helps another by word or deed,
let them both recognize in this the grace of God.

(St. Mark the Ascetic, *On the Spiritual Law*, Text 74,
p. 115, Vol. 1, Philokalia)

When we adopt this distorted conception, we not only get used to not resisting inwardly or outwardly (if it is appropriate) the praises and acknowledgment, but we also learn to enjoy them and feel "uplifted." That is why we constantly seek an *artificial* uplifting without understanding that the *true* upraising will come when we allow God to realize it inside us. While we should learn to seek humility, we constantly long to be first in importance and position.

"At the same time came the disciples unto Jesus, saying, Who is the greatest in the kingdom of heaven? And Jesus called a little child unto him, and set him in the midst of them, And said, Verily I say unto you, Except ye be converted, and become as little children, ye shall not enter into the kingdom of heaven. Whosoever therefore shall humble himself as this little child, the same is greatest in the kingdom of heaven" (Matthew 18:1-4).

The Inner Restoration of Christianity

When we receive praise we should *feel* and say, either outwardly or inwardly, "Glory be to God" for, *"Thine is the kingdom, and the power, and the glory, forever"* (Matthew 6:13). We cannot avoid conceit as long as we *believe in ourselves*; even the most balanced man, the most down to earth and "humble" person, will carry, imperceptibly perhaps, an air of *self*-confidence and not God-confidence, if he doesn't attribute everything to God. In that way he will carry a subtle pride which might be swelling from time to time. And this is the reason why we can never avoid the conflict that conceit breeds.

> "Nowhere will you find more rest except in humility. Nowhere will you find more tumult except in pride. Humble yourself in front of everyone and you will be raised by the Lord. But when you are raised by Him, continue to stay humble in order not to lose His Grace."
>
> (St. Dimitri of Rostov, *Spiritual Alphabet*, p. 37)

Yet, we might be afraid of humility, fearing that being humble means allowing everyone to take advantage of us. We are afraid that nobody will take us into account, and no one will respect us. In reality, however, true humility is related exclusively to an *inner disposition* of our soul and a *spiritual orientation*.

Despite what we show outside us, what matters is how we feel inside us. Our outward behavior might function as a means either not to exhibit pride or to be humbled, but real humility is an *inner state* which is experienced gradually and *is based exclusively on our relation to God*.

We don't need to pretend to be low and insignificant, because this pretension, instead of bringing us closer to the state of humility, on the contrary, removes us farther away from it. True humility brings forth an unprecedented strength which may also be perceived by the people around us, and then the respect we receive will be genuine, and not as a result of an egoistic demand, "I demand that you respect me!"

This strength is real because it's not related to anything outside, it's not derived by enforcement, it's not subjected to acknowledgment and disputes, it's free from approvals or disapprovals and from favorable or unfavorable situations. It's real and genuine *strength* because it's clearly *internal*. This strength derives from the deepening release from ourselves, but mostly from our deepening dependence on the Source of Strength, the Source of Love, God.

The state of humility introduces us to the Reality, to the real world of God where His Will (Love) reigns and where, for the first time, we begin Living. The more proud we are, the more *subjective* we become, living in our *own imaginary world*, usually believing that we don't bother or harm anyone. In that way, however, we limit ourselves from participating in the *real world,* and we exclude ourselves from the real Life, from Paradise.

In the most extreme form of pride, we become the centre of the universe, as well as God himself. We feel powerful and great, worthy of respect and recognition, and we might indeed manage to have, one way or another, our own way. In reality, though, we are completely cut off from anything real and beautiful, remaining enslaved in the prison of our "self" which we, ourselves, have created.

And strangely enough, we struggle furiously, without ever relaxing, in order to preserve this prison. That is why we seek constant acknowledgment, and fight with every inkling of disproval, because only in this prison do we feel safe. *Only in this prison of ourselves can we define our identity.* And in this narrow cell, of course, it's not possible for even one ray of light from God's Grace to enter, since it's full of us!

When, however, we realize the existence of this internal hell and desire whole-heartedly to be released from it, then we begin walking towards the bright direction that leads to our inner paradise. We begin walking towards freedom, to the Promised Land, to the holy and fertile land of humility.

And the inspirer and guide of this journey, of course, is always God. When He sees that we deviate and tend to be lost in wrong directions or return to our old enslavement, to our hell, He often hurries again to help us, but this time by depriving us of His Help!

"Divine Grace abandons us to some degree in order to ascertain how weak we are without it. In that way we are relieved from the egoistic self-confidence, we acquire humility and rely exclusively on mighty God."

(St. Theophan the Recluse, *Guidance in the Spiritual Life*, p. 122)

This kind of help aims only at one thing: in the deeper realization that without His Help we are desperately lost; *thus* we are led to always seek God's aid, literally, in our every step, because *this* Help is *absolutely* necessary.

"You will ascertain whether you have begun obtaining blessed humility: if you are seized by a permanent and fiery love of praying."

(St. Dimitri of Rostov, *Spiritual Alphabet*, p. 38-39)

The Inner Restoration of Christianity

When we begin tasting humility, even dimly, our *need* for Him cannot help but flow spontaneously from within as a prayer saying to Him whole-heartedly:

"Forgive me our Father, release me from ignorance and make me realize my nothingness so I can attribute everything to You. Guard me from praises because the others are not aware of my agony, weakness and inadequacies. From their kindness they see only Your Light in me and because of Your providence they are protected from my darkness, but I suffer from it. Forgive us our Father, clean us; enlighten us; save us from our false self; release us from our darkness and lead us close to You."

"You have humility? You have God. You have everything! You don't have humility? You lose everything!"

(St. Theophan the Recluse, *Guidance in the Spiritual Life*, p. 169)

"God Be With You"

> "Do not put your trust in yourself. Place all hope in the Lord, and His help will always be with you."
>
> (St. Theophan the Recluse, *The Spiritual Life*, p. 164)

If we taste the state of real humility and in that way all our hopes are based on God, then God will be with us; then we *allow* God to be with us. For as one friend of God has said: "God *is* with us, *we* are not with Him."

If God is by our side we can truly face ourselves with all our insecurities, hopelessness and weaknesses. All can be healed and transformed, if God is with us.

> *"Be strong and of a good courage, fear not, nor be afraid of them: for the Lord thy God, he it is that doth go with thee; he will not fail thee, nor forsake thee"* (Deuteronomy 31:6).

When we are with God, He reinforces and covers us with His Grace which transforms our sense of reality. When we are lost in weakness and worry, terrified in the thought of various possible enemies, Love can raise us up, urging us to transcend the narrow limits of ourselves and be connected with a very drastic Source of Energy and Force by which we can have access in a very simple but essential way: with prayer.

Sincere heartfelt prayer brings us in direct communion with God; it makes us feel Him with us: very deep inside us and right next to us.

We all know that in the difficult hour we always seek some kind of help. If certain people are with us we feel stronger, or even certain objects might provide us with the sense of additional strength. The truth is, however, that what really reinforces us, using the aforementioned means, is the secret aid of God which we receive rather limitedly, however, because in essence, we are closed to it, either because we don't acknowledge it or because we forget it.

Now, if God *strives* to help us in spite of our being closed to Him, imagine what He would do for us if we allowed Him to help us. And even more, if we called Him to help us. For this to happen however, that is, in order to be in this state of receptivity and remembrance, so the difficult (or the *easy*) hour won't make us forget everything, all these realities we have mentioned are necessary: humility, hope in God, remembrance of God, and mainly prayer.

So let's pray to be in a state of *receptivity*, that is, of humility and real hope, so we can allow God to be with us: "Our God! Give us the strength to not forget You; to turn to You and realize that despite the outcome of any trial, its real purpose and meaning is to not lose You, to remain with You, in Your Love! Since the deeper Meaning behind everything Is You!"

To struggle on our own is very different than to struggle along with God. In the latter case we don't have anything to fear, because everything is going to be alright.

When we struggle alone, however, we should know that, in effect, we *suffer in vain*. The only benefit is that at some moment, after repeated failures, we might realize the futility of our efforts and turn to God for help. We might even need many years before we understand that we are feeble without God, that man is helpless without God. As soon as we realize this, however, all can be fixed; because then we start to pray. And then the real struggle begins… to be with God no matter what.

It's certain that we all need reinforcement, and this may either come from men or from anywhere else, but when we are left "alone" to face our difficulties, from the smallest ones to the largest, then we have a unique opportunity to experience something completely different and stunning:

> *"Behold, the hour cometh, yea, is now come, that ye shall be scattered, every man to his own, and shall leave me alone: and yet I am not alone, because the Father is with me"* (John 16:32).

If "God is with us" we can surpass our trials calmly and peacefully, and whereas we might be passing through hell, we will remain in our inner paradise – the one of relation and communication with God, with Love.

> *"Though I walk through the valley of the shadow of death, I will fear no evil: for thou art with me"* (Psalms 23:4).

"Along with Athena, Move Your Hand"

"In the struggle to keep ourselves directed Godwards and to fight against anything in us that is opaque or that prevents us from looking in the direction of God, we can be neither altogether active nor passive. We cannot be active in the sense that, by agitating ourselves, by making efforts, we cannot climb into heaven or bring God down from heaven. But we cannot just be passive, either, and sit doing nothing, because God does not treat us as objects; there would be no true relationship if we were merely acted upon by him."

(Metropolitan Anthony of Sourozh, *Living Prayer*, p. 93)

But what is our essential work? What is our necessary and possible effort?

It is our disposition and desire; the acknowledgment of our *need*.

In reality we cannot do much. We can study, search, struggle and try, but all this aims deeper at this one and only thing: in being persuaded ourselves, that what we really want is Love, is God. All our efforts and labors are focused on a genuine desire to return to where we parted, or fell off. And after thousands of hardships, when we reach this one and only desire (Luke 10:42), and turn back (inwardly or upwardly), immediately God comes out or descends to welcome us (Luke 15:20).

"Blessed is he who knows in truth that we are but tools in God's hands; that it is God who effects within us all ascetic practice and contemplation, virtue and spiritual knowledge, victory and wisdom, goodness and truth; and that to all this we contribute nothing at all except a disposition that desires what is good."

(St. Maximos the Confessor, *Various Texts*, 28, Third Century, p. 216, Vol. 2, Philokalia)

This is all our work which, *as simple as it is, so difficult it seems*. Our work is to decide to return back with the whole of our Being and *thus* make our soul's soil fertile in order to accept Divine Grace, which will fulfill our desire by cleansing, enlightening and raising us to our lost Paradise.

In order to acquire anything we must first *desire* it deeply, because our lukewarm desire won't lead us anywhere, *"I know thy works, that thou art neither cold nor hot: I would thou wert cold or hot. So then because thou art lukewarm, and neither cold nor hot, I will spew thee out of my mouth"* (Revelations 3:15-16).

Next, we must diligently *try* for it, because without effort we can't have anything, *"And from the days of John the Baptist until now the kingdom of heaven suffereth violence, and the violent take it by force"* (Matthew 11:12).

Finally, we must *relax* and wait for it to come (or to be given), because our intense desire and effort might eventually become obstacles to it.

Our work is not for us to ascend a little towards God and for God to descend a little downwards so we can meet in the middle.

"A soul can never attain the knowledge of God unless God Himself, in His condescension, takes hold of it and raises it up to Himself. For the human intellect lacks the power to ascend and to participate in divine illumination, unless God Himself draws it up –

in so far as this is possible for the human intellect – and illumines it with rays of divine light."

(St. Maximos the Confessor, *On Theology and the Incarnate Dispensation of the Son of God*, First Century, Text 31, p. 120, Vol. 2, Philokalia)

Our effort is directed in cleansing our inner hearing in order to hear His Call, God knocking on the door of our heart, so we can respond and open, *"Behold, I stand at the door, and knock: if any man hear my voice, and open the door, I will come in to him, and will sup with him, and he with me"* (Revelations 3:20).

Nevertheless, even our cleansing is in essence a result of Grace's action. Our efforts and labors are being made for our sake and cannot really guarantee us anything. They take place to prove to *ourselves* the *extent* of our *desire* and prepare us to accept with gratitude and appreciation the Divine Grace. Otherwise, we could demand from God the payment of our efforts and coerce the coming of His Divine Action, which simply is not possible.

"Therefore do not be content with these efforts alone; do not rest in them as if they were what you have to find. This is a dangerous illusion. It is equally dangerous to think that in these labors there is merit which grace is bound to reward. Not at all: these efforts are only the preparation for receiving grace; but the gift itself depends entirely on the will of the Giver."

(*The Art of Prayer – An Orthodox Anthology*, p. 145)

The Holy Spirit will visit us as soon as It finds us ready and It will revive our spirit which cannot by itself ascend to God. God descends to it.

Our inner ground, however, must be fertile and cultivated for this coming, otherwise God's seed won't bear fruit (Matthew 13:18-23). Our efforts have to do with the right cultivation of our ground, and in spite of being our "own" they still lack results without God's help. So we owe everything to God, both our efforts and their results.

But this fact doesn't spare us from our personal responsibility and participation in this work. We are not led through this point of view to a fatalism in which we rest assured, saying, "God will take care of it" or "If it is God's will," thus finding an excuse to avoid whatever seems toilsome, unpleasant or painful.

> "So holiness is woven of these two strands. Thus, I entreat you neither to entrust everything to God and then fall asleep, nor to think, when you are striving diligently, that you will achieve everything by your own efforts.
>
> "God does not want us to be lying idly on our backs; therefore He does not effect everything Himself. Nor does He want us to be boastful; therefore He did not give us everything. But having taken away from each of the two alternatives what is harmful, He has left us that which is for our good."
>
> (St. Theodoros the Great Ascetic, *A Century of Spiritual Texts*, 68-69, p. 28, Vol. 2, Philokalia)

What we must do is offer ourselves *whole-heartedly* to the Divine Action of God which will resume our full treatment. But if we ourselves, first of all, don't acknowledge our disease, it will not be possible to cooperate with our soul's Doctor, or to accept any medical suggestion.

> "In order to attain communion with God and achieve the blessed state of divinization [theosis], we must first be healed. So, beyond all other interpretations, Orthodoxy is mainly a therapeutic science and treatment. It differs clearly from other psychiatric methods, because it is not anthropocentric but theanthropocentric, and also because it does not do its work with human methods, but with the help and energy of Divine Grace, essentially through the synergy of divine and human volition."
>
> (Metropolitan of Nafpaktos Hierotheos, *Orthodox Psychotherapy – The Science of the Fathers*, p.15)

This synergy, that is, cooperation between God and us, must continue to the last and cannot do otherwise. And our part is to be in a constant watchfulness so we can act according to the Divine exhortations and promptings, as we ascertain *gradually* that in these are hiding our highest benefits.

So what is demanded mostly from us is our disposition, our wanting more than anything God and His Will. So we will be led safely to the ability of perceiving and coping with the Divine directions in order to attain our aim: freedom from our "self" and a union with God, with Love, or in other words, return to the Lost Paradise.

This is, after all, what the example of Jesus Christ is teaching us, whose exclusive work and only care was to do the Will of His Father, because this was His only true capability as well as His true destination:

"*I can of mine own self do nothing: as I hear, I judge: and my judgment is just; because I seek not mine own will, but the will of the Father which hath sent me. [...]*

For I have not spoken of myself; but the Father which sent me, he gave me a commandment, what I should say, and what I should speak. And I know that his commandment is life everlasting: whatsoever I speak therefore, even as the Father said unto me, so I speak. [...]

If I do not the works of my Father, believe me not. But if I do, though ye believe not me, believe the works: that ye may know, and believe, that the Father is in me, and I in him" (John 5:30, 12:49-50, 10:37-38).

Jesus Christ

"With regard to Christ's love of man, I think that the Word of God suggests even this, that the Superessential proceeded forth out of the hidden, into the manifestation amongst us, by having taken substance as man. But, He is hidden, even after the manifestation, or to speak more divinely, even in the manifestation, for in truth this of Jesus has been kept hidden, and the mystery with respect to Him has been reached by no word nor mind, but even when spoken, remains unsaid, and when conceived unknown."

(Dionysius the Areopagite, *Letter III: To Gaius Therapeutes*, pp. 142-143)

After two thousand years, humanity is still struggling with the enigmatic figure of Jesus Christ: Who was Jesus? Was He God? Was He a man? Was He a God-man? Did He really exist? Is He an historical or a mythical person?

There are people who believe undoubtedly in the story of Jesus Christ as we learn it from the Gospels; there are people who feel that their reason is offended by Christ's story so they reject it altogether; and there are others who adjust it to the frame of their own reason and interpret it in various ways.

So there are different views, extending from seeing Jesus Christ's story as a nice tale, to the conception and application of a Divine Plan for all humanity.

What is remarkable, however, is that Jesus Christ is appreciated by the followers of every religion and by every man who is affiliated with any kind of spiritual path. For example, Buddhists, Hindus, Muslims, appreciate Jesus Christ, and accept, of course, His existence. All theist people try to interpret Jesus one way or another and include Him in their faith or world view, while Muslims, for example, are not necessarily interested in Buddha or Krishna, or Buddhists and Hindus, in Mohamed.

There are also some who dispute the historical existence of Jesus and consider the fact of Christianity as a well calculated fraud at the expense of humanity, which they attempt to prove in every possible way. Nevertheless, in the end, even the strongest opponents of Christ (and Christianity) cannot avoid or ignore Him, and end up persecuting Him (like Saul), acquiring thus a strange obsession with His personhood. So, we see that only a small part of humanity doesn't appreciate, in one way or another, Jesus Christ, and even that observation is concerned with Him.

Nevertheless, in order to be precise, we must admit that the majority of humanity, faithful or not, is not concerned *actively* in its daily life with Jesus Christ or His Teaching. It shows an intense passiveness or indifference in this possibility, even though at the same time it is always ready to absorb any new "evidence," serious or laughable, that comes up in relation to Christ and Christianity. And this proves its thirst for understanding, and consequently, the lack of personal inner experience in relation to the truth concerning Jesus Christ and Christianity.

The ones, however, who are more actively involved with Jesus often pose various questions in relation to His historical existence. And it seems rather reasonable, when you are dealing with a person, to first examine whether he really existed.

The Historicity of Jesus Christ

The whole issue concerning Jesus Christ presents a difference which we don't meet with in any other person in humanity. What differentiates the case of Jesus is the claim for His Divine nature. His human nature can certainly enter into a historical frame, but can this be with His Divine nature? Of course, not. So when we refer to the historicity of Christ, we refer inevitably only to His human nature. And this is because whatever has to do with His Divine nature cannot be examined with the physical or psychological eyes of the human historical view.

Here it's worth noticing the following: Even if we could prove the historical existence of Jesus Christ, it wouldn't follow automatically that the claims about His Divine nature are true. But if we could prove in some way the truth around the claims concerning His Divine nature, we would inevitably prove His historicity.

So, for someone who is seriously interested in solving the mystery of Christ, proving His historical existence would only constitute a very small progression towards the question of "Who or what was Jesus Christ?" – and even by so great a labor, who knows how much could actually be achieved through books, studies and researches.

Nevertheless, if our research would lead to proving the historical non-existence of Jesus, then we would have also solved the mystery around His Divine nature. So we ought to have a look at the issue of His historicity.

The Human Nature of Jesus Christ

Let's briefly examine some facts in relation to the date of birth and death of Jesus Christ; two rather important facts for placing a person historically.

With little research we will find out that the date of His birth is not clearly defined. According to the current data it is placed somewhere around 4 to 8 years *before* His established year of birth, due to some, as it seems, erroneous calculations by the monk and ecclesiastical writer Dennis the Little during the 6th century.

And as far as His date of birth is concerned, we can easily ascertain after a brief research that it is celebrated on the 25th of December, mostly for symbolic and practical reasons, while the real date remains unknown. The Gospels don't refer to any celebration of the birth of His human nature, neither did the first Christians celebrate it. On the contrary, they emphasized His Divine nature and Teaching, and this was their daily concern.

In relation to the date and year of His death, and consequently to the duration of His life, it's interesting to cite the writings of two eminent Fathers of the Church: St. Maximos the Confessor and Irenaeus of Lyons.

"The Lord appeared when He was thirty years old, and with this number secretly teaches those with discernment the mysteries relating to Himself. For, mystically understood, the number thirty presents the Lord as the Creator and provident ruler of time, nature, and the intelligible realities that lie beyond visible nature. The number seven signifies that He is the Creator of time, for time has a sevenfold character. The number five signifies that He is the Creator of nature, for nature has a fivefold character because of the fivefold division of the senses. The number eight signifies that He is the Creator of intelligible realities, for intelligible realities come into being outside the cycle that is measured by time. And the number ten signifies that He is the provident ruler, because it is the ten holy commandments that lead men towards perfection, and also because the symbol for ten is the first letter of the name taken by the Lord when He became man. By adding up five, seven, eight and ten you obtain the number thirty. Thus he who truly knows how to follow the Lord as his master, will understand why, should he attain the age of thirty, he will also be empowered to proclaim the gospel of the kingdom. For when through his ascetic practice he has irreproachably created the world of the virtues as if it were a world of visible nature, not allowing his soul to be diverted from its course by the hostile powers as he passes through time; and when he unerringly gathers spiritual knowledge through contemplation, and is providentially able to engender the same state in others, then he himself, whatever his physical age, is thirty years old in spirit and makes manifest in others the power of the blessings which he himself possesses."

(St. Maximos the Confessor, *On Theology and the Incarnate Dispensation of the Son of God*, First Century, Text 79, p. 130, Vol. 2, Philokalia)

Let's also review a passage from Irenaeus of Lyons which comes from his famous work, *Against Heresies*, where he exerts a severe polemics against the *heresies* of his time that were related to Jesus and His teachings.

"Being thirty years old when He came to be baptized, and then possessing the full age of a Master, He came to Jerusalem, so that He might be properly acknowledged by all as a Master. For He did not seem one thing while He was another, as those affirm who describe Him as being man only in appearance; but what He was, that He also appeared to be. Being a Master, therefore, He also possessed the age of a

Master, not despising or evading any condition of humanity, nor setting aside in Himself that law which He had appointed for the human race, but sanctifying every age, by that period corresponding to it which belonged to Himself. For He came to save all through means of Himself – all, I say, who through Him are born again to God – infants, and children, and boys, and youths, and old men. He therefore passed through every age, becoming an infant for infants, thus sanctifying infants; a child for children, thus sanctifying those who are of this age, being at the same time made to them an example of piety, righteousness, and submission; a youth for youths, becoming an example to youths, and thus sanctifying them for the Lord. So likewise He was an old man for old men, that He might be a perfect Master for all, not merely as respects the setting forth of the truth, but also as regards age, sanctifying at the same time the aged also, and becoming an example to them likewise. Then, at last, He came on to death itself, that He might be 'the first-born from the dead, that in all things He might have the pre-eminence,' the Prince of life, existing before all, and going before all.

"They, however, that they may establish their false opinion regarding that which is written, "to proclaim the acceptable year of the Lord," maintain that He preached for one year only, and then suffered in the twelfth month. [In speaking thus], they are forgetful to their own disadvantage, destroying His whole work, and robbing Him of that age which is both more necessary and more honorable than any other; that more advanced age, I mean, during which also as a teacher He excelled all others. For how could He have had disciples, if He did not teach? And how could He have taught, unless He had reached the age of a Master? For when He came to be baptized, He had not yet completed His thirtieth year, but was beginning to be about thirty years of age (for thus Luke, who has mentioned His years, has expressed it: "Now Jesus was, as it were, beginning to be thirty years old," when He came to receive baptism); and, [according to these men] He preached only one year reckoning from His baptism. On completing His thirtieth year He suffered, being in fact still a young man, and who had by no means attained to advanced age. Now, that the first stage of early life embraces thirty years, and that this extends onwards to the fortieth year, everyone will admit; but from the fortieth and fiftieth year a man begins to decline towards old age, which our Lord possessed while He still fulfilled the office of a Teacher, even as the Gospel and all the elders testify; those who were conversant in Asia with John, the disciple of the Lord, [affirming] that John conveyed to them that information. And he remained among them up to the times of Trajan. Some of them, moreover, saw not only John, but the other apostles also, and heard the very same account from them, and bear testimony as to the [validity of] the statement. Whom then should we rather believe? Whether such men as these, or Ptolemæus, who never saw the apostles, and who never even in his dreams attained to the slightest trace of an apostle?

"But, besides this, those very Jews who then disputed with the Lord Jesus Christ have most clearly indicated the same thing. For when the Lord said to them, "Your father Abraham rejoiced to see My day; and he saw it, and was glad," they answered Him, "Thou art not yet fifty years old, and hast Thou seen Abraham?" Now, such language is fittingly applied to one who has already passed the age of forty, without having as yet reached his fiftieth year, yet is not far from this latter period. But to one who is only thirty years old it would unquestionably be said, "Thou art not yet forty years old." For those who wished to convict Him of falsehood would certainly not extend the number of His years far beyond the age which they saw He had attained; but they mentioned a period near His real age, whether they had truly ascertained this out of the entry in the public register, or simply made a conjecture from what they observed that He was above forty years old, and that He certainly was not one of only thirty years of age. For it is altogether unreasonable to suppose that they were mistaken by twenty years, when they wished to prove Him younger than the times of Abraham. For what they saw, that they also expressed; and He whom they beheld was not a mere phantasm, but an actual being of flesh and blood. He did not then want much of being fifty years old; and, in accordance with that fact, they said to Him, "Thou art not yet fifty years old, and hast Thou seen Abraham?" He did not therefore preach only for one year, nor did He suffer in the twelfth month of the year. For the period included between the thirtieth and the fiftieth year can never be regarded as one year."

(Irenaeus of Lyons, *Against Heresies*, Book 2, Chapter XXII, pp. 391-392)

Even if we accepted unobjectionably that Jesus lived only thirty-three years we could still wonder: What does it really mean for us whether Jesus Christ lived thirty, forty or fifty years? Probably nothing. Would that change our struggle even a little? Obviously not. Would it shake our faith in the credibility of the Gospels due to their historical inaccuracy or inadequacy? It's true that the Gospels seem to be deficient in historical sufficiency and sometimes they might even contain obvious historical contradictions. From another point of view, however, perhaps this is not true if they are studied more carefully by historical researchers. But one thing is certain, that if we mention all these historical questions to someone who tastes and experiences the Word of Christ, the Word of the Gospels, on the one hand he will smile, thinking of his own experience, and on the other he will be sad, thinking of the lack of our experience.

Other issues that come up when we study the historical accuracy of the Gospels around Jesus' life have to do with His lineage, place of birth and many other facts, as well as with the occurrences of His life. So we begin wondering to what extent the evangelists gave care to their narrations in an exact historical character. Perhaps what interested them didn't have so much to do with the historical aspect of the human nature of Jesus Christ, but with the theological meaning of His Divine nature.

The Divine Nature of Jesus Christ

In this point our research gets much more interesting, reflecting on how this ineffable mystery, in case it is real, can be expressed in human terms and words. Is it possible in the few pages of the Gospels to convey this unintelligible fact of the birth of the Son of God in human language?

If we continue our research we will discover that the Gospels lend from various sources, mostly eastern as well as ancient Greek, many elements, symbolisms and images in order to convey this inconceivable mystery of the Son of God in a way that their narration will be accepted in their time, but at the same time, will be timely and equally alive in the passing of two thousand years.

We should also notice that if we study the story of other spiritual persons who belong to various traditions, modern or ancient, we will find out that many of them, if not all, wanted to spread a veil of mystery as far as their personal identity and history were concerned, in order to prevent their disciples from identifying with their human personality and direct them to their spiritual personality (which cannot be limited in any historical biography) so they can draw its fruits: its spiritual work and teaching.

So wouldn't this be even truer for Jesus Christ, who struggled to not allow people to identify with His human personality and therefore be blinded by it? *"Is not this the carpenter's son? Is not his mother called Mary? And his brethren, James, and Joses, and Simon, and Judas? And his sisters, are they not all with us? Whence then hath this man all these things? And they were offended in him. But Jesus said unto them, A prophet is not without honor, save in his own country, and in his own house. And he did not many mighty works there because of their unbelief"* (Matthew 13:55-58). Whereas he obviously aimed at making them understand His Divine nature: *"He saith unto them, But whom say ye that I am? And Simon Peter answered and said, Thou art the Christ, the Son of the living God"* (Matthew 16:15-16).

This point of view is reinforced by the words of Jesus himself: *"While he yet talked to the people, behold, his mother and his brethren stood without, desiring to speak with him. Then one said unto him, Behold, thy mother and thy brethren stand without, desiring to speak with thee. But he answered and said unto him that told him, Who is my mother? and who are my brethren? And he stretched forth his hand toward his disciples, and said, Behold my mother and my brethren! For whosoever shall do the will of my Father which is in heaven, the same is my brother, and sister, and mother"* (Matthew 12:46-50); emphasizing thus clearly the priority and importance of His Divine nature.

So as we understand that the lack of exact historical data in relation to His human nature is probably deliberate, what is left for us to deal with is His Divine nature. But here we are faced with a difficulty: human intellect cannot understand the things of God. Only the spirit can understand the things of the Spirit: *"But the psychological [psychic-ψυχικός] man receiveth not the things of the Spirit of God: for they are foolishness unto him: neither can he know them, because they are spiritually discerned"* (1 Corinthians 2:14).

In essence, only God Himself can reveal the things of God: *"He saith unto them, But whom say ye that I am? And Simon Peter answered and said, Thou art the Christ, the Son of the living God. And Jesus answered and said unto him, Blessed art thou, Simon Bar Jona: for flesh and blood hath not revealed it unto thee, but my Father which is in heaven"* (Matthew 16:15-17).

This is one way to acknowledge the Divine nature of Christ, that is, the personal living relationship with Him which is given by God: *"And as he journeyed, he came near Damascus: and suddenly there shined round about him a light from heaven: And he fell to the earth, and heard a voice saying unto him, Saul, Saul, why persecutest thou me? And he said, Who art thou, Lord? And the Lord said, I am Jesus"* (Acts 9:3-5). One other way is through His Teaching, through His Word: *"Thou hast the words of eternal life. And we believe and are sure that thou art the Christ, the Son of the living God"* (John 6:68-69).

> *"To understand the significance of the word, we must fulfill it. The commandments of the Gospel which are being fulfilled immediately start to transform, change and enliven man, his mode of thought, the feelings of his heart, his very body. "For the word of God is quick, and powerful, and sharper than any two edged sword, piercing even to the dividing asunder of soul and spirit, and of the joints and marrow, and is a discerner of the thoughts and intents of the heart"* (Hebrews 4:12). *The word of God contains in itself its [own] witness. […] A Christian who does not know the attributes of the word, denounces himself as being cold towards the word, ignorant of the word of God, or only possessing dead knowledge according to the letter alone."*
>
> (St. Ignatius Brianchaninov, *On Miracles and Signs*, Orthodox Life, Vol. 45, Nos 2-4)

> "The word acts in one manner, the signs act in another. The words act directly on the mind and heart, the signs on the mind and heart through the senses. The consequences of the action of the word are stronger, more powerful, more definite than the consequences from the action of the signs. When the word and the signs act together, then the action of the signs is left as if unnoticed, by reason of the abundant action of the word. This is clear from the narrative in the Gospel. Nicodemus was influenced by the signs, and he recognized in the Lord only a teacher sent by God (John 3:2). The Apostle Peter was influenced by the word and he confessed the Lord as the Christ, the Son of God."
>
> (St. Ignatius Brianchaninov, *On Miracles and Signs,* Orthodox Life, Vol. 45, Nos 2-4)

As we can see, we need the personal, living experience of the Word of Jesus in order to perceive who He was. The experience of others can simply inspire us, but can't make us recognize that, *"Thou art the Christ, the Son of the living God"* (Matthew 16:16).

Nevertheless, these God-given experiences, even when they're not felt personally, often convey a dynamic, a certain quality, which grants them authority that makes them a source of inspiration.

Witnesses

So here we could cite the experiences of certain people, starting with the narrations of John G. Bennett from his autobiography, *Witness: The Story of a Search*, in which he records his spiritual search:

> "The following week we met again at Kuru Cheshme and this time Sabaheddin's usual reserve in speaking of his own private convictions lifted, and he spoke about Jesus

Christ in a way no one had ever spoken to me before. He had, of course, been brought up as a Muslim. He had studied Eastern religions — especially Buddhism, but he had found no satisfaction except in the contemplation of Jesus Christ. His face lit up as he spoke of the love of Jesus for mankind. I could see that Divine Love was a reality for him, whereas it had been no reality for the Christian priest who had tried to teach me the meaning of the Christian faith.

"Mrs. Beaumont was obviously delighted to hear him speak in this way. She drew him on with the right interjections. He said that Islam was a great and noble religion and that he had never renounced its central dogma — that is, the Oneness and the complete Otherness of God. The Holy Virgin was for him as much a living reality as Jesus the Son of God. Only it was necessary to remember that no man ever could or ever would understand the true meaning of the relationship 'Son of God.'

"For me this talk was a marvelous experience. I had never until that evening taken religion seriously. The next day I remembered much of what he had said. But before the week was out, the impression had faded. It was not until much later that I realized that no one can transmit his faith to another. I had been deeply moved by what the Prince had said, but it had not entered the depth of me."

(John G. Bennett, *Witness: The Story of a Search*, pp. 42-43)

So much later, John Bennett reached a personal experience in relation to Christ:

"One day I was at High Mass, sitting behind the Choir as a guest of the Monastery, but in front of the rail at which communion was distributed to the laity. This means that the celebrant had to pass me as he brought the Sacrament. My thoughts were wandering, when I felt a shiver pass through my body. I became completely aware that Christ was coming towards me in the sacrament. I could feel Him go past and felt the deepest reverence and pure joy. As I knelt, I understood beyond doubt that God could be and was present in the host. I saw in a flash how the doctrine of the Real Presence is free from the anthropomorphism that so distressed me in most Christian theology. If God is pure Will, then He can manifest in and through any vehicle. I saw how the second Person of the Trinity must be manifested and indeed is a person by reason of manifestation.

"All these and many other understandings poured into my mind, while I felt at the same time joy and gratitude that this should be shown to me. Above all, I was aware of the Love of God as beyond all the limitations of existence – of 'name and form' – in terms of which we think. I was sure that this omnipresent love was able to reach me as the small being kneeling unnoticed in the aisle of the chapel."

(John G. Bennett, *Witness: The Story of a Search*, p. 353)

Next, we cite the experiences of the Greek author, Sophia Antzaka, as she describes them in her autobiography *Hieros Gamos* (*Sacred Marriage*), where she uses the third person giving her protagonist the name Th.:

"She sat up in her bed and wrote the following in her journal: "I am astonished by the "ideas" that are visiting me. In short, something insists on informing me that when Jesus referred to His Father, he referred to a Supreme Being and not simply in an abstract energetic outflow neither to electricity of high voltage nor to light or sound in their highest expression. [...] So how could I claim now that God is light, that is, a physical, material, cosmic power? Now God is a living conscious Being with conscious aims and intentions."

[...] "Soon however she woke up after a very lively dream. She saw the materialization of roses. [...] The dream had a strange influence on her. It introduced her into a region where the immaterial slips smoothly into the material, while the two worlds, the material and the immaterial, communicate unhindered.

"She didn't have the time to fully assimilate the dream when 'knowledge' visited her once more, bringing her new gifts. Th. leaned again upon her diary: 'The Supreme Being, or God, concentrates on some thought of His. And His thought is condensed due to His concentration. Creation probably took place in that way. Who knows, perhaps I never would have understood the act of Creation internally if I hadn't seen the dream with the roses. Now I understand without a hitch the thorny issue of the immaculate conception of Jesus. The Supreme Being just needed to concentrate on the thought or idea of an embryo in the womb of Mary for the materialization to take place by the articulation of thinking to sound, that is, to word. Christ was the Will of God, the Thought of God, the Plan of God, which incarnated. His mission, His role, had been conceived age-long until the moment of His materialization to earth came. My God, how could humanity of all ages dare to downgrade such supreme spiritual facts only because the materialistic mind of man can only grasp the material reality! Few are those who have transcended the limits of the materialistic mind in order to know firsthand the truth of another superior reality!' " (Vol. 7, pp. 203-205)

"The morning of Great Thursday Mrs. Xanthidou called her. It had been a while since she last saw her and she had missed her. They agreed for Th. to visit her this evening.

"Mrs. Xanthidou was a lady around 75 with remarkable outer and inner subtlety. Early on she had denounced Christianity because she didn't understand it and she had penetrated into the way of thinking and understanding of the Upper East. She had met Th. at a lecture years ago and she had been impressed by a question that Th. posed to the speaker. At the end of the lecture she approached Th. and asked her for a meeting of discussion. Since then they hadn't stopped seeing each other and Mrs. Xanthidou watched with evident excitement the inner unfolding of Th. as if her being was unfolding.

So that evening Th. was in the warm living room of Mrs. Xanthidou.

"I closed the windows so I won't hear the psalmodies" she explained to Th.

Th. smiled remembering her similar attitude.

"I was never able to get under the skin of Christianity" Mrs. Xanthidou continued. "Since I was little I was like that. And I cannot figure out how people pretend that they understand all these incomprehensible things that the Gospels say. Whereas the spring waters of the East are clear as crystal. Yesterday a religious friend of mine came to visit and brought me a book about Christ. "I brought it so you can approach Jesus" she said. "But I forbade her to proselytize me."

"Which was this book? Do you remember its title?" asked Th. with a sudden interest.

"I didn't even care to see the title, even though my friend left it in case I read it."

"She left it? Where is it?" asked Th.

"Behind you, in the library."

Th. got up. She found it at first sight. It was, *Christ* of Papini. On its cover was Jesus in His severe form. Th. looked at it with interest. There was no doubt. His form was telling her something. His eyes were absorbing her look.

"Mrs. Xanthidou, as you know I am like you. Only thing was that I turned within, towards myself, while you turned to the East. But if you don't have any objection I would like to read the Passion of Christ from this book. Take it as a biography."

Mrs. Xanthidou was a little puzzled with Th. but soon she recovered.

"This is the way I take it. Jesus was a special man and I accept him like that but I cannot accept Christianity."

Th. went through the pages searching for the Passion Week.

"Should I start, Mrs. Xanthidou?"

"I am ready, you can start."

Th. started. Was it Papini, was it her own opening to Christ that metamorphosed the little living-room of Mrs. Xanthidou into the garden of Gethsemane, into Praetorium, into Golgotha? Where did the furniture of Mrs. Xanthidou go? What happened to her strong resistance to the God-manhood of Jesus? What happened to her Eastern beliefs? Was it the vibrating voice of Th. that loosened all the closely-knit ties of Mrs. Xanthidou and dissolved her into tears? And where did the atheism of Th. go?

The skin under Th.'s eyes was burning by the lava of her tears. Her voice got hoarse from the sobbing while her solar plexus were writhing with delight, rejoicing for the food that fell into its abyss.

When Th. stopped reading, she couldn't distinguish clearly Mrs. Xanthidou, but neither could Mrs. Xanthidou distinguish Th.

"What was this tonight, Th.! What unheard of miracle!" Mrs. Xanthidou repeated again and again with a broken voice. "And when I remember what I said before you started reading!! Tonight, for the first time, I felt what Jesus Christ means. And you know what? I doubt whether all theses masses that are filling the churches tonight feel the slightest vibration."

Th. was nodding her head and at the same time she was wiping her tears. The vibration of her solar plexus was so intense that her tongue was still bound.

"Tonight a miracle took place here" Mrs. Xanthidou continued. "Here was the real temple, here came and stood between us the invisible Christ. Now the Eastern beliefs which have fed me from my early youth seem so cold to me!

Th. how can I thank you for insisting to read from this book I had scorned?" (Vol. 7, pp. 266-269).

"The tension increased, urging Th. to express herself by drawing. She felt the desire to draw in rough glass paper as she used to do in the past. She took a piece of glass paper and yellow chalk and committed herself to drawing. She knew that this was the only way for the tension to wear out. But the only thing that she wanted to draw was a bright yellow swirl, the source of everything, the Absolute, God. The condensation of the swirl was tremendous. Th. named her "painting" "The Swirl of the Universal Cosmos." Soon she felt relieved that her channels had opened again.

"Then, in a flash, her mind received the following: 'Jesus Christ, the Lord of thousands of millions of Galaxies, incarnated as a human being to save the inhabitants of an infinitely small planet in a remote corner of the Universe.'

She was filled with awe.

'My God, what an ineffable mystery!' she said to herself." (Vol. 7, pp. 270-271)

♦

"And what do you have to say about Christ, Buddha and their like?"

Something sounded wrong inside Th. She watched carefully and she perceived that her being had caught a huge mistake in E.'s formulation, a mistake that almost everyone commits.

"Jesus Christ, E., is a completely special occasion. In no way can He be compared with Buddha or with other perfected or enlightened humans."

E. was listening with surprise the atheist Th. distinguishing with these words, the Christ.

"I am explaining myself" Th. continued. "The other founders of religions were *humans*. I can see your question. Don't bother. You will ask me, why Jesus wasn't a human?"

"Exactly" E. agreed.

"If by human you mean a being with a carnal covering, surely he was. But I am referring to the inner origin of the perfected ones. But perhaps you aren't interested in the inner differentiations" she said and became silent.

So E. burst out.

"Are you kidding? This is exactly what I am crucially interested in. Please, Th. stop fooling around and continue. What were you thinking... stopping in the most key point?"

"Ok, relax, I am ready to continue. So there are beings (inner beings I mean) that descend from above and beings that ascend from below. The latter are human beings who after many and various efforts are being perfected. And in that way they become worthy of reaching into exo-human spheres. But their base, their origin, remains human. Is that clear so far?"

"More than clear. But talk to me about Jesus Christ. What happens to His case?"

"The exact opposite happens. He descended from the highest and holiest apartments and wore the human garment. His own base is heaven, not earth. He descended, he didn't ascend. He suffered damage, He was lowered, He became incomplete outside, while the others, the humans, became all the more perfect as they ascended. So let's say that some perfected ones established religions based on the truths they met in the higher region where they had arrived. Now, compare them with the religion that is established by someone – for example, Christ – who comes directly from the gulfs of the Father, who knows what the Father knows. Doesn't it follow that his religion will be different than the religion of others?"

"This sounds very logical" E. agreed, who still couldn't shake off the surprised expression she had after hearing Th. talking so thoughtfully about Jesus." (Vol. 9, pp. 53-55)

In this point it is worth noting the obvious interest of E. for the "case of Jesus Christ" as she says. The majority would react in such a way, because we are all burning, admitting it or not, to solve (or to have solved for us) the mystery of Jesus Christ.

Next, it is interesting to see how, despite her previous experience in *Vol. 7* where "knowledge" revealed to Th. the feasibility of immaculate conception, and in particular led her to admire: "My God, how could humanity of all ages dare to downgrade such supreme spiritual facts only because the materialistic mind of man can only grasp the material reality!" that nevertheless her materialistic mind keeps disbelieving in the possibility of immaculate conception and needs a new living insight:

"She half-sat on her bed and turned on the radio. She came up to the day's preaching. Someone was talking about the immaculate conception. She reached her hand to turn off the radio. She thought of the subject as unfeasible.

"Listen to this, immaculate conception, they say" she thought.

But her hand froze upon the button, as some subtle inner string, from the many that were freed from the anger covering them, started pulsating in accordance with the words of the preacher.

"Yes there is no doubt that my being is in accordance with immaculate conception" Th. ascertained with surprise.

She strained her ears in order to grasp anything relevant. And what she grasped assured her that the immaculate conception wasn't a myth but a tangible fact; that God-Word, a huge, invisible Entity had diminished in order to fit in a human womb borrowing from her a physical body. Instantly something speared her mind, like an illumination, and in its light Th. saw the Word or the Absolute as a conscious living Being and not anymore as a mass of energy. In another gleam she saw that the energetic conception was materialistic and mechanistic, comparing to the conception of a Being." (Vol. 9, p. 120)

And later on when her Being had assimilated the aforementioned possible reality, she opened to new "knowledge:"

"What interests me, now that I am living in this vibration, are not the miracles of Christ, His immaculate conception, His Metamorphosis and Resurrection, but His teaching. Even though I don't know much about the teaching of Buddha – but neither about the teaching of Jesus – some secret "knowledge" inherent in this level, informs me that the teaching of Buddha doesn't even touch the borders of the purity and perfection of Christ's teaching. The latter produces a harmonic effect in me, as if my essence was always inclined towards absolute purity – which is Christic!" (Vol. 9, p. 140)

And despite all these living revelations that are offered to her, she later reflects:

"I am a novice in the world of Christ" she pondered. "I accept some things while others I don't. I am a neophyte in the region of Grace, of total cleanliness and purity. I am also finding out that everything pales in front of the state of purity. [...] And anyway what has been revealed to me by the Miraculous world of the Living God? Nothing." (Vol. 9, pp. 149-153)

So her insights continue:

"Imagine, however, that the Living Christ descended and lived in such a mechanical system like earth's, that even in me produces a sense of suffocation and imprisonment! I see Him leaving his high Apartments of His Living Kingdom, crossing one by one the spheres or zones or heavens of the mechanical Creation. [...] so Christ, descending from zone to zone, from level to level, was subjected to alterations of His real nature since each mechanical sphere of Creation engaged and interpreted Him according to its own mechanical data, its own noosphere or intelligence. The last step, earth, almost didn't recognize Him since it ignores the Absolute, it mocks Its existence and substitutes It with the term Energy, in contrast to dense matter. This planet, that is, the texture and structure of its mechanical intelligence, doesn't acknowledge any higher creature than man and any other creator than the mechanical matter with its random combinations." (Vol. 9, pp. 153-154)

But her researching mind doesn't give up until her Being is permeated wholly beyond any doubt by the experience of truth:

"I discern in me the deep request of discovering the truth behind the mission of Christ. What Religion claims – even if it's real – seems to me prefabricated, naïve and incomprehensible. And as such, it provokes my aversion. I am ascertaining that in my case there is no room for outer intervention, that is, interpretation or guidance. No, this is out of the question. The truth, as enlightenment, should be direct, having as a conveyor my now mature being."

Soon Th. "saw" that the teaching of Christ, a teaching from the highest apartments of Absolute, presupposed the existence of Moral Conscience. Comparatively, the summit of Zen (Satori), Tao and Nirvana, hit her in the face as inexpressibly lower states." (Vol. 9, pp. 190-191)

"If it is proved that Christ was really sent to earth from high above for some mission, then all the other religions are not Divine, since they are concerned only with the moral or psychological purification of man and not with his theosis. I am burning by the desire of solving this mystery..." (Vol. 10, p. 31)

So after many painful inquiries, a different certainty begins permeating her Being:

"And the most important is that this Creator ceased to be just a Power, a kind of supreme, creative energy but is revealed to me as a living, conscious Being who handles powers and energies according to some ultimate Plan."

Th. stayed, still watching an imperceptible vibration in her depths.

"Yes" she said after a while. "Now I have to do with a Supreme, Living Being, with Its overwhelming reality. Now I can speak to this Being, while before I couldn't speak to Light, to energies, to the Creative Power. Ah, just now I am beginning to see that prayer – which angered me so much in all my life – is a means of talking to the Creator. It's a direct way of communication. Most High God, it's like I am starting to feel, sensitively, His Presence, His vibrating Existence, His supreme Wisdom, His Plan. It's like I am starting to conceive the saying that He knows the number of our hairs and that nothing can be done without His consent. This must be the so called Destination. My God, how much time was necessary in order to realize, finally, that my destination has a place in the general Plan of Destination of a Living Being. There goes my supposed (and non-existent) independence. From now on it is necessary to act and move consciously in the huge plexus of the Divine Plan. But I am lacking in clear vision both of the general Plan or Destination and of my own, in the great Destination. I need inspired Knowledge and Enlightenment about the Divine Plan, the Fall, the necessity of the incarnation of the Word to Earth, what would happen to Earth and the World if the Word hadn't incarnated, and so forth. I am starting to suspect that there must be a very serious reason behind the embodiment and death of the Word and in the fact that this dramatic occurrence had been betokened by various prophets long before it became a tangible reality. Everything unfolded according to a Plan. This gives meaning to everything. Nothing is independent, unconnected. Everything depends on the Living God and His Plan." (Vol. 10, pp. 50-51)

In that way she obtains a flash from the meaning of the "Divine Plan:"

"And the so called "Divine Plan" from Love must be emanating. It is a Plan of Restoration of the fallen Matter, of the fallen man, of the Spirit of Fall itself, to their initial place in the region of Spirit, for the re-starting of the interrupted co-function." (Vol. 10, p. 77)

All these passages might not offer any new "revelations" and much of their data, if not all, might already be known to us; the characteristic, however, which gives them a special value is their living quality.

We referred to experiences of certain people that we wouldn't place in the "traditional," as it were, Christians (one of them was a Muslim), otherwise some witnesses and experiences in relation to Jesus Christ by people who have been brought up in Christianity without ever questioning Jesus, might be considered prejudiced. But when they are derived by people who had disbelieved in or even denied the traditional beliefs of their religion, then they constitute probably a cause of making us think. They challenge us to face ourselves and really wonder whether we might pretend (to our own self) we "know" or "believe," since our faith doesn't transcend even our daily difficulties let alone remove the mountains (Matthew 17:20) of our egocentrism...

Personal Witness

For those who have never defied in their course of life the belief of their childhood, we could say that there isn't any problem with the faith that was implanted in us at the beginning of our formation, but it's not enough and it won't lead us very far; it needs renewal, we need to re-examine its foundations. Where is it based? Could it need some restoration which can be offered now by our personal experience and not by the narrations of other people's experiences? Should it be founded on experience so we can be certain that it won't give up on us at the first opportunity? And for those of us who have lost the belief of our childhood in the course of our life, the words of Christ will always be timely, *"Verily I say unto you, Whosoever shall not receive the kingdom of God as a little child, he shall not enter therein"* (Mark 10:15).

Especially in relation to Jesus Christ, if we study the Gospels we will see that even His own disciples, as well as John the Baptist, the forerunner of His work, had their doubts. Even though John the Baptist is charged with such an important work and a knowledge and faith far beyond our standards are obviously demanded of him, he is still feeling doubts, *"John Baptist hath sent us unto thee, saying, Art thou he that should come? Or look we for another?"* (Luke 7:20). In this point the answer of Jesus is very important, who refers John to His work and words, *"Go your way, and tell John what things ye have seen and heard"* (Luke 7:22).

Jesus never tries to convince anyone about His identity; He turns everyone's attention to His work and word. For He knows that the real and essential relationship with Him cannot be any other than the spiritual one, *"No man can say that Jesus is the Lord, but by the Holy Ghost"* (1 Corinthians 12:3). That is why only after someone has experienced His works and words, can he really be related in a relationship of Love with the Son of Love.

"I am the way, the truth, and the life: no man cometh unto the Father, but by me. If ye had known me, ye should have known my Father also: and from henceforth ye know him, and have seen him. Philip saith unto him, Lord, show us the Father, and it sufficeth us. Jesus saith unto him, Have I been so long time with you, and yet hast thou not known me, Philip? He that hath seen me hath seen the Father; and how sayest thou then, Show us the Father? Believest thou not that I am in the Father, and the Father in me? The words that I speak unto you I speak not of myself: but the Father that dwelleth in me, he doeth the works. Believe me that I am in the Father, and the Father in me: or else believe me for the very works' sake. Verily, verily, I say unto you, He that believeth on me, the works that I do shall he do also; and greater works than these shall he do; because I go unto my Father. And whatsoever ye shall ask in my name, that will I do, that the Father may be glorified in the Son. If ye shall ask any thing in my name, I will do it. If ye love me, keep my commandments" (John 14:6-15).

Almost everyone in the Gospels who acknowledged Jesus Christ to be the Son of God, had first personally experienced His works and words. And their faith was according to the depth of their experience.

"Every word of Christ shows us God's mercy, justice and wisdom, and if we listen gladly, their power enters into us. That is why the unmerciful and the unjust, listening to Christ with repugnance, were not able to understand the wisdom of God, but even crucified Him for teaching it. So we, too, should ask ourselves whether we listen to Him gladly. For He said: *"He who loves Me will keep My commandments, and he will be loved by My Father, and I will love him, and will manifest Myself to him*" (John 14:21). Do you see how He has hidden His manifestation in the commandments? Of all the commandments, therefore, the most comprehensive is to love God and our neighbor."

(St. Mark the Ascetic, *226 Texts*, 223, pp. 144-145, Vol. 1, Philokalia)

The products of our thinking process have a certain quality and specific results; the products of insight or revelation and mostly of *heartfelt experience* have a completely different qualitative taste and the corresponding results.

"Christ is hidden in the Gospel, and he who wishes to find Him must first sell all that he has and buy the Gospel (Matthew 13:44). It is not enough to merely find Christ through one's reading, but one should also receive Him in oneself by imitating His way of life in the world. For 'he who seeks Christ,' says St. Maximos, 'should seek him not outside but inside himself.' Like Christ, he should become sinless in body and soul, in so far as a human being can do this; and he should guard the testimony of his conscience (2 Cor. 1:12) with all his strength. In this way, even though in the eyes of the world he is poor and of no consequence, he will rule as a king over his will at all times."

(St. Peter of Damaskos, *Book I – The Fourth Stage of Contemplation*, p. 126, Vol. 3, Philokalia)

We know the saying of Jesus, "*Whosoever therefore shall confess me before men, him will I confess also before my Father which is in heaven. But whosoever shall deny me before men, him will I also deny before my Father which is in heaven*" (Matthew

10:32-33). But we often think that these words refer to an outer spoken confession, overlooking their much more significant *inner* meaning and its corresponding outer results. What we are called to do is to experience internally the reality of Jesus Christ by keeping His Word and in that way our whole life will consist of an outer witnessing of His Truth. Confessing Jesus Christ in our words while denying Him in our hearts or actions, certainly won't lead us anywhere. On the contrary, the practical response to His Word and call will provide us with the necessary personal experience and living taste of the Truth.

> *"If ye keep my commandments, ye shall abide in my love;*
> *even as I have kept my Father's commandments,*
> *and abide in his love"* (John 15:10).

The New Testament

"This book (with the four Gospels) is the mother of all books; the prayer of prayers. It is the guide to the Kingdom of Heaven. It leads man on earth to true knowledge and makes us worthy, while still in the body, to come 'in our heart,' face to face with God."

(Starets Parthenios, *Counsels and Sayings*, p. 95)

We use (in Greek) the expression, "Man's soul is an abyss." But what does this phrase really mean? Its essential meaning can be found in the fact that the soul of man constitutes indeed an immense and vast region which contains immeasurable depths and heights. One should have a map in order to travel in there and be led somewhere, otherwise he will be lost. The New Testament is this kind of map, a living guide.

"The Holy Gospel and the whole of the New Testament is the most trustworthy guide, the real guide of the Christian life, the safe beacon of the right path to salvation. All those who want to be saved obtain the knowledge on how to strive for their salvation from the New Testament."

(Theophan the Recluse, *Preaching Another Christ*, Part 4)

It is a very old map however, two thousand years old, which has been written in a "strange" ancient language, so its interpretation is not always easy.

"When you read Holy Scripture, perceive its hidden meanings."

(St. Mark the Ascetic, *On the Spiritual Law*, Text 26, p. 112, Vol. 1, Philokalia)

If this map promises to lead us to a definite destination, then each misinterpretation will inevitably lead to an irrelevant or opposite destination. And since this specific map seeks to lead us to Life, its misinterpretations could easily lead us to an imitation of Life, to some kind of "life," that is, to death.

"But it is not easy for everyone who reads the Gospel to understand it fully and thus walk safely on the path of salvation. Someone may read the Gospel, but interpret it incorrectly. For him the Gospel becomes an instrument of destruction!"

(Theophan the Recluse, *Preaching Another Christ*, Part 4)

Despite its age, possible damage and probable alteration, this map is still able to lead us safely to its promised destination, to the Kingdom of God, to Love. Yet, one of the basic conditions for this to happen, is its practical use, as is the case with every other map.

"It is not enough to be struck by the passages which appear to be so true, the struggle to become, at every moment of our life, what we are at the best moments must follow, and then we will gradually shed the superficial and become more real and more true; just as Christ is truth and reality itself, so shall we become more and more what Christ is. This does not consist in imitating Christ in his outer expression only, but of being inwardly what he is. The imitation of Christ is not an aping of his conduct or of his life; it is a hard and complex struggle."

(Metropolitan Anthony of Sourozh, *Living Prayer*, p. 100)

So one of the first demands is to acknowledge truthfully and from experience that this map refers directly to us.

"When reading the Holy Scriptures, he who is humble and engaged in spiritual work will apply everything to himself and not to someone else."

(St. Mark the Ascetic, *On the Spiritual Law*, Text 6, p. 110, Vol. 1, Philokalia)

Only when we start applying it, using it practically, do we begin understanding it. Otherwise, its directions and instructions will remain just information to us.

"The law of freedom [of the Gospel] teaches the whole truth. Many read about it in a theoretical way, but few really understand it, and these only to the degree to which they practice the commandments."

(St. Mark the Ascetic, *On the Spiritual Law*, Text 30, p. 112, Vol. 1, Philokalia)

We learn from the ones who went before us in this journey that this map can help us discover the most valuable treasure.

"The whole teaching of the Gospel is really a teaching about loving."

(Anthony Bloom, *God and Man, The Atheist and the Archbishop*, p. 14)

But this kind of outer assurance is not enough, nor can it establish within us the necessary faith and determination we will need many times during this inner journey in order to continue, despite the seeming or real difficulties.

"He who does not know the truth cannot truly have faith; for by nature, knowledge precedes faith. What is said in Scripture is not said solely for us to understand, but also for us to act upon."

(St. Hesychios the Priest, *On Watchfulness and Holiness*, Section 60, p. 172, Vol. 1, Philokalia)

We are obliged as we use this map to verify its *value* in every step through its *practical application*. In that way we will gradually believe in it since it will constantly reveal its abilities to us!

Many are wondering about the value of the New Testament as a work of art or holy text. But only when we see its narrated drama taking place in us, when we realize that everything in this work illustrates an aspect of ourselves, are we able to grasp some of its importance.

Only when we feel the Divine Word coming to raise our deadened soul as in the case of Lazarus, will we experience some of its meaning. When we see the Pharisee in us, as well as Peter, or Saul being transformed to Paul, we will perceive part of its greatness. When we see the two thieves on the crosses fighting within us in relation to the Divinity, we will begin suspecting the hidden treasures of this Holy Scripture.

When we realize how much we heard but didn't understand, we will taste what it means to "hear" but remain deaf. When a small part of the truth of the New Testament's message is revealed to us, we will marvel, seeing a little of its Light, and then we will know what it means to "see" but be blind.

We have to see the inner Pilate acknowledging something of the miracle and being informed secretly (from his wife, another one of our aspects!) that here is the Truth… but doing nothing about it; he is passively abandoned to the deaf and blind multitude in us which always crucifies the Word of God.

The most important, however is to understand the notion of the Virgin Mary in us. Our soul must become pure, clean, virgin and immaculate in order to conceive the Spirit. For only when she is pure and untainted can she come into contact with the Spirit so His Son can be born inside her. Only our virgin soul can consist in her purity of a fertile ground for the seed of the Father.

When we experience even the beginnings of this reality, we cannot help but stand in awe before this Holy Revelation of the New Testament and then we won't have any doubt that it is a Divine Work, the Word of God.

It is extremely important to have this personal experience, because if we decide to use this work in relation to our inner search, it must really play the part of a living guide.

> "Several spiritual writers say that we must try to discover Christ in us. Christ is the perfect, completely true man, and we can begin to discover what is true in us by discovering what is akin to him. There are passages in the

gospel against which we rebel and other passages which make our heart burn within us (Luke 24:32). If we single out the passages which either provoke a revolt, or which we feel with all our heart to be true, we will already have discovered the two extremes in us; in short, the anti-Christ and the Christ in us. We must be aware of both kinds of passages and concentrate on those which are close to our heart, because we may safely assume that they mark one point at least in which Christ and we are akin, a point at which a man is already – certainly not fully, but at least in an incipient way – a real man, an image of Christ. But it is not enough to be emotionally moved, to give complete intellectual agreement to this or that passage of the gospel; we must embody the words of Christ. We may have been touched, and yet abandon all we have thought and felt on the first occasion that offers itself for applying the discovery."

(Metropolitan Anthony of Sourozh, *Living Prayer*, pp. 99-100)

The story of Jesus Christ is a map for reaching to the union with God, to *theosis* and it wouldn't be given if we weren't capable of treading this path. And it is certain that many before us were helped (or saved) by this map, which is why its greatness is praised up and until our days.

The experience of others, however, is sufficient only to draw our attention to this guide of Life; we also need our personal witness. That is why all of us who want to make this inner journey must discover the Bible anew through a personal experience.

"For a true man it is a bad error not to know the scriptures."

(Evagrius of Pontus, *Maxims 3*, Maxim 13, p. 232)

And we should have, of course, a great longing for this inner journey, so the law of Christ can be applied, *"Ask, and it shall be given you; seek, and ye shall find; knock, and it shall be opened unto you: For every one that asketh receiveth; and he that seeketh findeth; and to him that knocketh it shall be opened"* (Matthew 7:7-8).

In that way this manhandled map will begin revealing its value. We must be careful, however, not to be misled by the ones who cannot see or hear, and whom we will meet both outside, but *mostly* inside us! Because for them it has been said, *"They seeing, see not; and hearing they hear not, neither do they understand"* (Matthew 13:13). Let's be watchful in relation to all these inner and outer false prophets who are constantly calling us to follow them, *"Many false prophets shall rise, and shall deceive many"* (Matthew 24:11).

We should emphasize that these words are much more important regarding our own selves than any outer voices. For we have many aspects inside us that belong to our false self, and despite the fact that they are deaf and blind, they want to lead us, they want to be our Real Self when they're not. These inner voices hasten to mislead us long before any false outer prophet has the chance.

We are in the dark and so we are blind. We need Light to see and walk in the straight path, far from any cliffs. But we let our false, blind self lead us, which always asserts control, *"Let them alone: they be blind leaders of the blind. And if the blind lead the blind, both shall fall into the ditch"* (Matthew 15:14).

Christ is urging us to follow Him, *"Follow me"* (Mark 2:14) and this is because His story, His personal journey, is a guide, a map to our lost treasure, to our Lost Paradise; it is the path to the rediscovering of the Kingdom of Heaven; it is a course of Love which leads to Love, to God.

The Inner Restoration of Christianity

The Inner Restoration of Christianity

Guidance

"The ways of the Lord are inscrutable [...] He alone knows how and why He has built the argosy of humanity, and the small boat of each one of us, such as it is."

(Starets Macarius of Optino, *Russian Letters of Direction*, Letter 376)

– My friend where are you going?

– I don't know; I have walked for many miles but there is darkness around me and I feel lost. Yet, something is drawing me intensely towards there... I need light to see and water to quench my thirst... I know I don't have much time left...

– Don't worry; I am coming from the place where there is light and water. I can lead you there. It's far but I know the way; come with me.

So just one step before reaching to a door leading to the light and water, one *unlocked* door which was *drawing him* for so long, he changed direction and began a long journey for *another* door.

In the middle of this journey he collapsed.

The fact is, that the existence of all outer teachers must aim to the awakening of the inner teacher, that is, to the contact with the Conscience; to the hearing of God's Voice inside us.

"The conscience is a great thing. It is the voice of the Omnipresent God in the soul. He who is in the world with the conscience is also in the world with God."

(St. Theophan the Recluse, *The Spiritual Life*, p. 264)

Each one of us is, in essence, accountable to himself, but basically to his Creator. And no one can use any outer excuse before Him to transfer responsibility, *"She gave me of the tree, and I did eat"* (Genesis 3:12); *"The serpent beguiled me, and I did eat"* (Genesis 3:13). For all of us receive our personal inner determination of boundaries and guidance, and in that way we are exclusively responsible towards it.

"When God created man He set a conscience within his soul. So that he may be governed by it as by a rule, and so that he may be guided in what to do and what to avoid."

(St. Tikhon of Zadonsk, *Journey to Heaven*, p. 20)

Yet, the truth is that we have a weird relationship with our Conscience. Many of us think we have an excellent relationship with her and that we act according to her precepts.

"Presumption can make it blind [the intellect], not allowing it to become what it supposes itself to be. What, then, shall we say of those who are enslaved to the passions, and yet think they have a clear conscience?"

(St. Peter of Damaskos, *Book I – Active Spiritual Knowledge*, p. 102, Vol. 3, Philokalia)

While in reality we might have repressed her in a dark corner of ourselves, imposing her strict silence.

> "Indeed, we ourselves are able, if not to see, then to determine what we are. Our conscience, the incorruptible judge, tells us. It may become suppressed with time, but it always manages to free itself from this yoke, and raises its voice even in those who are shameless."

> (St. Theophan the Recluse, *The Spiritual Life*, p. 68)

Or, on the other hand, we may have a relatively friendly relationship with her, without however getting along very well. We could say a "good long distance relationship."

> "You have an unsleeping guard, your conscience. When something evil is done, it does not let it slip by, and no matter how you try to justify it to your conscience, it will not cease evaluating everything in its own way: This is evil, that is evil."

> (St. Theophan the Recluse, *The Spiritual Life*, p. 145)

So, in order for the Voice of God inside us, for our Conscience, to take its appropriate place, we must restore our relationship with her.

> *"Do not do anything that your conscience prohibits, and do not omit anything that it says to do, whether great or small."*

> (St. Theophan the Recluse, *The Spiritual Life*, p. 180)

Naturally, as with everything else in our lives, for this restoration to happen we must desire it and see a benefit to it. The outer exhortation is not sufficient since the inner exhortation which comes all the time from our Conscience was also insufficient! No, we need again a personal witness regarding the benefit of responding to the precepts of our Conscience.

"Listen carefully, all the while, to the voice of conscience resounding in your heart. God will not refuse His help."

(Starets Macarius of Optino, *Russian Letters of Direction*, Letter 173)

If we begin trusting the Voice of our Conscience, realizing deeply that her precepts not only don't harm us and don't deprive us of anything real, but instead lead us to the most beautiful, great and God-pleasing things, we will truly want to establish the most profound relationship with her.

"Conscience is nature's book. He who applies what he reads there experiences God's help."

(St. Mark the Ascetic, *On the Spiritual Law*, Text 186, p. 123, Vol. 1, Philokalia)

In that way we will discover that no outer guidance can be compared with the quality of the inner one, because this comes from the One who knows our hearts, *"God knoweth your hearts"* (Luke 16:15).

"Neighbors are very free with advice, but our own judgment is best. If you want spiritual health, listen to your conscience, do all it tells you, and you will benefit. God and our conscience know our secrets. Let them correct us."

(St. Mark the Ascetic, *On the Spiritual Law*, Texts 68-70, pp. 114-115, Vol. 1, Philokalia)

If God hadn't bestowed us with His definite boundaries, He couldn't have any expectations from us, neither could we, from ourselves. The result would then be for everyone to seek the outer responsibility for whatever happens, which would naturally lead to a dead-end, for despite where we would place the responsibility, eventually it would get back to us since everyone would displace it. And in the end, of course, we would blame God for everything. Yet, the reality is much simpler.

"Each one has a measure and inner guide – his conscience."

(St. Paisius Velichkovsky, *Field Flowers*, p. 38)

This inner measure and guide has not been given to us in order to account for every straying of ours, this is just an unavoidable result of this Gift we have been granted. Conscience has been given, in essence, to *protect* and *lead* us to the highest good both for us and for everything around us. The ascribing of responsibility starts when irrationally and stubbornly we "desire" our ill. The supervision takes place when we head towards various cliffs. The remorse appears when we act against any creation around us. Our Conscience is one of our most valuable possessions since it is the *Voice of Love* within us.

Unfortunately, we don't appreciate her; we oppose and fight her; we are afraid of her because we feel threatened by her. So when we desire to restore our relationship with her, very often, despite our good intentions, we have a lot of difficulty in managing it.

"A good conscience is found through prayer, and pure prayer through the conscience. Each by nature needs the other."

> (St. Mark the Ascetic, *On the Spiritual Law*, Text 198, p. 123, Vol. 1, Philokalia)

That is why the outer aid and guidance is legitimate and usually indispensable. Until we restore our relations with our Conscience we will probably need the help of people who are better related with the Voice of God inside them.

"He who does not accept advice will never go by the straight path, but will always find himself among cliffs and gorges."

> (St. Thalassios the Libyan, *On Love, Self-Control and Life in Accordance with the Intellect,* Fourth Century, 42, p. 327, Vol. 2, Philokalia)

At the beginning of our course it's reasonable to feel the need for guidance. Before this point, we usually did whatever we liked, but always came to dead-ends. The Voice of our Conscience represented for us a limitation, a prison, or the supposed "right." But now we really feel how useful the contact is with Conscience, especially regarding this extremely subtle art of the unseen warfare. We acknowledge how important and necessary this inner guidance is, since we want to travel to the interior of our soul in order to discover the immense depths and heights of our spirit.

Much to our regret, however, we find out that it's not so easy to find access to our inner guidance, or to hear our Conscience after all we have done to her! So we need a new overall education and rearrangement, as well as new *Knowledge*, regarding this truly great work of our metamorphosis. That is why we should not hastily claim that we regained and restored our contact with our inner teacher, because there are plenty of conditions to be fulfilled before this contact is possible; we need to be trained in this inner art and also gain experience.

> "We should learn from examples provided by human arts and sciences. If we cannot accomplish anything in them by ourselves – in spite of the fact that they deal with things we can touch with our hands, see with our eyes and hear with our ears – but still need someone who will instruct us well and guide us, how can it be anything but foolish to think that the spiritual art, the most difficult of all the arts, has no need of a teacher?"
>
> (St. John Cassian, *On the Holy Fathers of Sketis and on Discrimination*, p. 104, Vol. 1, Philokalia)

But this stage, however, is not to be perpetuated. When the work of our inner cleansing and rearrangement shall truly begin, we will soon discover that the Inspirer of this inner renewing hastens to help us in every effort, as long as we are willing to respond to His Divine Action.

> "When you begin to work on yourself, you will see that all outward direction and instructions are only guidelines. What is really needed by the soul, or how best to act in a particular instance, each soul must decide for itself with the help of God's grace which guides it invisibly. A person who sincerely wishes to please the Lord and who has completely devoted himself to Him, will always end up doing the right thing, but he succeeds by humility."
>
> (St. Theophan the Recluse, *The Spiritual Life*, p. 169)

Our only aim must be to relate through our Conscience, that is, God's Voice, with Love; and then our further course and inner growing will be insured.

> "If the Lord makes you worthy of living in His presence, you will not need any teachings. This will teach you everything."
>
> (St. Theophan the Recluse, *Selection of Letters*, p. 87)

Yet, the deeper and stronger we are related to God's Voice inside us, the more responsible we become towards her. He who does not listen to the Voice of his Conscience is accountable for his deafness. But he who listens to her and disobeys her has much greater responsibility, *"Therefore to him that knoweth to do good, and doeth it not, to him it is sin"* (James 4:17).

This accumulating debt derives from our ungratefulness to the Gift of Conscience. It is due to the fact that we do not appreciate the aid of inner guidance which comes from Divine Providence. And when we do not appreciate the Light which is offered by this inner teacher, we lose it, which results in walking into the darkness risking to tumble at any time. While when we appreciate It, we can make a worthy use of It and in that way walk safely, following a *steady* course towards all Divine goods.

> "If a man does not carry out the will and law of God 'in his inward parts,' that is, in his heart, he will not be able to carry them out easily in the outward sphere of the senses either. The careless and unwatchful man will say to God: 'I do not want to know Thy ways' (Job 21:14), obviously

because he lacks divine illumination. But he who participates in that light will be confident and steadfast in matters that concern God."

(St. Hesychios the Priest, *On Watchfulness and Holiness*, Section 86, p. 177, Vol. 1, Philokalia)

The Inner Restoration of Christianity

Steadfastness

"He was prudent and kept the counsels and directions of the ones who had gone before him in this journey. But he was also exhausted. The road was long and the temptations many. He had met a lot of sirens[2]. So he deviated often and this was costing him a lot; he was losing energy, time and strength supplies. He was always returning to his path but each time more laboriously; the temptation was better disguised and more cunning, the siren was more alluring and seductive.

He had acquired wisdom, however, so he could feel and taste the deviations, which is why he no longer had any excuses. When he deviated, we couldn't say he chose to voluntarily, for a man cannot *choose* his destruction; we could say he let himself be carried away... And this was easy: he just didn't resist in the moment he should have, and opened a dialogue with the siren. Then, his captivity was almost certain. If some unexpected help didn't show up, he was carried away...

He was losing himself in his illusory paradise until it began to reveal its real face. After he had tasted it for awhile, the ephemeral "paradise" was sucking him in and turning into a hell. Then he would be disgusted, both by his "choice," that is, the fact that he allowed himself to be carried away, and by himself as well. At that moment, however, Help would be given, the strength to return to the search of the door leading to the Real Paradise. But each

---

[2] In Greek mythology, a sea nymph, half-woman and half-bird, who was believed to sing beguilingly to passing sailors in order to lure them to their doom on the rocks she sat on.

time there were more demands of him; his debt was accumulating.

So now he was feeling tired again, and that was because he had forgotten that *in this journey he need not rely on his own strength*. Whenever he forgot the Help, he felt his strength and believed in his strength... and in that way he soon felt tired... and thus he would let himself be carried away.

Now he had begun to believe in his own self again, and in that way he said to himself: "I am tired..." and at the beginning, felt this familiar, sweet sensation of letting himself be carried away by a siren after so much resistance to her, which is accompanied, however, by an imperceptible, bitter taste... a taste of death.

He gave himself once more to the temptation... but this time, as he was falling, his eyes caught a fleeting bright glimpse that flickered behind some kind of a curtain... something was hindering this Light from overwhelming everything... it was something like... a door...

"Yes..." he thought to himself as he was sinking deeper down... "This looks like the descriptions... it looks like the door... yes... which leads to..."

"..."

"Welcome!" said the familiar sirens.

"Thank you! It's nice to be back!"

Steadfastness means not to deviate; to stay firm in our course, and that is attained only when we are steadfast within us; when we are *internally* unshakeable.

Steadfastness means to *return* to our course no matter what. Even if we are lost, carried away, steadfastness will bring us back to our path. No matter how many times we fall, the same number of times we must rise up.

> "Do all in your power not to fall, for the strong athlete should not fall. But if you do fall, get up again at once and continue the contest. Even if you fall a thousand times because of the withdrawal of God's grace, rise up again each time, and keep on doing so until the day of your death. For it is written, '*If a righteous man falls seven times*' – that is, repeatedly throughout his life – '*seven times shall he rise again*' (Proverbs 24:16)."
>
> (St. John of Karpathos, *For the Encouragement of the Monks in India who had Written to Him*, Text 84, p. 318, Vol. 1, Philokalia)

Steadfastness is built *through struggling* with the deviations. And these deviations are, of course, related to our displacement from our proper inner state: the state of prayer, humility, faith, hope, silence, stillness, fullness, Love. We touch a beautiful and real inner state and after awhile we lose it, perhaps forever. This changeableness in relation to our essential inner state has become a second nature of ours which is very detrimental, so we need to know how to be steadfast in it. For this to happen, however, we must study ourselves through self-observation, directed attention and watchfulness. We must employ constant vigilance in order to perceive what gets us in and out of each inner state. We must learn the art of steadfastness: its function, condition and application.

Steadfastness means a silent mind, a clean heart, a composed eye and a slow, deep and calm *breath*. It means to not be scattered, to remain within, to remain in our center. Steadfastness requires a constant renewal of our attention and insight.

"Steadfastness and continuity of labor over oneself is an essential condition for success in the spiritual life."

(St. Theophan the Recluse, *The Spiritual Life*, p. 196)

Steadfastness: Not to let anything foreign enter into our mind and heart; not to respond to anything calling us to get out of our course, of *ourselves*, of God.

"Stay unshakeable in front of

inner and outer challenges.

Do not deviate. Stay firm.

And when you deviate

always come back to your course,

to yourself, to God."

We need to have a sense, however, of *who we are, what we are doing* and *where we are going*. We need to discover our inner path in order to be firm in it. Otherwise, there can be no steadfastness – in what will we remain steadfast?

If we have begun experiencing God-confidence, God-reliance and God-control, this is what we should hold onto without getting lost and sacrifice the things of God for the things of ourselves; Paradise for hell; Beauty for wickedness; and Freedom for enslavement and self-limitation.

Everything tends to deviate at a certain point; deviation is the natural course of all things. And this deviation can easily be observed in relation to our inner aims which constantly seem unfeasible. At one time they are in our sight, while at another time they seem utopian and unsubstantial.

> "Seek after your aim firmly;
>
> stand on a rock and become one with it.
>
> Stay uninfluenced by all the 'voices,'
>
> inner and outer ones.
>
> Hold your arrow steady
>
> and aim clearly at your mark."

Let's remain steadfast in what we *Are*, in our ideals when they constitute a part of our Being, even if no one else shares our efforts and inner values. And let's not search for external reasons for our falls and dejection; let's finally acknowledge that the reason can always be found in some personal *internal deviation* of our own. Whenever we find that we have deviated even a little, that something alien has entered within us and begun to seize us, let's hasten to be cleansed from whatever it is that has invaded. Let's *detach* from it without letting ourselves get lost in it.

> "Provide yourself with only one thing, strong courage: no matter what happens, stay with what you have begun. This alone must now be established and set for life by commitment and steadfast perseverance. No matter how life goes, whatever successes and failures there are, you should give all of this over to God's will."

> (St. Theophan the Recluse, *The Spiritual Life*, p. 164)

Steadfastness: Stay firm in spite of whether things go better or worse. God is always so clearly teaching us His Love, His Miracle, which is destined to remain unchangeable inside us under all circumstances, good or bad, pleasant or unpleasant, easy or difficult.

"Faith gives it [the mind] the wings of freedom. This freedom is apparent in a quiet firmness, unruffled by any circumstances, fortunate or unfortunate."

(Starets Macarius of Optino, *Russian Letters of Direction*, Letter 47)

When we walk on this spiritual path, we ascertain *gradually* that God is behind all the "settings" of our lives. And what He is teaching us is to perceive Him behind all things. In that way good and bad acquire a relative meaning since we discover that they are just means in the hands of God. So we are freed from the changeable state we experience all the time in which "things are well or bad," and all that remains is Love.

Steadfastness is necessary in this inner journey of return, because without it we will constantly tend to deviate, and mainly step backwards. The results are that we will be quickly exhausted and, of course, suffering uselessly, since we will constantly scatter what we have gathered.

"We gain nothing, therefore, by our decision to renounce earthly things if we do not abide by it, but continue to be attracted by such things and allow ourselves to keep thinking about them. By constantly looking back, like Lot's wife, towards what we have renounced, we make our attachment to it clear. For she looked back and was turned into a pillar of salt, remaining to this day an example of the disobedient (Gen. 19:26). She symbolizes the force of habit which draws

The Inner Restoration of Christianity

us back again after we have tried to make a definitive act of renunciation.

What does the Law mean when it commands anyone entering the temple, after finishing his prayers, not to return by the door through which he entered, but to go straight out through the opposite door without changing direction? It means that we should keep to the path that leads straight to holiness, not allowing any doubts to make us turn back. By habitually thinking about what we have left behind, we undermine our determination to advance and we are pulled in the opposite direction, returning to our old sins."

(St. Neilos the Ascetic, *Ascetic Discourse*, p. 236, Vol. 1, Philokalia)

On this road, determination is necessary and will grant us the freedom from our inner Egypt, for which we might even feel nostalgic when we meet various difficulties. It is certain, however, that if we don't retreat, and remain steadfast and faithful to our course, sooner or later we will be led to our Promised Land. So let's not forget that *"No man, having put his hand to the plough, and looking back, is fit for the kingdom of God"* (Luke 9:62). For this way of return, the straight path, the path of virtue, is eventually God Himself. He is the beginning, the middle and the end of the Way. God *Is* the Way.

"He that shall endure unto the end, the same shall be saved"
(Matthew 24:13).

The Inner Restoration of Christianity

Patience

"In your patience possess ye your souls" (Luke 21:19)

We often use the expression, "Patience has its limits." So whenever we are called to show patience, we want to know its limits: "Have patience," ... "Ok but until when?" But when we want to know the limits of patience, we show in effect, impatience. We are not patient, we just wait. Real patience doesn't have limits, or at least, is experienced beyond them when it transcends them by not expecting them.

> "If you want to be taught patience, plant a seed and watch its timeless and invisible growth."

Patience is experienced *in* time but *transcends* it. Otherwise, it is not patience but expectation. And expectation has truly very narrow limits.

We often feel despair in this demanding spiritual struggle when we think of patience and that is because we are used to wanting everything the moment we want it, while "You have need of patience, to do the will of God" (Hebrews 10:36). We see patience as some kind of torture which we simply have to endure; yet, the truth is very different.

Real patience doesn't exhaust. On the contrary, it reinforces and strengthens. The "patience" which is being practiced for the sake of some result or according to some expectation, is not, as we've already said, patience, but *waiting* which can truly be very exhausting. These are two entirely different things: Patience accepts and transcends time; waiting keeps counting it and tries to fill it.

Real patience is feasible only when it is related to God, and that's because only with God's help can we transcend the natural time limits. Only when we are patient for the sake of God and with the help of His Grace, can we break our self-limiting time limits. Otherwise real patience is impossible for us; we're just waiting and *showing* "patience."

So let's have patience for His sake and *with* His Grace!

For only this is the real and possible Patience.

The imaginary "patience" brings a sense of sufficiency, self-assurance and self-satisfaction which is followed by a natural, almost imperceptible retreat. This is due – especially in relation to our spiritual course – to the fact that we haven't yet deepened enough within ourselves, and *our desire for good hasn't yet overwhelmed our whole Being.*

"To those who are just beginning to long for holiness, the path of virtue seems very rough and forbidding. It appears like this not because it is really difficult, but because our human nature from the womb is accustomed to the wide roads of sensual pleasure. But those who have travelled more than half its length, find the path of virtue smooth and easy. For when a bad habit has been subjected to a good one through the energy of grace, it is destroyed along with the remembrance of mindless pleasures; and thereafter the soul gladly journeys on all the ways of virtue. Thus, when the Lord first leads us into the path of salvation, He says: 'How narrow and strait is the way leading to the kingdom and few there are who follow it' (Matthew 7:14); but to those who have firmly resolved to keep His holy commandments He says: 'For My yoke is easy, and My burden is light' (Matthew 11:30). At the beginning of the struggle, therefore, the holy commandments of God must be fulfilled with a certain forcefulness of will (Matthew 11:12); then the Lord, seeing our intention and labor, will grant us readiness of will and gladness in obeying His purposes. For 'it is the Lord who makes ready the will' (Prov. 8:35), so that we always do what is right joyfully. Then shall we truly feel that 'it is God who energizes in you both the willing and the doing of His purpose' (Phil. 2:13)."

(St. Diadochos of Photiki, *On Spiritual Knowledge and Discrimination*, Text 93, pp. 290-291, Vol. 1, Philokalia)

At the beginning we are "patient" trying to remain in the narrow limits of the straight path. In the middle we suffer when we have deviated involuntary from the saving limits of the straight path and we show true Patience until we return to it.

At the beginning, our "patience" is exhausting and a result of "violence." In the middle our Patience is effortless and eager. It is the time of strengthening and growing deep roots; it is the time of assimilating and understanding. But the most important thing is that it consists of the time when the truths we have experienced are *engraved* deeply and permanently in our soul.

The Inner Restoration of Christianity

Pain

"A wise man used to say: 'Everybody knows him but no one likes to talk about him. He has been my faithful companion even though I always tried to avoid him. Now I cannot do without him and I really love him. I used to see him as my deadliest enemy but now I consider him my best friend. He is my most beloved and most hated teacher. His name? ...Pain."

Only with pain is the truth engraved in our soul.

We wonder why we cannot act the way we think we should, and why the right thing often remains a nice theory, but a difficult act to achieve? It is simply because *the precepts of our spirit are not experienced by our soul*. On the contrary, the precepts of our carnal mind, of our egoistic mind, are engraved in our soul and in that way determine her. Therefore, a lot of pain is needed for these engravings to be removed and the same amount of pain is needed for new ones to be engraved.

Yet, before the old ones are removed we cannot engrave new ones. Or rather, we should not try to engrave the new ones because, *"No man putteth a piece of new cloth unto an old garment, for that which is put in to fill it up taketh from the garment, and the rent is made worse. Neither do men put new wine into old bottles: else the bottles break, and the wine runneth out, and the bottles perish: but they put new wine into new bottles, and both are preserved"* (Matthew 9:16-17).

Very often we cannot understand how the notion of a Most Merciful God can be reconciled with the notion of pain. And this is because we just can't understand the relation between love and pain.

Even though the things that move us most in life are, in effect, these two: *pain* and *love*. So the relation between them is simply: the one is the means to the other. The fruit of pain is Love; of *real pain* however.

There are *three kinds* of pain. Two of them are real and one is false.

The false pain is the pain of egoism. The two kinds of real pain are the inevitable, involuntary pain of life, and the voluntary pain.

The *false pain* is the subjective imaginary pain which comes from our pride, fear, insecurity, self-pity, self-justification, self-love, self-interest, vanity, vainglory, arrogance, greediness, lies to ourselves and others; in a few words, from our egoism. This kind of pain is pointless and harmful.

The *inevitable, involuntary pain* is the one which comes from unpleasant occurrences such as diseases, death, natural disasters and generally from all the inevitable misfortunes and hardships of life.

The *voluntary pain* is the pain which comes from undertaking this inner struggle, from deciding to walk the narrow path and taking up our cross. It may also come from deciding to take up, for awhile or longer, the cross of someone else, or in the case of Christ, *the cross of humanity*.

The two kinds of real pain can lead to salvation.

The false pain is clearly *pain in vain*.

Initially we must learn to *distinguish* the real pain from the false one. Next, we must realize that the false pain constitutes an obstacle to our development and salvation. We must *sacrifice* this kind of pain; we must deny and abandon it.

At the same time, we will realize that without pain nothing can be done. So we will perceive that we must, *through* the voluntary and the inevitable involuntary pain, get rid of the false one. We must get rid of the imaginary subjective pain in order to become worthy of the real objective pain. If we don't get rid of the false pain, we will never be able to become real disciples of Christ and take up our cross – our real objective pain – in order to learn from it and reach through it to Love.

Pain is the ladder leading to Love. Real Love can only be born through pain as the journey of Jesus Christ indicates: at the summit of His pain Jesus reaches the supreme heights of Forgiveness and Love (Luke 23:34).

Pain is the spud which prepares the soil of our soul to receive the seeds of Love. Only through pain, through the temptation we tasted and perhaps succumbed to through are inadequacies and weaknesses, can we have *com-passion* (co-suffering). The man who hasn't suffered, hasn't learned, and so he cannot *Be*.

Only when we experience real pain, can we understand the pain around us and in that way acquire *sympathy*. And only through transcending our pain, can we develop real strength, so we can also heal the pain around us. In short, only through the transubstantiation of pain can we acquire Real, Incorruptible, Powerful Love, *"According to the multitude of my sorrows in my heart, thy comforts have given joy to my soul"* (Psalms 94:19, Douay-Rheims Bible, Challoner Revision).

Through our distorted view we have great difficulty in understanding and accepting God's gifts as *gifts* and we usually perceive them as curses. And this is our basic problem: our ignorance of God and our ignorance of Love. If we had a living knowledge of God, of Love, everything would be much simpler for us, not necessarily easier, but at least more attainable. That is why we cannot understand the *gift of pain*; which is being given, on one hand, in order to be restored to our initial, natural beauty:

> "The person who truly wishes to be healed is he who does not refuse treatment. This treatment consists of the pain and distress brought on by various misfortunes. He who refuses them does not realize what they accomplish in this world or what he will gain from them when he departs this life."
>
> (St. Maximos the Confessor, *Four Hundred Texts on Love*, 82, Third Century, p. 96, Vol. 2, Philokalia)

And on the other hand, in order to appreciate this beauty so deeply that we won't fall again from its height:

> "You must know that only after much labor and sweat of the brow will you recover your richness. Nor is it to your advantage to attain this blessed state without suffering and great effort, for if you do you will lose what you have received."
>
> (St. Symeon Metaphrastis, *Paraphrase of the Homilies of St Makarios of Egypt*, 51, pp. 306-307, Vol. 3, Philokalia)

He who perceives the value of this gift will inevitably love it. So he will enrich his soul with one more virtue, the one of real and genuine sedulity.

> "Patient endurance is a continuous effort for the soul; it is born of suffering freely chosen and of trials that come unsought."

(St. Thalassios the Libyan, *On Love, Self-Control and Life in Accordance with the Intellect,* Third Century, 16, p. 320, Vol. 2, Philokalia)

This virtue will makes us undertake all the voluntary labors needed in order to be freed by the false pain of our egoism. When we have made a significant progress in this spiritual work, we will find that we are much more capable of "taking up," of *assimilating* a part of all this real pain that there is everywhere around us and visits us, either calling us directly to take up all our various crosses, or indirectly calling us to help our neighbors with their crosses.

There is no man who doesn't struggle. There are just some of us who struggle in vain for useless things and some others who struggle meaningfully for real things.

Pain is interwoven with life and no one can avoid it, whatever he might do. For some it is a curse, for others it is a gift. The truth is that it constitutes a necessary means for anything beautiful. As an Armenian proverb says, "Until you see trouble you will never know joy."

If we transcend pain, it will be a gift which raises us to the heights of Love. If we are lost in it, it will be a curse which will cast us to the bowels of hell. It is rather a paradox, but according to the instructions of Jesus Christ, whoever takes up his pain, *"If any man will come after me, let him deny himself, and take up his cross, and follow me"* (Matthew 16:24); will find rest: *"Come unto me, all ye that labor and are heavy laden, and I will give you rest. [...] For my yoke is easy, and my burden is light"* (Matthew 11:28-30).

The people who *Live* with pain are truly remarkable. Not the ones who "live," that is, who groan and shut down to everything around them, but the ones who truly *Live*. These are imitable, who are able, despite whatever *real pain* they endure, to not become lost in it, but remain open and be further opened to the Miracle of Life and Beauty. The ones who transcend their pain are initiated into the Miracle of Love. These are the people who have learned the art of *silent* pain. The ones who have learned to suffer silently, *"When ye fast, be not, as the hypocrites, of a sad countenance [...] When thou fastest, anoint thine head, and wash thy face. That thou appear not unto men to fast, but unto thy Father which is in secret: and thy Father, which seeth in secret, shall reward thee openly"* (Matthew 6:16-18).

When we start appreciating the *gift* of *real pain*, we also learn to transcend it. And then our reward cannot help but be our communion in the Kingdom of Love, our communion in Love.

Fear

"There is no fear in love." (1 John 4:18)

There is nothing for us to fear except God. And God is Love.

We walk on the path of Love when we *hear* our Conscience. To fear God means fearing *to not hear our Conscience, or to hear it incorrectly,* and thus fall off of the path of Love. Other than that, we really don't have to fear anyone or anything. If our Conscience is clear, everything is alright.

> "If you do not do evil to anyone, you will not be afraid of anyone."
>
> (*The Sentences of Sextus*, Sentence 386)

In reality, fear shows lack of faith, as well as egocentric weakness.

> "A fearful and slavish nature will not be able to partake in faith."
>
> (*The Sentences of Sextus*, Sentence 170)

Our basic physical fear is dying.

Our basic psychological fear is to be left alone.

These are the basic fears of egoism from which all other phobias come. In their extreme form they might appear with their exact opposite: wanting to die or wanting to be left completely alone.

If we had real knowledge of, and faith in, Divine Providence, we would neither be afraid nor worried, and we wouldn't take thought of anything, because we would know that the supreme Power which is Love, is taking thought for us, and therefore we are truly safe no matter what, and under all circumstances.

> *"Are not five sparrows sold for two farthings, and not one of them is forgotten before God? But even the very hairs of your head are all numbered. Fear not therefore: ye are of more value than many sparrows."* (Luke 12:6-7)

If we had a proper relationship with God, that is, with the Powerfulness of Love, what could we be afraid of?

"He who doubts God's help, will be afraid of his own shadow even without being tempted."

(St. Paisius Velichkovsky, *Field Flowers*, p. 125)

We could say that the only thing we should be afraid of, is again our "self:" our false egoistic self. But even *it* is not stronger than God. Therefore: We don't have to fear anything except God. And God is Love.

We constantly seek strength; ways to be strong. We want to be ensured against every possible danger, both for ourselves and for all those we love. The last place, however, where we turn in our search for strength is God, Love.

But why is there so much fear?

Fear of the political and economic situations, fear of the end of the world, fear for the environment, fear of other nations, of other religions, fear of the devil, fear, fear, fear. Are we afraid for ourselves? For our souls?

These fears are egoistic. And this is shown by the way we act when we are saturated by them. It is a way that is characterized by lack of love, sympathy and mercy. We could say that it is the way of the frightened animal which might become extremely aggressive when it feels threatened. So egoistic fear is an animal which, in its most extreme form, wants to destroy what it feels threatened by.

Or perhaps our motives are more unselfish? Maybe we are not afraid so much for our soul, for ourselves, but for humanity, for our children, our neighbor or for our environment? We could say that this fear is anthropocentric. But it is again, perhaps to a lesser degree, egoistic, because in an indirect way it still has to do with an extension of ourselves which might be expressed by our children (literally or metaphorically). And this time, it might be manifested even more aggressively, as it happens with a mother who is afraid for the life of her child and can literally become a wild beast.

So much anxiety therefore, so much fear, which is constantly revolving around ourselves or the extension of ourselves – our children and humanity or the environment. And once again, even the best of us, when we are saturated by fear, are ready to destroy what we feel threatened by.

Humanity has lost, and so it seems as though it never existed, the God-centric perspective of things, that is, the desire to save and be saved, not for our sake, not for our children's and humanity's sake, but for God's sake.

Indeed, Jesus Christ came and suffered for us, but we must suffer for Him. It's not reasonable to suffer again for us, it's not reasonable for everything to be revolving around us. And this is obvious in every human relationship of love: I sacrifice for you without you asking and expecting me to, and you sacrifice for me without me asking and expecting you to. *This is Love.*

The same should happen in our relationship with God. Christ is sacrificed for us and we are sacrificed for Christ. And then we want to be saved for the sake of God, not for the sake of ourselves. And correspondingly, we want our children, humanity and the planet to be saved for the sake of God.

If we are permeated by this God-centric attitude, we will discover that the fear will be lessened, it might even disappear. And our actions will be cleansed from aggressiveness and the blind impulse to destroy. It will be pervaded by prudence, clarity, determination, forgiveness, strength, mercy, patience and of course... Love.

Paraphrasing the words of St. Paul, "And if we are saved, but don't have Love, we are nothing" (1 Corinthians 13:1-3).

If we pay attention, we will ascertain that when we are exposed to the egocentric fear for the salvation of our soul or to the anthropocentric fear for the salvation of humanity, our soul is tainted and feels an intense urge for aggressiveness and a desire for *immediate action*, for the immediate distraction of the threat; or on the other hand, we feel within us an urge to hide, to disappear, we feel we don't want to know anything "about all that" and to have nothing to do with it.

When our agony is God-centric, it appears within us as a *calm strength* which is permeated by *trust,* and informs us, "Don't worry, everything is going to be alright" as long as God is with us and all is done as He wills.

We must give up our will even in relation to the salvation of our soul, of humanity or of nature, because as long as we have a will, we have egoism. And as long as we have egoism, we cannot save or be saved. We must trust and surrender to God's Will. And if we must have a will, let it be one and only, *"Thy Will be done"* (Matthew 6:10).

Nevertheless, the state of fearlessness that comes from the relationship with Love, doesn't mean recklessness. It doesn't mean lack of caution or being hazardous.

When fearlessness is mentioned, our mind usually tends to think of various dangerous situations, and we wonder, "Yes but if this or the other happens, isn't it logical to be afraid?" "If some snake appears..." and so forth.

Certainly we will be found in a state of fear when we come face to face with any dangerous situation, because we *must* be afraid. Fear in these cases is a function of alertness which releases additional energy into us, the so-called adrenaline, in order to cope with the given situation. Even in this case, however, if we forget Love, then the beneficial fear which is given again as a gift, will turn against us. Not being able to make a worthy use of the extra energy which it offers us, we will panic.

If, however, we remain in the state of prayer and contact with God while we confront any dangerous situation, then our fearlessness won't be disturbed. On the contrary, it will be reinforced by the energy of the *necessary fear* we'll experience at this moment which we will *use* by transcending it, that is, by *transmuting* it.

Fear in the face of a real and dangerous situation is the best thing we could have in order to face it, because it offers us an additional power. It can offer us speed, physical strength, acute senses, determination, courage and effectiveness. Not only for being "active" when faced with a situation, but also for being completely "passive;" we can grow wings on our feet or stand dead still, because this is what is needed.

If we don't make use of our *real* fear, however, in the face of a *real* situation, then it will turn, as we said, against us and seize us, making us even more vulnerable than before the threat. We all know that fear can be "smelled." And then whatever threatens us will use it against us, as would an angry dog, for instance, or someone who is planning to harm us.

So, in essence, there is real and useful fear which must be used as a gift, otherwise it becomes harmful; and there is also the imaginary fear which brings forth every kind of phobia and which is in every case detrimental and useless. For what we are afraid of is rarely going to happen as we fear it. Unless, that is, it becomes an obsession and we end up provoking it ourselves!

> "We ourselves create situations of fear with our faint-hearted thinking."
>
> (St. Paisius Velichkovsky, *Field Flowers*, p. 118)

And at the same time, there are so many things we don't expect which may happen at any moment, but it's not possible to constantly fear some non-existent thing which we cannot even imagine.

> "Let us not become enemies of ourselves by fearing the unexpected."
>
> (St. Paisius Velichkovsky, *Field Flowers*, p. 118)

In reality, fear is useful when we know how to use it and when we don't let it use us; it is again one of God's gifts, no matter how difficult it is for us to understand it.

Regarding the body, fear is a function of reinforcement and empowerment, if we are not lost in it. The reason that it is seizing us is simply because we don't know *how* to handle the *abundant energy* which it releases in us. So it overwhelms us and we consider it something bad when it is a Divine gift.

Regarding the soul, the only reasonable and valuable fear is the *Fear of God,* which doesn't mean to be afraid of being punished because we deviated, but of *not being punished*, that is, being left to deviate from the paths of Love. It functions as a means of awakening and vigilance. It doesn't aim to exhaust us, but to save us. It doesn't aim to limit us, but to free us.

So when we realize that fear constitutes, in effect, a gift of God, it assumes in us its proper place and performs its soul-saving function. In its highest form it is expressed as Divine Fear and can truly liberate us from all the imaginary fears and from all the acquired soul-destroying phobias.

> "Whoever goes in the fear of God is not afraid when surrounded by evil men, for he has the fear of God within him and wears the invincible amour of faith. This gives him strength to do all things, even those that seem to most people difficult or impossible. Like a giant among monkeys or a roaring lion among dogs and foxes, he is resolute in the Lord."
>
> (St. Symeon the New Theologian, *One Hundred and Fifty-Three Practical and Theological Texts*, 52, pp. 34-35, Vol. 4, Philokalia)

And that applies until we reach the valuable good of Love where every fear is abandoned, fear having served its purpose.

> "Thus the fear which characterizes those who are still being purified is accompanied by a moderate measure of love. But perfect love is found in those who have already

been purified and in whom there is no longer any fear, for 'perfect love casts out fear' (1 John 4:18)."

(St. Diadochos of Photiki, *On Spiritual Knowledge and Discrimination*, Text 16, p. 257, Vol. 1, Philokalia)

In this way we understand that nothing that exists in the Creation of God, neither pain, nor fear, nor anything else, is evil in itself, but becomes thus when it is used erroneously, that is, when it is not used *properly* and *worthily*.

So let's not be afraid of anything, because evil *in essence* doesn't exist. *We* create it, by *believing* in it due to our *ignorance*. Evil doesn't *really* have a substance of its own; it is only a lack of Love, as darkness is a lack of Light.

Evil

"Evil does not exist by nature, nor is any man naturally evil, for God made nothing that was not good. When, in the desire of his heart, someone conceives and gives form to what in reality has no existence, then what he desires begins to exist. We should therefore turn our attention away from the inclination to evil and concentrate it on the remembrance of God; for good, which exists by nature, is more powerful than our inclination to evil. The one has existence while the other has not, except when we give it existence through our actions."

(St. Diadochos of Photiki, *On Spiritual Knowledge and Discrimination*, Text 3, p. 253, Vol. 1, Philokalia)

The known problem of evil in the world: If God is good, how can evil exist?

Either God has created it, so He is not altogether good, or someone else has, so there isn't only one God. And if there is another God, is he equal in strength to the good God or not? If not, then why does the good God allow him to exist? And if the two Gods are equal in strength, which one of them created man? One of them? Or both, since man seems to be both good and evil? And why do we men feel a natural attraction towards what is good and an aversion towards what is evil? And anyway, what is evil?

These kinds of questions, even though they seem reasonable, belong only to our mind which can "philosophize" endlessly without ever reaching anywhere. For, on the one hand, one question begets the other, and on the other hand, none of these possible answers can be verified in any final way. So, this kind of intellectual search always ends up at a dead-end.

If we taste, however, the Love of God, then we begin to understand through personal experience the notion of evil and what place it may have in Creation. And then the answer to the question, "What is the place of evil in Creation, and where is it coming from?" – is, "In essence, none and from nowhere!" This will be the answer of the Love of God.

"Nevertheless, evil exists," is what our minds keep pondering, because if we take a quick look at the world around us, it is obvious. Yet, we are being taught that God is All-Good and that everything comes from Him since He is the Maker of All and Everything. And the same thing will be verified by our personal experience of God's Love.

"And in one word, all things existing are *from* the Beautiful and Good, *in* the Beautiful and Good, and *turn themselves* to the Beautiful and Good. Moreover, all things whatever, which are and come into being, are and come into being by reason of the Beautiful and Good; and to It all things look, and by It are moved and held together, and for the sake of It, and by reason of It, and in It, is every source exemplary, final, creative, formative, elemental, and in one word, every beginning, every bond, every term, or to speak summarily, all things existing are from the Beautiful and Good; and all things non-existing are superessentially in the Beautiful and Good; and it is of all, beginning and term, above beginning and above term, because from It, and through It, and in It, and to It, are all things, as says the Sacred Word."

(Dionysius the Areopagite, *On Divine Names*, Caput IV, Sec. X, p. 44)

So what is evil?

"It remains, then, that Evil is a weakness and a falling short of the Good."

(Dionysius the Areopagite, *On Divine Names*, Caput IV, Sec. XXX, p. 68)

That means that evil doesn't have any personal substance (hypostasis), it is not something *created,* but is, as it were, the negation of Creation. And since it hasn't any substance, not having been created as a thing in itself, this means that it doesn't exist!

"For, for the sake of the Good, are all things, both those that are good, and those that are contrary. For we do even these as desiring the Good (for no one does what he does with a view to the Evil), wherefore the Evil has not a subsistence, but a parasitical subsistence, coming into being for the sake of the Good, and not of itself."

(Dionysius the Areopagite, *On Divine Names*, Caput IV, Sec. XXXI, p. 68-69)

Evil is a distortion of good; it is a negation of good which doesn't aim at something evil in itself, but is due to a *twisted notion* of good.

"And the very man who desires the very worst life, as wholly desirous of life and that which seems best to him, by the very fact of desiring, and desiring life, and looking to a best life, participates in the Good. And, if you should entirely take away the Good, there will be neither essence, nor life, nor yearning, nor movement, nor anything else."

(Dionysius the Areopagite, *On Divine Names*, Caput IV, Sec. XX, p. 57)

Even though we can see clearly around us the results of evil, *in reality* we see the results of the *lack of good*. Since evil is nonexistent (without substance) and non-created, it is obvious it cannot *create* anything. Only good can create something, but the lack of good will have its consequences as well.

"There is no existing thing from the Evil, nor will the Evil itself be, if it should be evil even to itself. And, if it be not so, the Evil is not altogether evil, but has some portion of the Good, in consequence of which it wholly is. Now, if the things existing desire the Beautiful and Good, and whatever they do, they do for the sake of that which seems good, and every purpose of things existing has the Good for its beginning and end (for nothing looking to the Evil *qua* evil, does what it does), how shall the Evil be in things existing; or, wholly being, how has it been seduced from such a good yearning?"

(Dionysius the Areopagite, *On Divine Names*, Caput IV, Sec. XIX, p. 53)

So, we ourselves "create" evil when we have a *perverted notion* of good, and then act in the *opposite direction* of good. But let's emphasize again that this happens out of *ignorance* of the right direction and *not* for the sake of serving evil, which, in essence, cannot be served, since it doesn't exist as a creation in itself.

"How, in short, can evil do anything by its mixture with the Good?³ For that which is altogether without participation in the Good, neither is anything, nor is capable of anything."

(Dionysius the Areopagite, *On Divine Names*, Caput IV, Sec. XXXII, pp. 69-70)

So even though the All-Good Love has created a *"very good"* (Genesis 1:31) creation, evil can have a "place" in it as an opposite and delusive direction from the one of good; without, however, aiming at this opposition, it assumes it due to ignorance of the truly good.

"Evil then is privation and failure, and want of strength, and want of proportion, and want of attainment, and want of purpose; and without beauty, and without life, and without mind, and without reason, and without completeness, and without stability, and without cause, and without limit, and without production; and inactive, and without result, and disordered, and dissimilar, and limitless, and dark, and unessential, and being itself nothing in any manner of way whatever."

(Dionysius the Areopagite, *On Divine Names*, Caput IV, Sec. XXXII, p. 69)

---

³ In this point a correction in translation is necessary. The Greek text actually has it, "How, in short, can evil do anything? By its mixture with the Good. For that which is altogether without participation in the Good, neither is anything, nor is capable of anything." In the form of a question which receives the appropriate answer, this passage makes more sense, otherwise, when the answer is assimilated into the question, the meaning is, in essence, lost.

All these notions about good and evil could become clearer using some relevant illustration of this reality; the illustration of Light and darkness:

> "For we also say, that the air around us becomes dark by failure and absence of light, and yet the light itself is always light, that which enlightens even the darkness. The Evil, then, is neither in demons nor in us, as an *existent* evil, but as a failure and dearth of the perfection of our own proper goods."

(Dionysius the Areopagite, *On Divine Names*, Caput IV, Sec. XXIV, p. 64)

This spiritual view of things as unintelligible as it seems and perhaps even paradoxical in some way, becomes extremely simple and self-evident when we taste the perfection of God's Love.

> "Evil is not something positive. All existing things are in a sense good, from the point of view that they constitute a form of existence. They might, however, become evil through distortion, limitation, negation. In every evil thing there is a lack, a lessening of being. There is disharmony and anarchy. There is an offense to perfection. This is true both for disease and sin. So when the negation reaches its utmost limits, we come to what we could call the principle of evil, total evil."

(Lev Gillett, *Our Father... Lord Jesus Christ*, pp. 78-80)

Still, why does God allow, one way or the other, the existence of this perhaps *involuntary* but fallacious opposite direction to good?

Love indicates in each case the right and necessary direction which benefits everything; and correspondingly, everything, since it has been created by God, feels inherently in it the need to turn toward this direction.

"Goodness turns all things to Itself, and is chief collector of things scattered, as One-springing and One-making Deity, and all things aspire to It, as Source and Bond and End, and it is the Good, as the Oracles say, from Which all things subsisted, and are being brought into being by an all-perfect Cause; and in Which all things consisted, as guarded and governed in an all-controlling route; and to Which all things are turned, as to their own proper end."

(Dionysius the Areopagite, *On Divine Names*, Caput IV, Sec. IV, p. 37)

Let's imagine the best possible physical parents: They would raise us with all their love. They would offer us the best possible education. They would provide us with the best possible conditions to make a worthy use of our inherent talents and acquired virtues. And finally, if they were truly conscious parents, they would *let us choose* and discover our right path, after having offered us, of course, all the necessary indications to be able to turn safely towards it. Perhaps they themselves might be perceptive enough to know what could be the best course for us, but still, the *choice*, the *desire* for the right path should be our own; otherwise our love for it would be adulterated and enforced. In that way we would always feel miserable, even in our Paradise, since we would feel imprisoned and entrapped in it. And even if we didn't feel that way, in case our Paradise was given to us without us trying even a little to acquire it, this imposed offering would make us quite weak and incompetent, and even ungrateful for it.

So God creates us "in His image" providing us internally with what is most good and most high, and lets us *choose* our "in His likeness" inner path.

"All men are made in God's image; but to be in His likeness is granted only to those who through great love have brought their own freedom into subjection to God. For only when we do not belong to ourselves do we become like Him who through love has reconciled us to Himself."

(St. Diadochos of Photiki, *On Spiritual Knowledge and Discrimination*, Text 3, p. 253, Vol. 1, Philokalia)

The "image" is an ability and a tangible reality, the "likeness" is a possibility and a potential reality. Man who is potentially a God-man, that is a Child of God, can diverge from his natural destination and be led to the exact opposite (becoming an inhuman or sub-human) always thinking that he is in the straight path.

Those men, however, who have fulfilled their real destination as Sons and Daughters of God, cannot anymore act against His Will, and consequently there cannot be any evil regarding them.

"Some say that there would be no evil in the created world unless there were some power outside this world dragging us towards evil. But this so-called power is in fact our neglect of the natural energies of the intellect. For those who nurture these energies always do good, never evil. If this, then, is what you too wish to do, get rid of negligence and you will also drive out evil, which is the wrong use of our conceptual images of things, followed by the wrong use of the things themselves.

"In its natural state, the human intelligence is subject to the divine intelligence and itself rules over the non-intelligent element in us. Let this order be maintained in all things, and there will be no evil among creatures or anything which draws us towards evil."

(St. Maximos the Confessor, *Four Hundred Texts on Love*, 82-83, Second Century, p. 79, Vol. 2, Philokalia)

God informs us all the time within our Conscience what is to our benefit, but if we don't want to hear Him, He becomes silent. He constantly knocks at the door of our heart, but if we don't want to open, He stops "bothering" us. He always waits for us to return, but He doesn't search to find us in order to impose His Will.

Whoever wants to tread his personal subjective path, listening to the precepts of his own will, inevitably will turn from good to evil thinking it as good, with whatever consequences this fickle course might have.

Whoever wants to tread His personal objective path complying with the precepts of His will, might also turn from good to evil out of ignorance and weakness, but no matter what happens it will be beneficial and fortunate because it will contribute to his Good course.

"*All things work together for good to them that love God.*"
(Romans 8:28)

Happiness (or Good Fortune/Luck)

"As long as are you are not living in the spirit, do not expect happiness. Intellectual and physical life, when the course is favorable, give something like happiness, but it is a fleeting illusion of happiness, and soon vanishes."

(St. Theophan the Recluse, *The Spiritual Life*, p. 63)

Happiness (in Greek) means etymologically good fortune or good luck. But what does good luck mean? Things are going well for us? Well, but according to what?

If we earn a lot of money, but don't really care about money, then are things going well or not? Obviously not so well. Will we be happy then? Probably not. So whether things are going well or not, is always defined in relation to a certain object.

If our purpose in life is our material prosperity, whether this is related to our conditions of living or to the health of our body, then whatever promotes this cause is good for us, and thus means good luck and makes us happy. Whatever opposes and impedes this cause, we consider bad or *un*fortunate, and constitutes for us a *mis*fortune. Under these conditions, our fortune (luck) is "random" (or "accidental") and will sometimes be good and other times bad. So we can be happy sometimes and other times unhappy (unlucky and unfortunate).

Now, if our object in life, our purpose, is the union with God, the union with Love, then whether things are going well and therefore whether we have good luck, is again related directly to our cause. Whatever leads us towards this direction which we have determined as our meaning in life is therefore good, and whatever leads us towards another direction is bad.

But when we set the unification with God as our purpose in life, we realize gradually that our life (and our luck or fortune) is not anymore left to "luck" but is determined by a *particular* luck: what happens to us is what God wants to happen. And since what God wants to happen is good because He is All-Good – otherwise we wouldn't set union with Him as our purpose in life – then we always have *good luck*. This is because our luck will be determined by the Will of God, and His Will is the best for us whether this has a pleasant or an unpleasant taste. Beautiful and ugly, "good" and "bad" acquire a relevant meaning as we realize that *all is right* and in essence *beneficial* for us, since it comes from God and promotes our purpose in life, the union with God. So, no matter what happens we have good luck and therefore *happiness* (good fortune).

"Bear in mind, however, that real peace is not outside, but within our soul. It doesn't derive from outer conditions, but from our good inner alignment."

(St. Theophan the Recluse, *Selection of Letters*, p. 71)

So we will be happy apart from whether we are healthy or not, whether things are easy or difficult; regardless of the conditions and occurrences of life, since we will be able to use whatever happens worthily, and indeed that is the reason why God sends it. He sends or *allows* it to happen in order to approach Him even more, and in order to initiate us deeper into His Love.

"When God sees us, He always sees our entire life. And because He is an infinitely good being, He eternally seeks our well-being. Therefore, there is no cause for worry in any of the things which happen to us.

"I often thank God that he let me be blinded. I am sure that he let this happen for the good of my soul. [...]

"One must never part from the principle that God is infinitely good, and that all of his actions are in our best interest. Because of this, a Christian should always be happy, and never unhappy. Because everything that happens is God's will, and it only happens for the well-being of our soul. Well, this is the most important. God is infinitely good, almighty, and he helps us. This is all one must do, and then one is happy."

(A monk from the documentary *Into Great Silence* (2005) by Philip Gröning)

A *real* Christian cannot help but be always happy. For his source of happiness, of good luck, is in essence, *internal* and not external. His happiness derives from his relationship with God; it is spiritual, and so unalterable from outer factors, and not psychological (intellectual) or carnal, two dimensions of life which are subjected to constant alterations between "good" and "bad," "up" and "down."

Real happiness can be found in the transcendence of the *relevant good and bad* which brings us in contact with the absolute Good. This relationship with Good makes us truly fearless and brings forth within us a sense of tangible and essential happiness from which derives a sense of real Strength that nothing can alter, lessen or destroy; on the contrary, *everything contributes* to broadening and establishing it even deeper.

When we acknowledge our subjective limited "strength," that is, our real weakness, then we enter into the real state of humility which

The Inner Restoration of Christianity

allows us to be related to the Almightiness of Love and thus discover "our" essential Strength.

Strength

"He who is humble in heart is stronger than the strong."
(St. Mark the Ascetic, *226 Texts*, 107, p. 134, Vol. 1, Philokalia)

What does strength mean?

Is it strength to impose on everyone and everything around us? Or perhaps the desire to *impose* is a sign of weakness, which would indicate that we want to restrain something because it is too big for us; it is beyond our control and so we feel threatened by it. And that is why we try to *under*estimate it in order to control it.

Is it strength to always want to be first, to be the winners in relation to everything? Or perhaps our obsession with victory indicates an unappeased longing for the assurance that we are not weak?

In all human history various symbols of strength and weakness have appeared. Man always sought strength and admired the sense of power. So could we seek, after taking a brief look in the records of humanity, the strongest figure – mythical or real, divine or human – that has ever been recorded?

It is a difficult question because we could look to numerous examples: conquerors, kings, heroes, superheroes, gods, sons and daughters of gods. There are innumerable symbols of strength, all equally impressive; but is this true even when they are interweaved with the notion of *evil?* Could we say that some portion of all these might be very wicked, but at the same time strength inspiring? Is it possible for this to happen? Or perhaps the real sense of strength is mutually exclusive from any sense of wickedness? Could perhaps total weakness fool us for supreme strength? And could, correspondingly, total strength look like supreme weakness? It seems a paradoxical assertion and is still extremely true.

In our theoretical search for the strongest figure that has ever been recorded by humanity, we would hardly ever think of Jesus Christ. Still, the story of Jesus is a story of objective and essential all-mightiness. Christ is a real symbol of strength which truly surpasses every other known record which might be referring to the notion of *strength.*

But still, what does strength mean?

If we examine the story of Jesus Christ in order to investigate the notion of strength, we will see a paradox: Jesus is crucified by His persecutors and is seemingly defeated. His persecutors mock Him for his "weakness" saying that if He was truly the Son of God, He would obviously do something to escape His torments instead of accepting them as an ordinary, helpless and weak man, *"And they that passed by reviled him, wagging their heads, and saying, Thou that destroyest the temple, and buildest it in three days, save thyself. If thou be the Son of God, come down from the cross"* (Matthew 27:39-40). But their mockery is very reasonable and their unfaithfulness to His strength justified, since these are totally related to their idea of *what strength means.*

Yet, who is the really strong in the story of Jesus Christ? His persecutors who felt threatened by Him and wanted to destroy Him because they weren't able to understand Him or because they suspected His greatness? Or Jesus, who was capable of enduring everything, the unfair accusations, the cruel torments and His crucifixion, without ever being touched internally by any of these things, remaining unshakeable in His inner state of Love? Which of these two illustrations consists of a symbol of real strength?

Even though the answer is clear, we ought to admit that we still have difficulty in perceiving *this* concept of strength. And that is because our perspective, being distorted, remains external; that is, we look from outside to inside instead of inside to outside. Appearances keep deceiving us.

This is shown by the example of Peter who still believes in the outer imposition and the use of outer strength, *"Then Simon Peter having a sword, drew it and smote the high priest's servant, and cut off his right ear"* (John 18:10); then, by contrast, in the greatness and the healing energy of inner strength which transcends everything, *"And Jesus answered and said, Suffer ye thus far. And he touched his ear, and healed him"* (Luke 22:51).

If we proceed a little deeper, we will be truly shocked by the following thought, "How strong should one be in order to endure being mocked, tortured, unfairly treated, manhandled, crucified and still not lose his Love, not generally and vaguely, but specifically towards his own torturers?"

Real strength is not to be found in the ability of imposing ourselves and winning, but in supporting, accepting and giving way. Real strength is not to be found in having the last word, having our way and controlling things, but in the ability to forgive, love, help and serve, *"He riseth from supper, and laid aside his garments; and took a towel, and girded himself. After that he poureth water into a bason, and began to wash the disciples' feet, and to wipe them with the towel wherewith he was girded"* (John 13:4-5).

It is true that initially the sense of strength that derives from our negative emotional states seems sweet, like when we are having angry outbursts or when we are outraged with someone and we declare, "I will *never* forgive you for this," feeling that the other person is hanging from us and our eventual decision for acquittal.

If we are honest with ourselves we will have to admit that these ugly inner states are accompanied by a strange "sweet" and underlying sense of power. We must know, however, that this illusory strength, sooner or later, will reveal its real bitterness and then its taste will be truly unpleasant. For this sense of "strength" constitutes in reality an *inner isolation*, an inner hell, which naturally throws us out of the Light. And then we are left all alone within us, trying to convince ourselves that we are strong and don't care about anyone and anything, while in essence we tremble, facing our absolute weakness and loneliness.

So whatever figure may have existed or was conceived by human imagination, when it symbolizes a notion of strength according to which one is imposing himself and destroys in the name of his "power" and authority, trying to conquer and subordinate everything, then it indicates, whether we realize it or not, absolute weakness, total insecurity and utter fear.

Strength is not to be found in being able to take away the life of someone, but in being able to forgive the one who is taking it away from us; it is not to be found in being able to control anyone or anything, but in it being impossible for anyone or anything to control us *inside* ourselves. *Omnipotence* means being able to remain untouched by anything happening – by transcending everything. But this can happen *only* in one way: through inner self-mastery, or more appropriately, *God-mastery*.

True strength is in the one who can stop or ignore his random and unchecked thoughts which try to discourage, threaten and terrify him, and even bring him nightmares; it is in the one who can keep his emotions from running wild like untamed horses, risking throwing him any moment from various cliffs, or roaring like an angry lion threatening to devour himself as well as everything around him.

He who can control his own inner world, cannot be controlled by anyone. So he is almighty, and no one can harm him because our *real* Life is our inner world.

The *only* way, however to truly control our inner world and keep it unaffected by whatever happens, is through the help of God. If our self-reliance does not derive from God-reliance, then its value is relative and in no case can it reach the borders of almightiness which is an *exclusive* attribute of Love.

Only Love can control our uncontrolled thoughts and can tame our untamed emotions. And only She can provides us with all the *energy* we need, not to impose on anything, but to transcend everything. And the way to have access to this super-human strength is of course one: prayer, the relationship with God, *"Then cometh Jesus with them unto a place called Gethsemane, and saith unto the disciples, Sit ye here, while I go and pray"* (Matthew 26:36). *Every time* we turn sincerely to Love for Her to reinforce and console us, we will gather *true Strength*.

The Inner Restoration of Christianity

Consolation

"Seek true rest in God. All human things are temporary and changeable. All divine things are everlasting and unchangeable."

(St. Dimitri of Rostov, *Spiritual Alphabet*, p. 28)

Why do we constantly seek consolation from men and only rarely from God? Simply because we don't know Him well enough. We can say to a man: "You are my only consolation, only you can understand me...." And then this man will become without our knowing, our "god." Yet, it is certain that there will come a time when we will say that he has let us down as well, and we will seek consolation elsewhere. We rarely believe, however, that God can constitute a real consolation for us.

So why is this happening?

If we tell our complaints, problems, worries, difficulties, needs, even absurdities, to a friend, brother, parent, he (or she) will understand, support, feel us; he might even cry with us, while God... We feel that God might judge, rebuke or even punish us. We will feel guilty towards Him when we just want some consolation, not another heavy guilt. So we believe that God won't *feel* us. He will sit unruffled, inexpressible and unmoved, announcing His fair but severe verdict, like a fair but immovable judge who is not touched by our hardships, complaints, indignation or discontent. Ok, if we implored, if we begged and cried, then He might give in; but we don't want to cry, we want to complain or be consoled, even if we know that the problem, in essence, is in us. So we know that God isn't going to respond.

That is why we turn to a man, who is… human; he has passions and is able to feel us, offer us some words of consolation, "Yes, I know, it's difficult, I understand you…." While for God nothing is difficult, He doesn't have weakness, so how can He understand us? He has only demands from us. Consequently, we turn elsewhere for consolation and without knowing, we seek for another "god" in friends, companions, groups, entertainments, interests, carriers, aims, and so forth.

"In times of great sorrow and unbearable pain, our soul, seeking a way out, turns many times with real desperation, to earthly consolations. It seeks in them the antidote for pain."

(St. Dimitri of Rostov, *Spiritual Alphabet*, p. 26)

The truth, however, is that all these "gods," at some point, will betray us; they will abandon us and will disappear because they are not imperishable, they are limited in their abilities, duration and power.

"The consolation that the perishable things offer to man is also perishable."

(St. Dimitri of Rostov, *Spiritual Alphabet*, p. 26)

And then we might begin to realize that God at least has infinite strength and duration; then we might remember that He was always there for us, under all circumstances, no matter how low we had fallen – and we cannot swear that this would happen with anything else below Him. He always supports us and never denies us or sends us away. It is just for our own benefit, for our spiritual growth, that He expects more and more from us, as *we* do in effect from ourselves. Still, His love, interest, compassion and assistance don't ever change.

So God always constitutes our ideal consolation, our only real consolation, even if we cannot acknowledge or perceive it. Like a small child who often believes that his parents don't care enough for him and may seek refuge and consolation even in imaginary friends, in the same way, we often disbelieve and reject God, creating imaginary "gods."

He, however, as a loyal and proper parent, is always there. Full of self-denial, He watches, teaches, helps, loves and takes care of us. And if we could acknowledge this and turn to Him for consolation, it's certain that He would do what's infinitely best for us. If He should give in, He would give in; if He should be severe lest we fall off a cliff being deaf and blind, He would be severe. And if He had to shake us intensely to wake us up to see that our next step is fatal, He would do just that without minding at all what our opinion of Him would be or whether we would think badly of Him and reject Him once more. And this self-denial is the demonstration of His real love for us. So let's turn for help and consolation to Him. We often say: "I don't have anybody to talk to, to care about me and my problems." But we all have God.

> "Tell [Him] every little part of your need, and ask personal help for everything. This will be the most genuine prayer."
>
> (St. Theophan the Recluse, *The Spiritual Life*, p. 301)

"Talking to someone" won't help us that much. We will often hear *human* solutions, usually very different ones according to with whom we are talking, while God will always tell us something much subtler, penetrating, constructive and liberating. For He, in effect, is our only *true consolation*.

> "Be always with the Lord. Whatever happens to you, take refuge in Him; reveal your soul to Him; lay your burdens on Him; tell Him about your pain."
>
> (St. Theophan the Recluse, *Guidance in the Spiritual Life*, pp. 149-150)

We should talk to Love, present to Her all our issues with awareness and we will see that *She* will always offer us wise solutions and will comfort our troubled heart and confused mind.

> "When you want to resolve a complex problem, seek God's will in the matter, and you will find a constructive solution."
>
> (St. Mark the Ascetic, *226 Texts*, 195, p. 142, Vol. 1, Philokalia)

Quite often, various thoughts darken our minds, creating sorrow, indignation and restlessness. We might be overwhelmed by troubles, worries, complaints, anguishes, fears and inner chattering. So when we ascertain that despite all our efforts to find a solution to these or cast them from our minds and they persist in seizing us, let's try to put them all in our prayer, in our communication with God. Let's turn to Him and tell Him clearly what is tormenting us.

If we do this honestly and properly, that is, as if we are really standing before Him – which is true – then one of these two things will happen: Either we will realize (with God's help) the vainness of our thoughts and they will retreat or disappear as if they never existed, and we will quiet down, wondering how these futilities could have troubled us; or we will realize (with God's help) what is hidden behind these thoughts, troubles and agonies, and the reason they keep upsetting us and are not willing to go away. In this case, we will really "hear" a subtle inner voice telling us: "But this is not the real reason you get upset, is it?" And then we will acknowledge that we probably get upset because of some aspect of our egoism, and not so much because this or the other happened. So we will have to wonder: "What is the real reason for my worrying? What is truly troubling me?" And if we are honest with God, one of our thorns will be revealed to us. Indeed, the trigger may be external, but the cause of the sorrow and the pain or upheaval will be internal.

> "When under the pressure of stupid [irrational] thoughts, we will find relief and joy by rebuking ourselves truthfully and unemotionally, or by confessing everything to the Lord as to a human being. In both these ways we will always find tranquility, whatever troubles us."
>
> (St. Hesychios the Priest, *On Watchfulness and Holiness*, Section 138, p. 186, Vol. 1, Philokalia)

Despite what is happening, whether what is bothering us is really important and truly unbearable, or unimportant but the teaspoon of water has become an ocean for us, if we turn to God we will gather genuine strength and consolation. There are many ways to be helped, but the Divine one is the most effective.

"When human help appears, the Divine One withdraws. Once a hermit was served by angels, but when people approached him and began helping him, then the angels withdrew."

(Starets Parthenios, *Counsels and Sayings*, p. 90)

Real help exists and is given only from God. Anything else below Him is just one of His *channels*, *means* and *organs*. And we should know that it is impossible to request true help and not receive it. If, however, we just ask for "help," that is, convenience, then His response will again be related to our essential benefit. If we ask for help that in the long run will harm us, He will simply deprive us of it for our benefit, and in that way He will have helped us all the same.

Let us turn to Him and we will discover with astonishment that there is no other consolation which is more *direct*, more *effective* and more *reliable* than His own. So if we learn to turn for reinforcement and consolation to God, we will also have to learn to be still (in *hesychia*) so we can hear His response and receive His help.

Hesychia (Stillness)

"When the heart has acquired stillness [hesychia] it will perceive the heights and depths of knowledge; and the ear of the still intellect [nous] will be made to hear marvelous things from God."

(St. Hesychios the Priest, *On Watchfulness and Holiness*, Section 132, p. 185, Vol. 1, Philokalia)

Quietness and unquietness; stillness (hesychia) and worry (lack of hesychia); worry we know too well and nobody desires it, stillness we all need, but often consider it an outer state and rarely seek it as an inner reality, even though it's obvious that since worry is an inner state, the same will go for stillness.

We all think we know how worry is created: its reasons are always external. We have great difficulty in perceiving that any kind of worry is due, in effect, to *internal reasons,* and basically to *one* internal reason: the fact that we are not related sufficiently to God. By saying "worry" we don't mean a state of vigilance and alertness which might be necessary for dealing with any possible or real event; we mean a state of agony, anxiety and upset in which we "lose" ourselves.

If we are honest, we will observe that we are constantly "worrying about something...." And all the time we think that "*if* this or the other happened" *then* we would stop worrying. We always justify and explain our "worries" without ever understanding that worry is our permanent inner reality, and what changes it is simply its object. Also, we don't really know that if we could be in *another* state, in the one of stillness (hesychia) then the same objects wouldn't provoke us to such upheaval, tension and anxiety. But what is this state of stillness (hesychia)?

It is an inner state of peace in which we have the ability to be related to God, of hearing His Voice and in that way gather guidance, knowledge and strength. It's not a state of denial, indifference, insensitivity or self-hypnosis, but an extremely *vivid* state of *receptivity*.

> "Some people maintain that hesychia in the way described by the Fathers is inaction, not action. In reality the opposite is the case. Hesychia is a very great action in invisibility and silence. The person is in repose and stillness in order to speak with God, in order to allow himself his freedom and to receive God Himself."
>
> (Metropolitan of Nafpaktos Hierotheos, *Orthodox Psychotherapy – The Science of the Fathers*, p. 324)

This hesychia is an inner state which is attained and *endowed* by God after a lot of inner struggle, and allows us to be related to life in the best possible way. It allows us to *Live* in life without constant worry, fear, anxiety or waiting for the worst. Yet, we like to believe that our inner upheaval, weakness and worry are totally justified "with all these things happening." Or we reach the point of even claiming that if you do not worry, if you are not anxious, then you do not live, because all these are part of life, which is true, but they are part of "life" not Life. For in reality all this is just a reassuring excuse for the fact that we don't have a truly established relationship with God. When something "alarming" is happening or is about to happen, immediately we are cut off from any notion of Faith, Hope, Strength, Knowledge, Trust and of course, Love. We lose everything, we lose *real Life* and then we claim that this loss is also a part of "life."

"We should worry only over one thing: how to manage not to spend our present lives aimlessly and vainly, that is, without spiritual struggle and prayer."

(St. Paisius Velichkovsky, *Field Flowers*, p. 99)

And when we cannot be meek, strong, kind, beautiful and real, we become violent, weak, harsh, ugly and fake, claiming that these are part of "life" and that a peaceful life would be very boring. We say this without ever having tasted it, since we cannot attain it! And here the proverb fits very well: "The grapes are sour, said the fox, when he could not get at them." In this way we seek Life in its opposite, and we end up "living" instead of Living.

"But if he says that those are inimical to peace, and good things of peace, who rejoice in strife and anger and changes and disturbances, even these are controlled by obscure images of a peaceful aspiration; being vexed by tumultuous passions, and ignorantly aspiring to calm them, they imagine that they will pacify themselves by the gratification of things which ever elude them, and they are disturbed by the non-attainment of the pleasures which overpowered them."

(Dionysius the Areopagite, *On Divine Names*, Caput XI, Sec. V, p. 116)

What is the reason, however, that inner stillness is truly such a hard-attained and rare God-given state? We don't have inner quietness because our attention is constantly turned outwards. When we look inside from outside, we cannot avoid being in a constant turmoil, since everything outside is *changing* and very often the events of our life are truly difficult. But if our attention is turning outside from inside, things are completely different. We learn that *"The kingdom of God is within you"* (Luke 17:21). What does this mean?

It means that we have inside, within our heart, a Divine place where we can be. If our attention turns *first* inside and *then* outside, we will have stillness. If it turns first to the Kingdom of God where everything is quiet and full of Love, without changing by external occurrences, then we will be starting with stillness and everything else will follow.

God tells us, *"Be still, and know that I am God"* (Psalms 46:10), as well as, *"Seek ye first the kingdom of God"* (Matthew 6:33) and all shall be added. From these two promptings, derives the following reality, "God first and then everything else," that is, *"Stillness first and then everything else."* This reality however is feasible only if we reverse the direction of our attention and turn first inwards and then outwards. If we are able to do that, we will always be in *hesychia*, for when we turn deeply into our heart, we discover a place of total stillness, peacefulness and strength, in short, the Kingdom of Love.

But is the direction of our attention truly that important? And in what sense?

"Attentiveness is the heart's stillness, unbroken by any thought."

(St. Hesychios the Priest, *On Watchfulness and Holiness*, Section 5, p. 163, Vol. 1, Philokalia)

Attention is one of the most valuable properties we have at our disposal. Attention can be a saving gift for us, as well as the cause of our sentence. If our attention is used by *us*, it can save us from all kinds of evil and can offer us all good things. But if our attention uses *us*, then it can truly lead us to all kinds of misfortunes.

When *we* don't use our attention, it uses us; that is, it is drawn by anything, and in that way draws us along with it. It becomes a prey of all things and so are we. Above all, however, it is not functioning in the soul-saving way that it should; it does not stand as an unsleeping guard at the entrance of our heart checking *what enters* into it. So since our heart's guard is sleeping, our valuable inner kingdom becomes an unfenced vineyard where anything alien and harmful can enter.

All events of life – anxieties, tensions, fears, negativities – everything is entering unchecked into our heart, and thus upsets us. Consequently, we are in a constant turmoil, always saying, "But this or that happened, and this or the other might happen," without understanding that we are responsible for allowing all these things, all these real and imaginary events to enter into our heart, simply because our attention is either missing or drawn uncontrolled by everything.

If, however, we had attentiveness or *nepsis*, that is, watchfulness, then we could check to see what wants to enter into our heart. And if we considered it beneficial we would permit it, if not, its entrance would be forbidden.

"Watchfulness [nepsis] is a continual fixing and halting of thought at the entrance to the heart."

(St. Hesychios the Priest, *On Watchfulness and Holiness*, Section 6, p. 163, Vol. 1, Philokalia)

In our state, the idea of control at the entrance of our heart seems of course strange and perhaps unfeasible. This watchfulness, however, is a necessary condition for every spiritual progress and is required in order to be led to the state of *hesychia*, of this indispensable stillness which constitutes the foundation to "know God."

"Watchfulness [nepsis] is a way of embracing every virtue, every commandment. It is the heart's stillness and, when free from mental images, it is the guarding of the intellect."

(St. Hesychios the Priest, *On Watchfulness and Holiness*, Section 3, pp. 162-163, Vol. 1, Philokalia)

When we are in the state of attentiveness or nepsis, then the random association of thoughts do not appear in us, neither do their consequent feelings and unavoidable sensations. This means that if some event, person or anything else which grieves, annoys or worries us, comes to our mind and doesn't manage to steal *our* attention, then we discover that it cannot bring along its associative train of thoughts and feelings, but instead collapses, which is very impressive. Yet, if we come out of the attentive state, that is, if it steals our attention, then it will carry us along with it.

An image, a name, an occurrence, a memory, can trigger, as we said, an associative chain of thoughts which will carry us along and then we will quickly be led to the corresponding feelings and sensations that these associations will provoke. This is a "random" changeable state which makes us feel happy in one moment and sad in the next. We feel brimming with kindness and joy, and next thing we know we are angry and furious. Our mood is altering according to *what happens*. So we become prey of any random influence, good or bad, and naturally we are at the mercy of every temptation.

In essence, when we are in this state of lack of attentiveness, we sleepwalk on a stretched rope where we live all kinds of dreams: different scenarios, intense adventures, glories and failures, loves and hatreds, and so forth, we "live" everything but we don't Live anything. However, when we come out of this dreamy state – which seems extremely realistic when we "live" it – we often marvel at its content and it looks completely unrealistic, as it happens with our night dreams as well, no matter how acute its influence was on us.

If we come out of this dreamy, random, associative and without attentiveness state, and enter into the attentive state, then nearly nothing of the previous "facts" can affect us. The same images and references to names, events, occurrences, might now leave us untouched. Even if they still exert some influence on us, they *don't* carry us away, leading us wherever they want, and they *don't* make us worry, as before.

Only this kind of attentiveness or *nepsis* can ensure our staying in a quiet, safe, sober and essential state through which is possible every real sense of *Life*.

> "Watchfulness [nepsis] is a spiritual method which, if sedulously practiced over a long period, completely frees us, with God's help from impassioned thoughts, impassioned words and evil actions. It leads, in so far as this is possible, to a sure knowledge of the inapprehensible God, and helps us to penetrate the divine and hidden mysteries."
>
> (St. Hesychios the Priest, *On Watchfulness and Holiness*, Section 1, p. 162, Vol. 1, Philokalia)

And, of course, the essential benefit of this state of stillness, which is attained through *attentiveness*, is that it provides us with the ability to *pray* and to *contemplate* God.

"We must have faith, endurance and hope, and also that inner peace which the Greek fathers call *hesychia*. Contemplation requires this silence, which cannot be defined as either activity or passivity. It is a serene watchfulness."

(Anthony Bloom, *Courage to Pray*, p. 43)

For only in this state of hesychia is it possible to hear God. Only through the state of stillness can we truly have a two-way communication with God in which one will hear the other!

"The hesychast, the person who has attained *hesychia*, inner stillness or silence, is *par excellence* the one who listens. He listens to the voice of prayer in his own heart, and he understands that this voice is not his own but that of Another speaking within him."

(Kallistos Ware, *The Power of the Name*, p. 1)

There is a particular state of separation of the soul from God which we could name, *"You don't hear me."* It is a state in which God tells us: "You don't hear me; I am talking to you and you keep saying your own stuff. Hear me!" And our own stuff is always words, thoughts and feelings of worry, upset, complaining, indignation, negativity and tension. But God is telling us: "Be still, be calm, *listen*... things are not as they seem... Love!" And in this state of separation we spend almost our whole life, not to say our whole life with the exception of some moments. This is our daily, ordinary and familiar state. It has to do with every moment when we are not particularly happy, particularly grateful, but a little bit troubled, a little bit vexed, a little bit bothered, a little bit displeased, a little bit bored, a little bit... anything.

We are not completely separated from God, because we can hear Him saying to us: "You don't hear me." He whispers to us: "Smile, relax, be grateful, be happy... Love!" He is telling us: "Be in the state of Love, in prayer, *be* with Me, Hear Me. Leave from sloth, complaints, worry, ungratefulness, tiredness, discontent, annoyance, and come Here, in the beauty of the moment, in the miracle of the moment, in Love... for if in the next moment you lose all of this which you don't appreciate now, this that you are used to, bored by, annoyed by, then you will cry bitterly... That is why I am telling you... Do not worry... Be still... and Hear Me!" So when God tells us: "You don't hear me," we should respond whole-heartedly: "Forgive me!" And we should re-enter into real prayer, in the communication with Him, that is, we should be transferred to *gratitude*, to *hesychia*, which allows us to hear Him.

This is a very subtle reality because we often feel that we function normally and that we are alright, but without knowing it, inside us we chatter unceasingly, we are in anguish and *disquiet*. If we try at these moments to breathe slowly and deeply, we might perceive our state. And perhaps we will hear God telling us, "You don't hear me..." For how is it possible to hear Him when our mind and heart is full of fear, anxiety and all kinds of inner dialogue?

As we grow, we begin to realize that this state of anxiety is completely natural until there comes a point where, when we manage not to be anxious or at least try not to be anxious, then in the eyes of other people and perhaps even to our own eyes (!) we might seem insensitive.

This is extremely important, because very often we come face to face with our whole false self, which resists with all its might and claims its right to worry. Using of course our voice, it hastens to say: "Is it possible not to worry when these things are happening?" "Is it possible to be relaxed in this or the other situation?" And when he himself gives the answer: "No, it's not possible..." Then it "relaxes:" "Ah... ok... I got nervous for awhile, I was worried... ok, everything is alright." As incredible as it seems, *this is* our reality!!!

If we ever happen to be still... then we are really stressed!

If we ever relax... then we really worry for being so relaxed!

Certainly something is wrong with us!

If we happen to be in a state of quietness, peacefulness and calmness, all the inner and outer voices will rush in to "wake us up:" "But how is it possible not to get angry?" "But how can you not worry?" The truth is, however, that our Real Self is calm; he is in a state of Love and can *hear* the Voice of God.

In the *state of hesychia*, which is an inalienable right of our Real Self and a necessary reality for us, our mind is not troubled and our heart is not agitated. But this stillness frightens us; because we perceive it as a "void."

We are afraid of the "void" and so we constantly try to fill it with activities, people, interests, cares and concerns. Yet, God also needs some space to enter into us and be with us. He needs this "void," this voluntarily created "void" of stillness. It remains a fact, however, that only when we stop being excessively occupied with ourselves are we able to quiet down. And we could truly say that where our *self* stops, there Stillness begins. For Stillness is God.

When our self gets out of the way, there is room for Him. And of course the same is true with every other thing in our lives. Even if we manage to stay in a relative stillness, it is known that the devil doesn't tempt us only from the left, but also from the right. This time its challenge will come through the exhortation to worry, for example, for the others: for our children, friends, companions and whatever we love. And our weakness, that is, losing again our contact with God, will turn it to a virtue! "I am not worrying for myself, but I worry a lot for one or the other..." Yet, worrying for the other people is very often a form of *conceit*, in contrast to the *trust* to others which indicates appreciation and respect.

When we genuinely care for someone, our Real Love for him is essentially proved when we transcend our personal worries in order to be able to be in a state of stillness and thus communicate with the Omnipotent and Omniscient God who will inform us how to act in relation to him and will provide us with every strength to do what His love is showing us.

So would we prefer to be in a state of restlessness in relation to the one we love and thus be unable to offer him any real help, or to remain quiet in a direct communication with the Almightiness of Love, in order to offer him any possible help?

And if we claim that it is possible, even in the state of worry, to hear God inside us and that we have truly experienced this, we should know that this is simply an *illusory sensation* which is due to our slow perception. For the truth is that we will be able to *hear* God only during the slightest interval when we have quieted down within our disquiet. As soon as we surrender even a little, saying: "I cannot stand this agony any longer, talk to me God" we might come into a subtle, imperceptible stillness and then and only then, it will be possible to hear, even faintly. The more quietness there is, the more clearly we will hear.

Worry and disquiet are like yelling while someone is trying to talk to us. Is it ever possible to hear him? But the first second we stop yelling – perhaps because we got tired – that is, as soon as we quiet down, only then we will be able to hear what our interlocutor tries to tell us; especially if his voice is *quiet* and *subtle* (and *at the same time* dynamic and commanding) as God's Voice is. For His voice is not imposing, compelling and domineering; it needs the proper conditions to be heard, the right soil to flourish.

In order to hear the Voice of Love inside us, we need to give Her our attention. As long as our attention is diverted and carried away by various outer and inner voices, it won't be able to hear this other Voice. When we regain control of our attention, we will be able to silence all these voices and be still, to know God.

One condition for this stillness is silence. These are two terms which express, in effect, the same thing and are completely interrelated since there cannot be one of these states without the other.

"Intelligent silence is [...] a companion of stillness."

(St. John Climacus, *The Ladder of Divine Ascent*, p. 158)

Silence

"Many words equal poverty"

Silence is an inner state which cannot really be explained with words, which is rather paradoxical, talking about silence... but is something that must be experienced. Only silence can reveal its value to us and explain its function.

Only silence can teach us silence.

Nevertheless, here we will use rather many words in order to examine silence as a method and attitude, and not so much as a state. Still, let us not forget the words of a wise saint who is reminding us not to fall into the passion of talkativeness when speaking about silence:

> "I would prefer not to write too much about this [Word on Talkativeness and Silence], despite the urgings of my wily passions."
>
> (St. John Climacus, *The Ladder of Divine Ascent*, p. 159)

The attitude of silence aims at leading us into a state of silence, so silence is both a means and an end. The state of silence is a necessary condition for spiritual life and one of its strongest foundations. Correspondingly, its lack is the root of many evils.

There are many different aspects of our life where the attitude of silence can be applied. Here we will examine it in relation to some specific forms of our communication: counsel and criticism, spiritual discussions, our general talk and our internal chatter.

Counsel and Criticism

Let's begin with the counsel (and criticism) we either offer or receive, and let's examine the first part of this form of communication.

Giving advice without being asked is, in essence, an egoistic act. It derives from *our* personal desire to give, without taking into account if our neighbor has the necessary inner room to receive. This *unwanted* and *untimely* offer comes, in effect, from *our* need to feel useful, great, virtuous, and even wise or as "teachers."

We must be very careful when we attempt to advise our neighbor, because we must mainly take into consideration *his* state of receptivity and absorption and *not our desire* to help and save. People have room and are receptive only when they are in a state of need. It is only then that they want, and only then that they are able to accept and receive. It's impossible for someone who is thirsty to not ask for water to quench his thirst.

In short, let's not pull anyone by the hand in order to lead him to the Light, for if he is not participating willingly toward this course, the result will be dragging him into the ground, since he will either resist or he won't make any kind of effort. And in this way he will become injured and full of wounds, and will be in a worse position than before. That is why we should closely examine the purity of our motives, because the difference between coordinating with the inner reality of our neighbor, with his benefit as our motive, and obeying our subjective urgings to "help", and counsel our fellow men, is very subtle.

We need real discernment in order to be aware of the *right moment*, the *right way* and the *right words* which are the prerequisite for the flourishing of every beneficial talk. But if we haven't been granted this gift of the Spirit, this Divine charisma of discernment, then we should usually act according to the rule of not offering counsel if we haven't being asked persistently to do so:

> "No responsibility rests with a counselor for his advice, if he has given it with the fear of God and with humility, not of his own accord, but because he was asked and urged to give it. [...] We will observe that the Fathers forbid us to give advice to our neighbor of our own accord, without our neighbor's asking us to do so. The voluntary giving of advice is a sign that we regard ourselves as possessed of spiritual knowledge and worth, which is a clear sign of pride and self-deception."
>
> (St. Ignatius Brianchaninov, *The Arena: An Offering to Contemporary Monasticism*, p. 53)

Now, if God enlightens us, making us carriers of His Word, then there is often a debt to transmit this light and not hide it (Matthew 5:14-16). Yet, we should never imagine that *we* will save the world or even one man. This is only God's work.

> "When we think we know how to correct people, it means that we still have a lot of pride inside of us."
>
> (Mersine Vigopoulou, *From I-ville to You-ville*, p. 81)

Still, in reality it's not so important what we say, but *what we do*.

> "The faithful do not speak many words, but their works are numerous."
>
> (*The Sentences of Sextus*, Sentence 383)

And in a latter stage, it's not so important what we do, but *what we are*. So let's not take pleasure in giving counsel, but let's try instead to *be* the counsel.

A very important issue having to do with giving advice is the one of *criticism,* in relation to which it is important to know that there is either discernment or judgment.

Discernment tries to take into account all the data concerning a person or a situation, and realizing that this is impossible, its conclusion is not emotionally colored, positively or negatively, but it is as impartial and objective as it gets, far from any personal opinions and views. Discernment doesn't judge, so it neither condemns nor acquits, it just ascertains. Discernment is aware of its limitations, so reserves itself; it doesn't jump to conclusions, and is able to remain *silent*.

Judgment, instead, thinks it knows whatever it needs to know. It jumps to conclusions and verdicts, and it's pretty sure of the correctness of its decisions. Judgment is unrelenting, limited and one-sided. It can *never* be silent; it will always find a way to express its conclusions.

> *"Judge not, that ye be not judged. For with what judgment ye judge, ye shall be judged: and with what measure ye mete, it shall be measured to you again. And why beholdest thou the mote that is in thy brother's eye, but considerest not the beam that is in thine own eye? Or how wilt thou say to thy brother, Let me pull out the mote out of thine eye; and, behold, a beam is in thine own eye? Thou hypocrite, first cast out the beam out of thine own eye; and then shalt thou see clearly to cast out the mote out of thy brother's eye"* (Matthew 7:1-5).

Discernment is always based on a preceding self-knowledge. What it sees and perceives in others, it has already more or less perceived in itself. Discernment is based on a preceding cleansing, on an inner catharsis. The eyes of discernment have be cleansed by God; that is why it has been said that discernment is a gift of the Spirit.

The eyes of judgment are still tainted. Judgment looks always outward, and is completely blind in relation to whatever concerns it. Its eyes are never turned inward.

If we ponder on how the inner world of a man is being formed, and how many things contribute to this formation, we realize that all possibilities of judgment disappear and all possible accusations of our neighbor seem an outrageous sin.

The childhood of a man, his family, friends, relatives, teachers, education, environment, country, age, the events of his life, even the moment of his birth, are just a few of the factors which contribute to his formation. So how is it possible for us who can't know but only an infinitesimal part of this data, to judge a man?

Only God can know even the slightest detail in relation to the existence of a man, and so only He can judge a man. This realization can help a lot in the limitation of judgment and the consequent appearance of discernment and *silence*.

Let's examine next the second part of this form of communication which has to do with receiving counsel and criticism.

This is an issue which troubles us very often and very intensely, and it's a cause for many conflicts and tensions. Its solution, however, is very simple, and is again related to our self-knowledge and inner growth.

When our fellow men criticize us (or counsel us) this criticism might be right or wrong. If we have enough self-knowledge we won't have difficulty in recognizing which one of these is true. In case the first is true, we should be thankful and grateful to our neighbor for becoming a means by which we are informed by God of something important for us.

"Do not shun the person who opportunely berates you; but go to him and he will show you how much evil lies hidden from your consciousness. Once you have swallowed the bitter and nauseous draught, you will taste the sweet nourishment of health."

    (St. Ilias the Presbyter, *A Gnomic Anthology*, Part I, Verse 33, pp. 37-38, Vol. 3, Philokalia)

If the criticism is wrong, we can just let it pass by, or even use it to our benefit to deepen our self-knowledge and our real self-evaluation.

So, in both cases there is no need to be resentful, talk back, defend or attack. And if we cannot recognize whether our criticism is right or wrong, we can simply keep it on the side and evaluate it in the future when we will acquire more self-knowledge.

The only one in us who is not benefited by any kind of criticism and counsel, is our egoism. Only egoism is indignant with every "unfavorable" criticism – while it enjoys praises – and is always ready to battle any remark which might not approve it.

That is why when we are exposed to criticism or are given counsel, let us learn... *simply to hear*. We should *increase our receptivity* in criticism, fair or unfair, cruel or kind, elegant or harsh. And generally we should learn to *hear more*, not be in a hurry to talk.

In this point we should pay close attention to our attitude towards unfair criticism. For when we are exposed to fair criticism, even if we resent it in the beginning, later on, we can recognize its truth. Towards unfair criticism however, most of us cannot remain untouched and are quickly driven out of the attitude or state of silence. We fall then into the trap of mentioning or even reflecting on what *we are doing*, what *we* offer, *how good we are*, and so forth. But if we mention the good we do, it ceases to be truly good and turns into a self-interested offer.

> "If you do good to one person, you may be wronged by another and so feel injured, and say or do something stupid, thus dissipating by your bad action, what you gained by your good action."
>
> (Evagrios the Solitary, *On Prayer, 153 Texts*, 137, p. 70, Vol. 1, Philokalia)

If we know ourselves, what we do and who we are, then we won't have need of any external or internal defenses and acknowledgment of ourselves. We won't seek to be liked by men, but to be liked by God. That is why we don't really need to give explanations all the time. We don't need to justify or defend ourselves, especially when we truly feel unfairly treated; except when our explanations have to do with the *benefit of our neighbor*. Only in this case is it worthy to explain ourselves, in order that our fellow man not be entrapped in his wrong and negative judgment.

> "When you are reproved, you ought either to remain silent, or else gently to defend yourself to your accuser – not indeed in order to gain his approval, but to help him rise up in case he has stumbled by reproving you in ignorance."
>
> (St. Ilias the Presbyter, *A Gnomic Anthology*, Part I, Verse 35, p. 38, Vol. 3, Philokalia)

And if we deepen in the spiritual order of things, we will find out that there is a secret communication of the souls. It is much better to pray silently for the one who wrongs us and thus communicate internally (secretly) with him, than losing time and energy constantly explaining and defending ourselves, risking in that way to fall into the traps of our egoism. So let's learn to pray when we feel our known communication stalemates.

> "Pray as heartfelt as you can. Your hearty and well-intentioned prayer won't leave their souls indifferent – for souls communicate in secret – and it will not be fruitless."

(St. Theophan the Recluse, *Guidance in the Spiritual Life*, p. 68)

We should be careful, though, because all of what we have said so far, does not refer to negativity and *closing up,* and to the superficial "silence" which is accompanied by discontent, annoyance and ceaseless inner dialogues that result in explosions and outbursts, but to genuine inner silence.

All our chattering, external and internal (and mostly the internal one) is nothing more than a result of egoism and self-love, self-admiration and pride, murmuring and self-pity.

So let's begin to be silent externally in order to learn to be silent internally when we face any kind of criticism or counsel. In that way we will be able to recognize their truth or untruth, having always in mind that what we truly long for is to please God and not to be approved by men.

> "If a man is treated with contempt by someone and yet does not react with anger in either word or thought, it shows he has acquired real knowledge and firm faith in the Lord."

(St. Mark the Ascetic, *226 Texts*, 124, p. 135, Vol. 1, Philokalia)

Spiritual Discussions

A very important subject in relation to our talking is the spiritual conversations, that is, the conversations which have to do with the Spirit, with God, *"God is a Spirit"* (John 4:24). There are certain necessary conditions in order for these discussions to take place. One of them is our inner cleanness:

> "If you are polluted on account of impure works, do not speak about God."
>
> (*The Sentences of Sextus*, Sentence 356)

Another condition is the preceding experience and application of our words:

> "May your pious works precede every word about God."
>
> (*The Sentences of Sextus*, Sentence 359)

Otherwise, our words are empty and vain, and thus particularly dangerous:

> "It is not a small danger for us to speak the truth about God."
>
> (*The Sentences of Sextus*, Sentence 352)

In general, if we take pleasure in talking about spiritual matters, giving counsel, spreading knowledge and teachings, then we won't be able to hear in us what God wants us to say, because *our* desire will come between us and the word of God:

"The true word about God is the word of God."

(The Sentences of Sextus, Sentence 357)

We might have difficulty in realizing that it is possible for God to talk through us, but the opposite belief, that *we* are in a position to know the things of God and talk about them, results from egoism and pride, *"For it is not ye that speak, but the Spirit of your Father which speaketh in you"* (Matthew 10:20).

"Do not say anything about God before you have learned from God."

(The Sentences of Sextus, Sentence 353)

The proper inner state to have a spiritual discussion, that is, to talk about the things of God, is to have the sense of His presence. It is very simple, we should never have spiritual conversations, that is, talk about God, *as if He is not Present.*

"Speak concerning the word about God as if you were saying it in the presence of God."

(The Sentences of Sextus, Sentence 355)

And we should always pay attention, of course, to what way we talk about God:

"It is better for you to be silent about the word of God, than to speak recklessly."

(The Sentences of Sextus, Sentence 366)

And to whom we talk about God:

"Do not wish to speak with a crowd about God."

(*The Sentences of Sextus*, Sentence 360)

The truth about God is valuable and, in essence, beyond (or above) human reason, so it cannot be offered massively, neither can it be understood if it is not experienced. So it cannot be an object of arguing. In reality, it can be taught only by God Himself within us. That is why the Word of God must often be transmitted in various indirect ways in order for our inner soil to be prepared, *"And with many such parables spake he the word unto them, as they were able to hear it"* (Mark 4:33). And later on we will be able to receive it more directly, *"And when they were alone, he expounded all things to his disciples"* (Mark 4:34).

We have been given a very important command of silence in relation to spiritual insights and teachings: *"Give not that which is holy unto the dogs, neither cast ye your pearls before swine, lest they trample them under their feet, and turn again and rend you"* (Matthew 7:6).

This command is referring especially to our inner life. Whatever miraculous experiences we have internally, but also externally, we should perceive them as something holy or valuable like pearls, and therefore take care of them as such. If we scatter them here and there, not only we will be poorer, but we will also meet a particular enmity and resistance by the people who are not interested or are even opposed to the things of God, *"But the psychological (psychic-ψυχικός) man receiveth not the things of the Spirit of God: for they are foolishness unto him: neither can he know them, because they are spiritually discerned"* (1 Corinthians 2:14).

Nevertheless, there is a necessity for the Word of God to be made largely known, *"And this gospel of the kingdom shall be preached in all the world"* (Matthew 24:14). A great amount of discernment is needed, however, when we talk about the things of the Spirit, something which we can easily ascertain if we try to talk about God among people who are either not interested or opposed to spiritual matters, or might have a different "spiritual" perception! We find out then that men are easily transformed to wolves: *"Behold, I send you forth as sheep in the midst of wolves: be ye therefore wise as serpents, and harmless as doves. But beware of men: for they will deliver you up to the councils, and they will scourge you in their synagogues"* (Matthew 10:16-17).

Still, this shouldn't discourage us and make us lose heart in the face of indifference or enmity, in the case where we are called to transmit something from the truth of God: *"Fear them not therefore: for there is nothing covered, that shall not be revealed; and hid, that shall not be known. What I tell you in darkness, that speak ye in light: and what ye hear in the ear, that preach ye upon the housetops"* (Matthew 10:26-27). But we should always have in our mind and heart, and in our whole Being, the Love of God as the motive of our words:

"If first your mind is persuaded that you have been God-loving, then speak to whomever you wish about God."

(*The Sentences of Sextus*, Sentence 358)

For when we love someone, we know how to talk about him: what to say, how to say it and to whom to say it. Our love for him wants to protect him, never exposes him or talks inappropriately about him; it doesn't reveal to unsuitable people things that need to be silenced; it doesn't create confusion and turmoil in his name, or negative impressions; it has always tremendous respect for him, measuring its every word about him. And if we need to remember the attitude of silence in relation to every subject, and not chatter or talk to no use, how much more carefully should we measure our words when we talk in relation to God:

> "A scientific knowledge of God causes a man to use few words.
>
> To use many words when speaking of God, produces an ignorance of God."

(Select Sentences of Sextus the Pythagorean, Sentences 99-100, p. 62)

General Talk

> *"Set a watch, O Lord, before my mouth; keep the door of my lips"* (Psalms 141:3).

Our daily speech is extremely important and affects decisively all aspects of our life. It is one of our favorite occupations and we often have a sense of duty in relation to it. We feel uncomfortable and awkward remaining silent amongst one or more people, because silence seems to indicate dislike between people, and in general, we are not used to it.

We do not realize how harmful unnecessary talk is, and how many evils we could avoid if we kept an attitude of silence as much as possible, *"But I say unto you, That for every idle word that men shall speak, they shall give account thereof in the day of judgment. For by thy words thou shalt be justified, and by thy words thou shalt be condemned"* (Matthew 12:36-37). These words might seem harsh, but if we examine how many sufferings are caused to human relationships and therefore to the whole of humanity by our incessant talk, then we might realize the value of *silence*.

Conflicts, disputes, jealousies, quarrels, assaults, crimes, misunderstandings, turbulences, and so forth, are created by our inability to be silent when we need to be silent, and by our fervent desire to talk and talk and talk.

So we need to examine the value of our talk: its meaning, intentions and purposes, if we are to reach the discovery of the golden silence.

> "Talking needs great attention. You ought to think about the place and the time that you speak, for what purpose, whom you are addressing, what is your motivation and the result of your talking. Before you talk, think on all these things. The silent one thought about these things. And that is why he became silent."
>
> (St. Dimitri of Rostov, *Spiritual Alphabet*, p. 47)

One thing that needs to be particularly examined is our tremendously harmful, completely mechanical tendency to talk about the faults and inadequacies of other people, as well as the general talk about other people which consists, in large part, of our daily conversations.

Let's not occupy ourselves so much with what other people do, what they say and what they are; they are what they are. Our real issue is what we do and what we are. What we seek is freedom from our "self." We don't need to be constantly correcting others, keep telling them what is right and what they should do, but to learn to turn our *attention* to *us* and to our own "virtue"...

> "Most of the time, instead of watching over ourselves, we have our eyes on what other people are doing."
>
> (Mersine Vigopoulou, *From I-ville to You-ville*, p. 90)

If we stop being busy and bothered ceaselessly about other people, about what they say or do, whether it concerns us or not, we might even learn to assimilate and transform our *real* annoyances. What we need to learn first is to cut off every outer manifestation of our annoyance and then move on to our inner world.

> "The first step toward freedom from anger is to keep the lips silent when the heart is stirred; the next, to keep thoughts silent when the soul is upset; the last, to be totally calm when unclean winds are blowing."
>
> (St. John Climacus, *The Ladder of Divine Ascent*, pg. 146)

In general, our response to whatever we hear or whatever happens around us, is very important and may have either extremely beneficial or harmful results. If we are initiated into the art of silence, it is certain that the latter one will lessen and the former will increase.

> "While it is a skill to speak, it is also a skill to be silent."
>
> (*The Sentences of Sextus*, Sentence 164b)

It is self-evident that the art of silence is indissolubly connected with the art of talking. Real silence doesn't refer to some kind of negative "introversion" which results in an unfitting and noxious "silence."

> Speak when it is not proper to be silent, but speak concerning the things you know (only) then when it is fitting.
>
> (*The Sentences of Sextus*, Sentences 161-162)

We are impressed by the fact that talking consists of an art, and we constantly defend our right to lack of taste, vulgarity and negativity, "This is how I talk, whoever likes it or not!" In reality, however, our talk can be a beautiful work of art as well as a source of discord and negativity. But our egoism is offended when it hears that we should, "Learn how to talk!"

Our word could be garnished and become very edifying. It could be enriched with genuine forgiveness and heartfelt thanks, two real pearls that are rare in our speech. Our talk would be more beautiful if it was calmer, more impartial and objective, and not so "personal," so identified and "intense."

Still, all this effort to cultivate our talk requires a specific condition in order to be genuine and really successful, and not feigned and artificial. We need to realize that our talk should be, for the most part, for *the sake of other people*. We should talk for the sake of others and *not for the sake of ourselves*. Nevertheless, sometimes it might be useful and beneficial to talk for the sake of ourselves, out of our need; perhaps even to hear our own words and perceive something from them. Still, our first concern should again be the inner state and receptivity of our listener.

This art of silence and talking needs long-lasting training so we can be released from our mechanical and egoistic tendencies: from talking the way we like, whenever we like, wherever we like, and saying whatever we "like." And then we might begin hearing that calm inner "voice" which notifies us each time what to say, to whom and how. And the more we become silent, the more we will hear. One Armenian proverb says: "Speak little and you will hear much." It's important, of course, what we hear and to what kind of company we expose ourselves, but it's certain that if we don't know how to remain silent when we are in the company of men where we could benefit much by listening, the inability to be silent will cost us a lot.

"When you are with believing persons, desire to listen rather than to speak."

(*The Sentences of Sextus*, Sentence 171b)

So in the beginning, as we are re-trained in order to learn the art of silence and talking, it is certain that we will find the rule: "Few words are best" to be very useful.

Internal Chatter

All that we just said is related to an attitude of silence and constitutes in some way the first external step. The aim is for the external silence to be gradually transferred internally.

"So first let us force ourselves to be silent. Then from this silence is born within us something which leads into Silence itself."

(Kallistos and Ignatios the Xanthopouloses, *Method and Precise Cannon for those who choose the Hesichastic and Monastic life*, 100 Chapters, 16f, pp. 39-40, Vol. 5, from the Greek text of Philokalia, publ. by To Perivoli tis Panaghias)

Initially, external silence will very probably create more internal chatter. Whatever we have learned to express externally, all verbiage and jabber, if we stop reproducing it on the outside we will probably reproduce it inside us. So because of the external silence, our already excessive internal chatter might be increased. But this has an advantage. In that way we will be able to acknowledge it more easily and admit its existence.

Since we are very voluble externally and we don't have time for silence, we don't have the chance to ascertain what happens internally. As soon as we become silent externally, we will perceive another level of chatter, equally harmful and exhausting, as well as extremely poisonous and soul-destroying, which takes place inside of us.

The internal chatter includes all our inner dialogues, explanations, defense against criticism and accusations, calculations and measuring of our offers, goods, virtues and the corresponding lacks of people around us; it includes our daydreaming, scenarios, fears, insecurities, suspicions, talking about the past and predicting the future, and whatever else there is inside us which talks unceasingly, jumping from subject to subject, holding us in a constant state of *disquiet* (lack of *hesychia*).

In reality, the only inner dialogue which should take place inside us is the one of prayer, the one of Divine communication, which is rendered impossible in the midst of all this chattering.

So the meaning of all these observations is to taste the external silence and ascertain its benefits in order to reach the inner silence which will lead us to the *state of silence*. When we are in the state of silence, even if we talk, we don't disturb silence, because we are not the ones who talk, but God is talking through us (Matthew 10:20). Our talk will be like a bow which stretches, throws its arrow and returns to its silent state, being composed again.

When we are in the state of silence, our talk doesn't produce disharmony, doesn't taint the silence, but flows harmonically, always fulfilling a work, always aiming to a target. In the *state of silence* there can be *prayer* which also shouldn't be characterized by chattering (Matthew 6:7). Only in the state of silence can we hear God's Voice inside us.

There will always be something which will be challenging us to come out of silence. Yet, if we remain in Silence, then we will go even deeper in Her and we will listen to Her voice whispering to us:

"Plunge into Silence, plunge *deeply* into *Silence*... plunge into Silence so you can hear Me."

"Silence is Golden"

The Inner Restoration of Christianity

Loneliness and Solitude

"You should love silence, isolation, conversation with the Lord, who will be your guide and teacher."

(St. Theophan the Recluse, *Selection of Letters*, p. 60)

Real silence begets genuine solitude. Genuine solitude means association with God. Often we don't understand people who choose to become monks or even less so, hermits, simply because we don't know God.

"A monk is one who is separated from all and united with all."

(Evagrios the Solitary, *On Prayer, 153 Texts*, 124, p. 69, Vol. 1, Philokalia)

Monks don't differ essentially in anything from laymen. They certainly differ in the means, but not in the end.

"No matter where we are and what our circumstances may be: in solitude or in company, in a monastery or in the world, everywhere and at all times we must keep them, His commandments. This is never easy."

(Starets Macarius of Optino, *Russian Letters of Direction*, Letter 92)

The truly spiritual aims and purposes are always internal, while anything external remains just a means.

> "The desert includes those living in a monastery or in the world who are attaining their salvation. For everyone the most important rule is to cleanse one's heart of the passions."
>
> (St. Theophan the Recluse, *The Spiritual Life*, p. 240)

The real aim of monks and laymen cannot be other than this pure and genuine solitude which gives us the possibility to associate with God.

> "Strictly defined, the word 'monk' means a recluse, a solitary. Whoever has not withdrawn within himself, is not yet a recluse, he is not yet a monk even though he lives in the most isolated monastery."
>
> (*The Art of Prayer – An Orthodox Anthology*, p. 54)

Therefore, genuine Solitude has to do with an inner state and not with an external way of life. External isolation may help in the creation of internal seclusion, but by itself is not worth anything.

> "When your prayer has gained such stability that it keeps you always face to face with God in your heart, you will have seclusion without being a recluse. For what does it really mean to be a recluse? It means that your mind, enclosed in the heart, stands before God in reverence and feels no desire to leave the heart or to occupy itself with anything else. Seek this kind of seclusion and do not worry

about the other. Even behind closed doors one can wander about the world, or let the whole world invade one's room."

(*The Art of Prayer – An Orthodox Anthology*, p. 252)

Our worst psychological fear is, as we have already said, the one of loneliness. We tremble at the thought of being alone and this fear doesn't include only our associations with people, but all things. We constantly fill our time and space simply to avoid being alone with ourselves.

"If you think of the number of empty minutes in a day when we will be doing something because we are afraid of emptiness and of being alone with ourselves, you will realize that there are plenty of short periods which could belong both to us and to God at the same time."

(Metropolitan Anthony of Sourozh, *School for Prayer*, p. 90)

We are afraid of our loneliness simply because we don't know that in effect we are never alone and that if we begin learning to be alone with ourselves, at some time we might also learn to be alone with God.

"[…] even though you are by yourself. You would not have realized you were alone, because you would have realized that the Lord is close by."

(St. Theophan the Recluse, *The Spiritual Life*, p. 252)

Still, despite our ceaseless efforts to fill our time and space in order to not be alone, very often we cannot avoid the feeling of loneliness. Even in the midst of a crowd or in the company of our most beloved people, we might feel alone. Even in the midst of a particularly "full" and active life, we might be chased by the feeling of emptiness and loneliness. If, however, we begin experiencing the presence of God in our lives, we will discover that our relationship with God fills us to such a degree, that whether we are completely alone or in our most active state, we feel an essential fullness and a genuine solitude which excludes all sense of loneliness, that is, of estrangement and confinement.

Whenever we feel, for example, that "It is very beautiful, but such a pity not having anyone to share my joy with; such a pity rejoicing on my own," that simply means we ignore God, who is by our side. And of course, we ignore also the truth that in the company of God there is a healthy, quiet, steady and not ephemeral, subtle fullness.

"Rush to take advantage of these chance moments of solitude for undistracted sojourning with the Lord and sweet conversation with Him. Solitude in the spirit is sweet. I hope you will taste this sweetness sometime, so that you will desire it as Paradise on earth."

(St. Theophan the Recluse, *The Spiritual Life*, p. 252)

While associating with anything else, if God doesn't participate, it will only fill us for a space of time and then we are left "empty" and "alone" again. And then we seek the object of our desire again, in order to refill us. So we keep seeking more and more of it, because it can no longer fill the void of our loneliness, until we exhaust it or are exhausted by it; and then we start seeking for something else to replace it. That is why in our relations with everything, even with our beloved ones, there is very often this sense of satiation, of void and intense loneliness.

The association with God, however, is different; it is more relaxed, more subtle, uplifting, ethereal; that is why it seems as though it is slipping away. But when there are the conditions for it, that is, the abolition of egocentrism, it becomes our sole assured reality, our sole constant in life without, at the same, time losing its sublime, heavenly character.

But what does association with God mean?

What does it mean to be in the company of God?

To *be* with Him?

We cannot, for example, imagine God dancing; we cannot imagine Him enjoying music. But still, the Creator of melody, movement and beauty, would stand in wonderment before these marvels? We think that we are their creators and that God remains foreign to them. So we are constantly self-admiring. We say for an artist, "Wow! He is a god!" "He paints incredibly!" "He plays unbelievable music!" And God is nowhere to be found, because He probably couldn't understand any of these things.

So that is what it means to be in the company of God: to dance with God, to listen to music with Him, to be entertained with God; to associate with God by praying unceasingly; to be in a constant communication with Him whatever we do.

Let's not isolate God from our life; let's not limit Him to only one small aspect of it. We should let Him participate in all our activities. In the same way we want to share with our loved ones all the aspects of our lives, good and bad, pleasant and unpleasant, serious and funny, let's learn to share everything also with Love, with God, who is calling us inside of us and is able to overwhelm our Being.

Whenever we feel lonely, incomplete and unsatisfied, we are simply cut off, self-limited, closed to the Love of God.

The sense of loneliness constitutes in reality an *offense* to God. When we realize deep in our hearts that we continually offend God by claiming that we feel lonely when He is constantly by our side, then an apologetic disposition towards Him will inevitably be brought forth within our spirit: "Forgive us for ignoring You by constantly feeling all alone, when You Are always at our side and inside us!"

It is true that virtue is a solitary path. For it is a rough and difficult-to-understand *inner* path. In the path of the lost we have a lot of company, many companions. For it is an obvious, tangible and "easy" path. In the path of the lost there is no real struggle, there is rather an unimpeded tumble. When we walk in the path of the lost we are generally accepted, and while we are never left alone in it, we constantly feel very lonely.

In the path of virtue we meet a lot of resistance, accusations and mockery. Often when we walk this path people *don't understand* us, they misunderstand us. In that way, we might be left alone without ever feeling lonely.

The things of the spirit are hard to understand, because we don't experience them. That is why they often seem to be anything from alarming to foolish (1 Corinthians 2:14-15).

Now, we cannot really grasp the difference between loneliness and solitude. And while most of the time we feel alone and are possessed by an intense sense of loneliness, we like to imagine ourselves as solitary, free and independent men. When, on the other hand, we meet some genuinely solitary man, we often consider him unsociable, alienated, weird, and even mentally ill.

And it's true that as soon as we decide to be left alone, to quiet down in order for some space to be created in us so something new can enter, those in our close environment are immediately disturbed by worries, and may feel "threatened." When we cultivate our "sociability" and participate in the "public affairs," then all is well, even if we don't feel well. Even if we declare that we don't see anything but a dead-end in our occupations, nobody worries for us as long as we participate in the daily procedure of "life."

As soon as we get out of the current even a little bit; as soon as we try to stop being carried away, filling our time and space – the inner and outer ones – with activities and distractions, then people around us will probably start worrying. And of course all the *well-intentioned* counsel and criticisms will begin: "You don't have a life! What's wrong with you?" "Aren't you bored all by yourself?" "What's the point in being alone?" And if we respond to these questions with words like prayer, stillness, spirituality, association with God, then it's almost certain that the worry for our environment will be intensely increased, and soon various unfavorable comments will reach our ears, "She is not well... I worry about her," while the reality is very different.

> "The desire to be alone shows your good inner state. You can be isolated daily. As soon as you have a little time at your disposal withdraw to your room, try to descend with the mind into the heart and there stand before the Lord. Praise Him, thank Him, ask Him spiritual goods."
>
> (St. Theophan the Recluse, *Selection of Letters*, p. 76)

We cannot understand the concept of solitude, because we are afraid of going past our "void." We all feel inside us a sense of emptiness or a sense of loneliness which is *immediately related to our separation* from God. That is why instead of experiencing and transcending this "void," we constantly try to fill it in order not to feel it, since its sense of *loss* is very painful.

So we keep seeking external excitement to feel "alive," indefinitely postponing our inner journey, thinking that "life" is "out there." But if we were truly Alive, we wouldn't need external excitements *to feel "alive."* The truth is that the deeper we go into ourselves, the deeper we are opened to Life: to people, to nature and, of course, to God.

One of the most essential messages of Jesus Christ which is either forgotten or neglected, is that the Kingdom of Heaven is inside us. But this message is not one of closing, limitation, "introversion" in a negative sense; it's not a message of excluding life, but a message of abundant Life. Only when we discover our inner wealth, our inner treasure, God *inside us*, are we able to also relate with God *outside us*, and with the miracle outside.

As long as we remain empty internally, not deepening inside us, we can only relate superficially with Life, and will only see what our external and limited sensations allow us to see. If we don't deepen within us to discover our *subtler sensations*, our higher or deeper sensations, then we won't have at our disposal – or they won't function – the senses necessary to perceive and to receive the Life behind "life," the Miracle, genuine Beauty, Silence, Love or God, behind all appearances.

We think that life is to be found in tension, activity and upheaval; stillness frightens us, silence seems boring, and in that way, without knowing, we have "life" but we lose Life which passes us by; that is why when the end of "life" approaches, we are afraid, we feel it's not enough, we feel that we "lived," but wonder with sorrow, "That was all?"

When we are shallow, that is, when we don't live *through* our Depths, we cannot embrace Life. We cannot contain its greatness, even if we imagine that we "live" at the *utmost*. And that is because we just don't have the necessary inner space, since we have not deepened. The deeper we go within, the more space we acquire to contain the miracle outside us.

When Saint Paul refers to the law of the flesh and the law of the Spirit (Romans 8) he refers, in essence, to the law of the surface and the law of the Depths. Our body is not undervalued in any way by Saint Paul; it just symbolizes, and indeed is, our most external part in contrast to our spirit, which is our core and deepest part. These two are parts of a unified total, but when the external determines the internal, that is, when the surface determines the Depths, then "life" determines Life. When the internal determines the external, that is, when the spirit determines the flesh, then Life determines death.

Saint Paul is clearly not against our body, but he refuses to be a slave of his more superficial parts. He refuses to be a slave of his more external parts, that is, of his carnal and psychological mind, because he acknowledges that his freedom is to be found in the "enslavement" to his *deeper*, *spiritual* self. His freedom is found in being his *Real Self* which he discovers to be *one* with God, "*Not I but Christ liveth in me*" (Galatians 2:20). He surrenders to his depths so God, Love, will determine his Life; so he won't be surrendered to the surface and end up being a helpless prey to superficial and external elements. Surrendering himself to God, he chooses, in a few words, his freedom.

Entering inside us means *opening* to the real world outside us, to real Life outside us. If we just turn to the world outside without first having entered inside, then we will be lost, we will disappear, because the world will enslave and swallow us; it will steal our soul, "*For what is a man profited, if he shall gain the whole world, and lose his own soul?*" (Matthew 16:26).

When we begin entering into our inner world, experiencing Stillness, Silence and Solitude, we find that our life begins filling with Life. All kinds of real Feelings and essential Sensations will flow from this inner source of Life, and our life will be more full, intense, active, miraculous and more magic than ever. Time will be transformed and minutes will become hours, hours will become days, days will become weeks, weeks will become months, months will become years and years will become *eternity*. So when our Life reaches to its end (or to its real beginning...) sooner or later, whenever this might be, it will be impossible to feel, "That was all?" For we will have lived a Life of fullness, *"I am come that they might have life, and that they might have it more abundantly"* (John 10:10).

Real solitude begets essential fullness. And correspondingly, there cannot be any essential solitude without genuine inner fullness.

Fullness

"All of them unto Thee do look, to give their food in its season"

(Psalms 104:27, YLT)

All and everything is a carrier of energy.

All things constitute sources and receivers of energy.

All life is a continuous energetic inter-feeding.

There are innumerable sources of energy as well as the *One Source of Energy* which feeds all the rest; the One Source of Life which *feeds* everything with life.

We derive energy (life) from food, air and every kind of impression we receive. Ideas, thoughts, discussions, music, movies, events, people, nature – everything creates impressions on us and thus provides us with energy.

How come we feel "uplifted" after an edifying conversation, listening to certain music or learning some good news? And how come we feel "down" by watching gloomy shows, negative movies, listening to disharmonic music, participating in conflicts and unpleasant conversations? Because all these, and anything else that exists or happens, carry with them some kind of *energy*.

Now, we could say generally that there is positive energy and negative energy, the latter being, in essence, *absence* of positive energy, just as darkness is absence of light. We can live with both kinds of energy; it is just that with the positive energy we Live while with the negative one we "live."

For example, we can be fed with bad food and thus preserve our bodies, but we will be in a bad physical state, even if we can't realize it directly, or we can be fed with healthy and nutritious food, offering our body qualitative energy. The same goes for our soul. We can feed her with bad and harmful food, with negative energy of every kind, or we can feed her with positive and qualitative energy. The difference is in the *quality* of life we want to live.

Usually we cannot *discern* between these two completely different kinds of energies, so we feed our souls or our bodies with what comes in handy, or just what is offered. So our sensations, physical and psychological, lose their refinement and become gross and slow in perception. They can no longer perceive the *qualitative difference* between what really nourishes and benefits us, and what only *seems* to nourish us, but actually harms us and provides us with some quick and easy energy that at the same time is detrimental and destructive.

We try to discover and taste the *essence* of life – that is, the *energy* of beauty, joy and happiness – that is why we can't stop consuming: foods, music, shows, clothes, drugs, alcohol, sex, human relationships, travels, carriers, and so forth. In essence, one way or the other, we are constantly trying to discover and enter into the Kingdom of Heaven.

We try to taste and live in this uplifted, beautiful, powerful, joyful, substantial inner state of fullness without, however, having the right qualifications, without the proper inner clothing. So we *imitate* the Kingdom of Heaven and very soon we are thrown out of it, "*And the king having come in to view those reclining, saw there a man not clothed with clothing of the marriage-feast, and he saith to him, Comrade, how didst thou come in hither, not having clothing of the marriage-feast? And he was speechless. Then said the king to the ministrants, Having bound his feet and hands, take him up and cast forth to the* outer *darkness*" (Matthew 22:11-13).

That is why we say afterwards, "Happiness doesn't last very long" "Nothing good lasts forever." We feel that beauty is fleeting and ephemeral, but this is due to the fact that we just haven't discovered and tasted the real Beauty. Not the "beauty" which fills us for awhile and leaves us later, emptier than before, but the Beauty which not only cannot be lost, but every time we taste it, comes to be added to our former experience in order to enrich it.

Everything is thus created in order to feed and be fed with *qualitative* energy. It has been created in order to be in a communion of Love. For us, however, this can happen only when we stand properly before all things; when we see everything in its *proper place* and act correspondingly.

Food, music, physical workouts, shows, works of art, books, activities, work, human relationships, relationships with animals, nature – everything offers energy.

Yet, not one created thing which can feed us can be compared with the Creator of everything. And if all that exists constitutes sources of energy for us, then how much fuller would the Source of all energy feed us?

If we discover this Source of energy, which for every man can be found *internally*, then we will relate to every other source of energy completely differently. Through the *sense of void* that we experience, we become unconsciously voracious organisms which consume incessantly in order to be full, to feel complete. This inner deficiency is responsible for all our egoistic *greedy acts* (energies) which aim at *our own* energetic feeding; whether these are expressed violently and criminally, or with more refined ways and through relationships of "love," or better, dependence.

Yet, if we experienced a sense of internal fullness instead of emptiness, then our external feeding wouldn't aim at our voracious satiation, but would constitute the expression of an essential communication, of a constructive inner-feeding.

As we would ask, so we would receive.

As we are fed, so we would feed.

In order, however, for a genuine offer on our part to take place, which doesn't aim at some kind of exchange, but is given freely since it has been received freely, *"Freely ye have received, freely give"* (Matthew 10:8), we need to be related with the sole inexhaustible energetic Source of Love which feeds everything. If we are related with this Source inside us, then we will feel truly full, and therefore realize that only through this inner state of fullness can we have essential relations.

At the bottom of our heart, this is the reality that we all long for: healthy relations with everything; that is, *inner fullness which begets a healthy external interaction*, communication, interchange and association.

We like to imagine that we are experiencing this reality, that we are internally full and do not relate to anything around us out of our need or because of our void, but out of love. Soon, however this illusory reality falls apart and then all the tensions, conflicts, attempts of control and imposition begin.

This is the main rule of our life from which we cannot escape, simply because we don't realize that our sole true hope of salvation is found in God. He is the one essential Source of fullness. Only through an established and living relationship with Him, can we have real relations of Love which won't degenerate into relations of use and abuse, relations which we all detest deep down: both using, and being used. For both of these are sides of the same coin and constitute a wheel that keeps turning…

Deep down we all seek fullness, *inner fullness*. But when we remain turned outwardly, out attention is carried away by the idols and the mere *reflections* of the Source, and thus we seek an *external fullness* which bears and is born by egocentrism. As long as our attention turns outside, we will remain imprisoned in an endless vicious cycle.

We need to break this vicious cycle by turning our attention within, to God. For this is our only real destination: The fullness of Love. This is why we were created. And only through this inner fullness and wholeness can we truly love, because then it's not we who love but God inside us, who Is Love.

For only Love can love; and God is Love (1 John 4:16).

So now we can better understand the reason for this constant sense of emptiness, loneliness and dissatisfaction, which overshadows all our activities, all our relations and all our "life." It is the result of a need for internal fullness which can be achieved only through our relation with the Spirit.

Usually, when we hear about the notion of *fullness*, not wanting to acknowledge our inadequacy, we undervalue it. We equate it with a state of indifference, alienation and deadening, of scorn and cruelty, which is not human. We feel that our "normal" reality is threatened, so we think, "And what does it mean to be full? That you don't care about anything? You don't want anything? You don't have feelings? You don't have needs? But I have needs; I like feelings and psychological fluctuations, that's the way man is… otherwise you are not alive…"

Yet, in other cases we often say that we are worn out and disappointed from "life." We explain how tired we are from the psychological fluctuations, instability, recurring sense of vanity and emptiness, relations of dependence, use and need, and alas, to the one who will point out this contradiction! We will immediately claim, "I like contradictions; these are part of life too!"

We downgrade the notion of fullness – simply because we don't live it – to a negation of life, when the state of fullness is the only real Life. Outside of it, there is only a constant, endless effort of life, a continuous attempt for things and situations to happen so we can feel satisfaction, full, *alive*. But whenever we want to *feel* alive, that means we don't live. So we spend most of our lives *trying* to live! And this *endless effort to live*, we called it life!

Yet, our fullest possibility for Life, internal and external, is born exclusively through the contact and relation with the Source of Life, and not out of some *effort* to live. Our effort can only be directed at being released from "life," in escaping from the death we call "life" in order to be related with Life. And this effort shouldn't scare us. The effort to get rid of the "void," loneliness, dissatisfaction, death and "life," won't deprive us of anything. Instead, it will offer us *everything*.

> "The life in which you are careful with yourself is not meant to be one that deprives you of all comfort, giving nothing in return. On the contrary, such a life, with the unceasing memory of God and obedience to one's conscience, is in and of itself a tireless source of spiritual joys to which earthly joys may be compared like absinthe to honey. You will have to deprive yourself of a few outward things. Everything must happen inwardly. It is possible to take part in everything, and yet to be apart from it. Outwardly you are doing one thing, but inwardly something else is taking place."

(St. Theophan the Recluse, *The Spiritual Life*, p. 184)

Our relation with the inner Source of energy and the inevitable inner fullness, will make it possible for us to Love and *thus* Live. Unfortunately, as much as this discredits our picture of ourselves, *it is not possible to have any relationship of Love with anything, if this does not come from a sense of inner fullness*. It will just be a relationship of need and not of Love. And this we can easily ascertain by seeing how much space and freedom we allow to the ones we claim to love. How steadfast is our love? And to what degree do we love the ones who cease to be interested in us, who cease to "love" us and estrange from us or even turn against us?

So let's observe *our* "love" and examine its fruits when it is not coming from the Source of Love, and then we can "compare" it with the attitude which Love Herself has towards us when we forget Her, when we turn against Her and when we betray Her, finding other new "loves."

The Inner Restoration of Christianity

"What Shall be Able to Separate Us from You?"

"Who shall separate us from the love of Christ? Shall tribulation, or distress, or persecution, or famine, or nakedness, or peril, or sword? As it is written, For thy sake we are killed all the day long; we are accounted as sheep for the slaughter. Nay, in all these things we are more than conquerors through him that loved us. For I am persuaded, that neither death, nor life, nor angels, nor principalities, nor powers, nor things present, nor things to come, nor height, nor depth, nor any other creature, shall be able to separate us from the love of God, which is in Christ Jesus our Lord" (Romans 8:35-39).

Being united with God isn't related to any situation, person or event. It is something completely personal and has to do with whether we consider and feel that God is everything for us and whether we consider or feel that there is anything more important to us than Him that we would allow to come between us.

It is the same as with a true union of marriage, which essentially isn't related to anything outside it, and nothing matters except whether the two companions truly desire each other. In such a case, nothing can break them apart; their relationship is unassailable by anything external and constitutes the foundation and starting point for everything. The relationship is first and then everything else follows. If something takes precedence over it, then it's more important than the relationship, and can come between them.

The same goes for our relationship with God. If God is first in our life – since we recognize Him as the most important thing, as the foundation and starting point, as our essence – then nothing can come between us and nothing can hinder our union with God. So naturally, whatever we let come between God and us, separates us from Him, carries us away from His Kingdom and becomes our god.

What does idolatry really mean?

Idols are all the possible reflections of the Divine, as well as all His imitations which can substitute in His place within our heart and become our gods, thus stealing our soul. Our god can become family, love affairs, music, nature, work, pain, happiness, money, football, every kind of addiction, and more or less, whatever else might take first place in our hearts. And whatever takes the place of God within, *steals our soul,* in essence, since we *give it* our heart. *"For what is a man profited, if he shall gain the whole world, and lose his own soul?"* (Matthew 16:26).

Gaining the whole world doesn't only mean to gain power, fame and money. There is another, much simpler and seemingly innocent aspect to all this. Gaining the whole world might mean to be socially capable, have a lot of interests, a good occupation, a nice family or relationship, enough friends and plenty of acquaintances, being admired, loved, appreciated, and all is fine... but God is nowhere to be found! We might be tainted by an imperceptible form of egoism, but other than that we are kind, pleasant, not particularly antagonistic, giving; perhaps if someone hurts us we become somewhat aggressive, but then again, within acceptable limits. Therefore we are the "best" and we have gained the whole world!

We can gain the whole world with a nice, moral, human life, having, of course, some human weaknesses, without even being extremely blameworthy in anything, yet all this without God... so again, we lose our soul! And why should we lose our soul?

"For where your treasure is, there will your heart be also" (Matthew 6:21).

All of the above facts of life constitute a treasure which can be, and is, lost; so if our heart is given to it, it will be lost along with it.

> *"Lay not up for yourselves treasures upon earth, where moth and rust doth corrupt, and where thieves break through and steal: But lay up for yourselves treasures in heaven, where neither moth nor rust doth corrupt, and where thieves do not break through nor steal: For where your treasure is, there will your heart be also"* (Matthew 6:19-21).

In the same way, if our treasure is in the heavenly goods, in Love, which cannot be corrupted, lost or stolen, our soul will be there also, and thus she won't be lost. That means if we do all the aforementioned, but our heart is given to God first, then *nothing that is of worth can be lost,* and so our soul is saved.

On the contrary, if our heart is not given to the heavenly treasure of Love, then everything will be able to steal our soul. And what does it mean, in essence, to steal our soul? It means to suck all our energies, from our lowest physical energies to our most refined psychological energies. So without knowing, we sell our soul to the perishable goods of this world.

We can lose our soul through everything, whether it is good or bad. If we observe ourselves honestly, we will soon realize that anything can steal our heart; even the God-pleasing things when they are cut off from God and become, themselves, our gods:

> "When another monk was practicing inner prayer as he journeyed in the desert, two angels came and walked on either side of him. But he paid no heed to them, for he did not wish to lose what was better. He remembered the words of the Apostle: 'Neither angels, nor principalities, nor powers shall be able to separate us from the love of Christ' (Rom. 8: 38-39)."

(Evagrios the Solitary, *On Prayer*, *153 Texts*, 112, p. 68, Vol. 1, Philokalia)

And also the negative things which, by definition, claim God's place in our hearts and grab it, not willing to let it go even when we desire to turn away from them.

This we can easily verify when we attempt to be released from some type of addiction. Each time we try to cut off an addiction, however harmful this might be, we have the taste of an extreme bitterness, something very unpleasant, and in that way we always claim the "one last time." But the "one last time" is, of course, one of our biggest illusions! For every "last time" is a contract for the next time. It is another small deal with the devil. The only way to break the vicious cycle of the "last time" is to not give in to the "last time" and bravely taste the bitterness, the emptiness, the desert, after our release from the Pharaoh of Egypt. For this desert is the necessary stage of cleansing in order to enter into our Promised Land, to return to our Lost Paradise.

And we should be certain that whenever we escape from some hell of ours, our real Paradise is expecting us. Whenever we reclaim our soul from some addiction, we regain our Power, our Vital Energy. For our addictions suck all of our energy and strength. They hold our soul locked up in them.

For this release to be feasible however, we should first of all desire it. We must realize that we have literally despised our birthright for a pottage of lentils (Genesis 25:34). For the truth is that we like our addictions, we "love" them. We like our chains because they offer us safety and above all "fullness." It might be a false, outer, ephemeral "fullness" but nevertheless it has the *taste* of fullness.

There is a distorted sense of freedom when we are lost in an addiction, because the more we are lost in it, the more we exclude everything else around us, and so we imagine ourselves free from everything; except from the object of our addiction.

So we, ourselves, are to blame for not wanting to break our beloved chains, and that is because we have forgotten the real Paradise, our real Freedom: God, Love.

Yet, if essentially, we begin observing our life and our various forms of addictions, our various "gods" and our imaginary paradises, then we will realize what is being hidden behind of all these "loves" of ours. When we *think* we want something, we usually get literally *mad* about it. Later on, however, when it proves that it wasn't something special for us, we forget all our former madness and turn immediately to the next object of our desire. Each time we believe that *this time* we found what we were looking for, what we need, what we feel missing from within us. And each time we *lose ourselves* in order to obtain it, out of fear of not losing it, and so the object of our desire and effort *becomes our god*.

That is why if we don't get to the point of perceiving how this whole mechanism of our addictions works; how we are *constantly enslaved, just in different objects*; and if we don't learn the whole range of our false "loves," we won't ever be released from them, nor will they ever cease to carry us away and dominate us. If we don't reach the point of being angry with our passions, small or large, they're not going to stop claiming us, since we will be related to them with bonds of desire, secret lust and "love."

This is the reason that anger, wrath and hatred have been given to us, in order to direct them in a *healthy way* against the *inner enemies* of our soul. They constitute some of our weapons in this *inner battle* of freedom.

"Our incensive power can be used in a way that is according to nature only when turned against our own impassioned or self-indulgent thoughts. This is what the Prophet teaches us when he says: 'Be angry, and do not sin' (Ps. 4:4) – that is, be angry with your own passions and with your malicious thoughts, and do not sin by carrying out their suggestions."

(St. John Cassian, *On the Eight Vices*, p. 83, Vol. 1, Philokalia)

If man can reach to the point of ignoring angels in order that nothing come between God and him, how much more should he hate low addictions that come between Love and him?

And we should completely hate, irreversibly, the enemies of our soul, otherwise their roots will remain in us and with time they will find ways to grow again and reclaim our "love." If we are not completely disappointed by the false paradises which our jailors promise us, they will again charm and captivate us. That is why positive anger, constructive fury, and healthy hatred against them cleanse our soul and cut off even the memories, that is, the roots, of these alluring thieves of our soul.

In this point, however, it is important to realize that we are completely responsible for the creation of all these idols, false gods and addictions. Even if we are carried away by another person, by a situation or a temptation, by all kinds of sirens and illusions, deep down it is our fault for being carried away, because we carry in us that element which responded to the outer occasion.

We carry the *causes* of our addictions. Or formulated another way, we are responsible for not being in the necessary inner state so as not to be drawn by the outer occasions which will eventually create their future causes inside of us. Since we haven't created a healthy relationship with Love inside us, we create *outside us* all kinds of unhealthy relationships with all kinds of "loves."

We might not realize it, but we all have many small gods, many small addictions. We worship innumerable small idols which we constantly justify and defend. And we usually reprobate those who have more obvious, "bigger" and deadlier addictions, and we can easily see in them that they are wasting their lives and that their addiction is stealing their soul. We are unable, however, to realize that they lose their soul because of one large devil, while our soul is claimed by hundreds of smaller demons.

As we've already said, however, the various outer prompts are not really to be blamed for our inner enslavements and addictions, for the only one to be blamed is our false, limited "self;" that is, our egoism.

"Alas, what shall I do? Where shall I flee from myself? For I am the cause of my own destruction. I have been honored with free will and no one can force me. I have sinned, I sin constantly, and am indifferent to any good thing, though no one constrains me. Whom can I blame? God, who is good and full of compassion, who always longs for us to turn to Him and repent? The angels, who love and protect me? Men, who also desire my progress? The demons? They cannot constrain anyone unless, because of negligence or despair, he chooses to destroy himself. Who is then to blame?"

(St. Peter of Damaskos, *Book I – The Second Stage of Contemplation*, p. 112, Vol. 3, Philokalia)

As long as our relation with life remains egocentric or anthropocentric, we will lose ourselves in it. We will be lost in everything, whether pleasant or unpleasant, good or bad, beautiful or ugly. Everything will be able to come between God and us to steal our soul. We will be in a constant state of dependence from everything, as well as in a constant state of alienation from God, from Love.

If, however, our relation with life is *metamorphosed* in a God-centric relationship, then we will be able to relate in a healthy way with every God-pleasing thing and refrain from anything useless, harmful and detrimental.

We will turn to the sole healthy Dependence which will set us free from all other unhealthy addictions. For indeed our aim is not to be independent, but absolutely dependent, not on men or any other thing, but on God alone. The truth is that it's impossible for man to be completely independent, despite what we like to imagine for ourselves.

There are *a lot* of addictions which steal our soul and thus hurt and enslave her, leading her to destruction and self-condemnation; and there is the *one* and *only* Dependence which saves her, *"Thou art careful and troubled about many things: but one thing is needful"* (Luke 10:41-42). The absolute Dependence on God offers us our perfect Freedom.

Freedom

"Our soul is in an evil state, rebelling against its own Maker and unwilling to be subject to His Kingdom. It is still sold into bondage to hordes of savage masters, who urge it towards evil and treacherously contrive to make it choose the way which leads to destruction instead of that which brings salvation."

(St. Maximos the Confessor, *Various Texts*, 41, First Century, p. 173, Vol. 2, Philokalia)

God doesn't deprive us of anything by indicating some prohibitive directions. In reality, He saves us, because these paths lead only to cliffs. We are not deprived of anything by resisting our temptations. On the contrary, we are deprived of much when we succumb to them. We are deprived of the beauty of the Divine Grace; we are deprived of relationship with God's Love, since we choose to taste other "loves."

The illusion that "sin is sweet" or that "the forbidden is charming" comes only from deprived people who have never truly tasted God in them, have never essentially responded to His call, and have never supped with Love and Beauty. If, however, we want to defend ugliness, we will always *deify* our limited and ephemeral satisfactions and seek them incessantly, since we will conceive them as sweet and charming.

There are a lot of gradations between the garbage (physical and psychological) with which we can be fed and the ambrosia which is the food of gods. He who tastes the ambrosia cannot surely feel that he is deprived of the garbage. And if for some reason he *falls* to the garbage, he cannot but feel that he is deprived of the ambrosia.

So let's not be jealous of all those who are "free" to taste all temptations, but feel sympathy for them for their "freedom." Let's "envy" the ones who are *free* from all temptations and captives of Quality, Beauty and Love. The former ones have anything they want, but are deprived of all. The latter ones have nothing, but taste everything.

Enslavement to God offers us a real and essential freedom from all, and thus a *healthy* and *beautiful* relation with it. Surrendering to God breaks our earthly chains and thus we are able to rise with His help to heavenly inner heights, instead of crawling to the earth of our passions, fears and weaknesses.

> "Whatever you honor above all things, that which you so honor will have dominion over you. But if you give yourself to the domination of God, you will thus have dominion over all things."

(Select Sentences of Sextus the Pythagorean, Sentence 7, p. 54)

Dependence on God fills our soul with Light and releases her from all tensions and upheavals which might darken her.

> "When the soul surrenders with all its powers to the Lord, to the Sun of righteousness, she is bright, joyful and peaceful. When she is given to anything else, earthly, its brightness diminishes. The more she is distracted, the more darkened she becomes."

(St. Theophan the Recluse, *Guidance in the Spiritual Life*, p. 154)

There is a vast difference between the state of enslavement to anything and the state of surrendering to God; between "freedom" to do whatever we want and Freedom from all wants.

Initially, this very free, bright state appears and disappears imperceptibly, like a soft wind blowing. As we keep surrendering to Love, however, our *inner freedom* strengthens and becomes unshakeable. Yet, its preservation and permanency are a long road which is based on the growth of *real gratitude* in us. It will never be possible to *completely surrender* to the Spirit, to the Light, and thus gain our total freedom from all and everything, if we don't feel an *immense gratitude* for the Love of God.

Until we feel and experience the Perfection of God's Love, we will continue being prodigals searching for other paradises, other gods and "loves." When we begin tasting His Perfection, we will inevitably experience the real gratitude which will give us the possibility to surrender to Love, and thus be saved and freed. Then our soul will ascertain with certainty:

"Thank You, because gradually and very slowly,

I am discerning behind everything

the greatness of Your Love,

the plan of Your Salvation,

Your Perfection."

The Inner Restoration of Christianity

Perfection

"Be ye therefore perfect, even as your Father which is in heaven is perfect." (Matthew 5:48)

Why do we constantly try to defend ourselves and justify or acquit ourselves in relation to anything that might happen? If nine or ten people have a good opinion about us and one of them doesn't, why are we haunted by this one opinion, and want to change it at all costs? Why, when something goes wrong, do we immediately search for who is to blame? Why do we always wonder: "Is it my fault?" – waiting in agony for the answer: "Ah, it's ok, it's not my fault."

Why, when someone starts saying good things about us, do we become silent, we listen attentively without interrupting, and we hardly ever disagree with him, while if he makes "negative" remarks about us, we assume a defensive attitude at once? We frown, we begin interrupting him, raising our tone of voice, claiming that *this conversation makes us very tired*, there will be a lot of tension, we talk simultaneously, not hearing each other, and we will probably counter-attack, since we feel attacked. Why, when someone says "good" things about us, he seems extremely loveable and when he says "bad" things he becomes our enemy?

And why do we constantly care so much about what others do?

Why, in general, are we in a constant state of *comparison* with each other?

It is simply because we carry within us by nature, the command, *"Be ye therefore perfect, even as your Father which is in heaven is perfect"* (Matthew 5:48). And this inner prompting determines our *whole life*: our every thought, word and action; and unfortunately haunts us because we are not conscious of it and we don't understand it.

We have been created for perfection, for *completion*; and the depth or height of perfection (completion) is, in essence, what animates, urges and *evolves* us. But what does perfection mean? Perfection means to be our Real Self: that is, to be united with God and everything else in a communion of Love. Perfection, however, is not something static; it has gradations, as striking as this seems.

"There is no complete perfection in this incomplete age [aeon] but rather an 'incomplete perfection.' "

(Kallistos and Ignatios the Xanthopouloses, *Method and Precise Cannon*, 100 Chapters, 43, p. 69, Vol. 5, from the Greek text of Philokalia, publ. by To Perivoli tis Panaghias)

For example, even if we reach to the state of perfection which is possible for us, the issue of its permanency will immediately come up. So we will keep learning from life and God, and keep being tested, keep struggling, experiencing sorrows and pains, and evolving. And even if we reach the point of making the state of perfection permanent within us, we still have to function with a living reality. We have to experience it daily as something new and alive, not as something of the past, consolidated and consequently dead.

If we are united with Love, we will constantly renew this union and go deeper in it. It is not possible to have been united with Love yesterday, then recall the past today, or project it into the present. Our yesterday's union should begin anew today. Consequently, real perfection doesn't aim to a static end, but to a continuous beginning, to a constant deepening and a *perpetual* completion.

Age, conditions and generally the various data of our lives, set measures and standards for our present possible perfection. We say of someone, "He is very mature for his age." But if this person grows up and doesn't evolve in his maturity, in older age he might not be so mature anymore. The same goes for perfection. A young man who has inevitably lived as many experiences as his age allows him, cannot have the same possibilities of perfection that a man of double his age can have (taking as a fact that both of them will make use of their life's data).

So one can be perfect at a certain age as much as is possible in it; and this level of perfection won't be sufficient in an older age, as he will have to be "more" perfect, more complete. His past perfection will have to be cultivated and evolve.

Perfection is not something crystallized and fossilized; consequently, it is always possible for every one of us. We just need to take into consideration all our life's data and judge our completion (perfection) according to it.

The command "Be perfect" assumes a much deeper, practical and vital meaning when it is applied to every phase and every moment of our life. It becomes a very live prompting which urges us to aim to our highest potential and fulfill it to its best possible degree. The level of our present perfection cannot be the same as tomorrow's, because the facts that constitute our existence today will be different tomorrow.

All of our unconscious inner anxiety to be constantly perfect in an impossible and unfeasible way, is due precisely to our erroneous concept of perfection. Our inability to accept or admit that despite our God-pleasing efforts we keep making mistakes, is due to this sterilized notion of perfection.

And because of the fact that we haven't yet realized or understood, in essence, this prompting for a *living perfection*, we end up comparing ourselves with each other, as well as constantly being occupied with what others do; *unconsciously demanding* of them to be perfect according to our incomplete notion of perfection.

So through this new, live and essential understanding of the concept of perfection, of completion (because perfecting means completing), we end up with the inevitable conclusion that perfection is clearly a personal matter, and it cannot in any way be a standard for comparison between us.

Perfection is determined theoretically according to some general measures that include everybody, but in practice it is measured by completely personal (inner and outer) standards. In this essential and practical sense, there cannot be *any kind of comparison between men*. Each one of us has completely different data, experiences, education, chances, possibilities and abilities, in one word, *talents*, and therefore, if we want to compare with each other it's like comparing incomparable types, like apples and oranges. Indeed we are all men (like apples and oranges are both fruits) and deep down we all aim at the same target, but the personal data between us differs to such an infinite degree that all comparison becomes, in effect, impossible.

That is why the only possible comparison that can exist regarding man is personal and internal. Any concept of higher and lower, superior and inferior, deeper and more superficial is valid only in relation to our inner world. We are superior or inferior, better or worse in relation to ourselves, in relation to our inner reality and our inner levels. The only legitimate concept of comparison between us and perhaps of antagonism (or better, *syn-agonism*) could be the one which is characterized by the spirit of emulation which would aim in helping us perceive the general human potential, and thus inspire us to aim to the ideal fulfillment of our *personal* potential. So we can reach where *we ourselves* can reach, physically, psychologically and spiritually. So *we can attain our own perfection*, our own completion. And thus fulfill our destination in this life and do our duty and our *unique* work.

Work

"The first divine decree about man is that he should be in living union with God, and this union consists of living in God with the mind in the heart: thus anyone who aims at such a life, and still more, anyone who participates in it to some extent, can be said to fulfill the purpose in life for which he was created. Those who seek this living union should understand what they are trying to do, and not be troubled at their lack of achievement in any specially important external feats. This work by itself embraces all other action."

(*The Art of Prayer – An Orthodox Anthology*, p. 193)

Each one of us has a destination in this life, a reason of being and a place in the Divine Plan. Now, our destination is both an inner and an outer one. Our inner destination is universal and common to all. Our outer destination constitutes our personal, subjective fulfillment of the objective Divine Will.

In order to exist and live we are fed with physical, psychological and spiritual energies, so the reasonable consequence of our being is to be also energetic sources of feeding, that is, to give from what we receive. We receive energy freely and we ought to give energy freely.

Our contribution is in two levels; it is of two kinds; one is internal and the other is external. Our internal contribution is determined by what *we are* and the external by what *we do*.

Our inner destination is the inner work of Love and we share this destination in common with all men. Our outer destination has to do with the external manifestations of the inner work of Love, and is immediately related to our *place* in the Divine Plan.

Our inner work could also be named "the Kingdom of God," which does not, however, belong to this world, *"My kingdom is not of this world"* (John 18:36). That means that it is an *inner kingdom*, an *inner state*, which after being attained will surely have its external results, *"Ye are the light of the world. A city that is set on an hill cannot be hid. Neither do men light a candle, and put it under a bushel, but on a candlestick; and it giveth light unto all that are in the house. Let your light so shine before men, that they may see your good works, and glorify your Father which is in heaven"* (Matthew 5:14-16).

Jesus Christ doesn't come to fight and conquer some external enemies or oppressors, but the inner enemies and oppressors. The enemies of the Kingdom of God that Jesus proclaims do not belong in this external world, *"If my kingdom were of this world, then would my servants fight, that I should not be delivered"* (John 18:36).

Nevertheless, it is true that the inner work that Jesus comes to perform is destined to exert its inevitable and necessary outer impact. For it's a fact that in all historical times known to man, there has always existed some external Babylon. That is, a society which was sick because it wasn't connected with real Love, but worshiped false "loves." Yet, the existence of every external Babylon had its cause in the existence of the corresponding internal one which dominated the hearts of its people. The outer Babylon never creates the inner one, the opposite is what is happening. That is why Jesus Christ doesn't come to fight the external Babylon, but the internal one, that is, our inner oppressor, our "self."

And it is obvious that we don't need the Son of Love to teach us about the external disease and unfairness which is self-evident, but about the internal one which constantly slips away from us and we usually go through our whole life without ever noticing. We need the Son of Love to teach us that our own "self" is our worst enemy and that *only* God can heal and free us.

So our primary work is the internal one which is related to our *voluntary participation* in this inner struggle to be cleansed, enlightened and freed, which means to attain *theosis*. And correspondingly, *each stage* of our inner work will also be reflected externally, providing its own contribution in this human world which constantly *falls* ill.

So we should never forget that the inner work is of utmost importance, while the genuine external work always reflects the results of the internal one. On the contrary, when we perform an outer work without the necessary inner conditions, our work becomes unscrupulous and even harmful.

> "As the holy fathers say, when the intellect forgets the purpose of a religious observance, the outward practice of virtue loses its value. For whatever is done indiscriminately and without purpose is not only of no benefit – even though good in itself – but actually does harm."
>
> (St. John of Damaskos, *On Virtues and Vices*, p. 340, Vol. 2, Philokalia)*

Initially, we have difficulty in realizing the truth of this perspective and indeed it constitutes a *temptation* for us to be devoted to an external work, putting in second place our inner duty. But our inner reality is infinitely more important than our external one.

> "Activities are not the main thing in life. The most important thing is to have the heart directed and attuned to God."
>
> (*The Art of Prayer – An Orthodox Anthology*, p. 235)

If this wasn't true, then we would be very good and happy in the event we were to procure all external things. We would feel complete if we had food, roof, clothes, physical freedom, money, etc., but we see a lot of people who have these things and are still very unhappy; and that is because they are slaves of their inner Babylon. And on the contrary, we can easily find people being deprived of much of the aforementioned, but having God in their hearts and having discovered Love inside them, they are happy and free.

Our real problem is not outer Babylon, because it cannot touch us when God has entered our soul and when Love reigns in our heart. And as much as we claim to ache for the sufferings which every outer Babylon causes to all of us, we cannot avoid the sin of pharisaic hypocrisy as long as we carry an inner Babylon.

> *"Woe unto you, scribes and Pharisees, hypocrites! For ye make clean the outside of the cup and of the platter, but within they are full of extortion and excess. Thou blind Pharisee, cleanse first that which is within the cup and platter, that the outside of them may be clean also. Woe unto you, scribes and Pharisees, hypocrites! For ye are like unto whited sepulchres, which indeed appear beautiful outward, but are within full of dead men's bones, and of all uncleanness. Even so ye also outwardly appear righteous unto men, but within ye are full of hypocrisy and iniquity"* (Matthew 23:25-28).

When our concern is to heal others, society or humanity before having healed ourselves, there are two inevitable and dangerous consequences. Firstly, this attitude exhibits the existence of some egoistic sloth, who, not willing to face its huge inner unclean stables, prefers to turn its attention to the inner uncleanness of others and declare the necessity of their cleansing. But if this attitude is crystallized in us, we will be entrapped in it, and in the long run we will become unable to receive any personal treatment, thus remaining enslaved in our incurable uncleanness.

And secondly, if the *power* to "heal" and "save" others is given in some way to us without first having received our inner Divine treatment, then it is absolutely certain that we will prove to be very bad and dangerous doctors and saviors, since we won't have any real knowledge regarding the diseases of human nature, and most of all, we won't have any skill of Love in order to handle the surgical tools we might be given.

As long as we want to change the world externally without having changed ourselves internally; as long as we want to be released from outer Babylon without having been released from the inner one, and as long as we want to heal without having been healed, the only thing we will achieve will be to perpetually fall into the same traps and mistakes which we want to avoid and correct.

This what the story of Jesus Christ is teaching us, for when Jesus comes to serve humanity, He faces the devilish *temptation* to obtain all the powers of this world, "*Again, the devil taketh him up into an exceeding high mountain, and sheweth him all the kingdoms of the world, and the glory of them*" (Matthew 4:8), through which He could offer and help, while His other choice was to travel upon a colt, "*Fear not, daughter of Sion: behold, thy King cometh, sitting on an ass's colt*" (John 12:15) and perform an inner work of Love, by worshiping and serving only Love, "*Thou shalt worship the Lord thy God, and him only shalt thou serve*" (Matthew 4:10). But the fellow men of Jesus wanted also to make Him a king, because they couldn't perceive the greatness of His *inner* work and anticipated an outer, superficial work, *"When Jesus therefore perceived that they would come and take him by force, to make him a king, he departed again into a mountain himself alone"* (John 6:15).

Yet, this outer work would be temporal and limited, perhaps even egoistic, since it would concern only the specific circumstances of time and place where Jesus Christ lived and acted. Nevertheless, the possibility of this external work was a constant challenge for Jesus since he had to continually refuse the outward, devilish dictates for grandness and be subjected to His inward, Divine promptings for humility.

So he performed an inner work that was unknown and seemed to have failed externally, but eventually spread into the whole world, *"And this gospel of the kingdom shall be preached in all the world"* (Matthew 24:14), and still exerts its strong impact after two thousand years, having established, in essence, its place in eternity.

That is why we shouldn't lose sight of our inner, unseen warfare, and shouldn't be misled by diverting our attention away from the *inner* battlefield.

Each one of us has a positive and beautiful place in this life; we have some essential part to play to fulfill a true purpose which can be accomplished only when the *necessary inner conditions* are realized. At some point, each one of us should answer, by treading our inner path to our personal question: "What is the purpose and meaning of my life?" And this answer can be found only within us. Afterwards, we will be able to take conscious care of what belongs to our care; we will be able to offer what we should offer.

And there are a lot of things in this world that need to be cared for: men, children, animals, forests, nature, science, technology, education, family, community, all nations, and the whole world. But we can easily imagine the creation of an outer chaos when our societies are composed by people imprisoned in an inner chaos. Let's imagine, for example, teachers without real moral education, greedy ecologists, scientists with no Conscience, preachers of Love full of negativity, merciless brothers and heartless parents. So it becomes obvious that we ought to first take care of our internal, to seek the things of God, and then *inevitably* the care of our external will follow. What do we expect to achieve, if our heart is not clean? What can we offer without *inner* wealth? What kind of works can we perform without Love?

> "Virtue is not true virtue when it is not within the heart. Therefore correct your heart and your will, and you shall be good and your outward deeds will be good, for the inward is the beginning of the outward. [...] Pure streams flow from a spring when the source itself is pure. Likewise good works come forth from the heart when the heart is good, but there cannot be good works without a good heart, just as from a putrid and noisome spring nothing else can flow but putrid and noisome water."
>
> (St. Tikhon of Zadonsk, *Journey to Heaven*, p. 59)

If our highest priority is not given to our inner battle, we will be inadequate in our personal role, that is, if we ever discover *what our real role is* in this life. For it's a very common case, and at the same time a very unpleasant one, to try and play the part of someone else; a role that doesn't fit us. It's like trying to put a puzzle piece in the wrong place. Apart from this being essentially impossible, if we insist, we will create a disharmonic result.

So it is sufficient to give to our inner battle daily, that is, *to perform our inner work of Love*, and soon our outer work will make its appearance, for there will be the right conditions for it. It's impossible to perform any essential external work without the necessary foundation of the internal one. And in the same way, it's impossible to perform our inner work without this having some outward reflection.

"Instead of concentrating upon external behavior, all those who work on themselves must have as their aim to be attentive and vigilant, and to walk in the presence of God. [...]

"Think as little as possible about external ascetic feats. Although they are necessary, they are nothing but a scaffolding inside which the building is erected. They are not the building itself; the building is in the heart. Turn all your attention, then, on what is to be done in the heart."

(*The Art of Prayer – An Orthodox Anthology*, pp. 170/238)

If we go deeper into this concept of offering in life, we will find out that we have, as we already said, two kinds of contributions in this world: one external and one internal. One is coming from what we *do* and the other from what we *are*. What we do certainly affects life, but what we are affects it even more.

A hypocrite philanthropist, despite his good works, continues to taint life and humanity by what he is on the inside. If we walk in mud and enter a house we will carry it inside. Isn't that so? In the same way, if our soul is not clean, we will carry its uncleanness wherever we go – regardless of our claims that the uncleanness of our soul is a personal matter and doesn't concern anyone else. This is not true! It concerns everything around us and it's very contagious, because it leaves its prints wherever we go. What *we are* exerts much more impact and it's much more important than what we do.

And if it's true that our inner uncleanness can contaminate everything around us, since we constantly carry it with us, then it's equally true that our inner purity will be as "contagious," even if it doesn't have a very obvious expression.

What matters above all is our *Being*. The inner work of some people might never be made known externally, but will serve its purpose marvelously by its existence, by simply *Being*.

> "The fragrance of a costly aromatic oil, even though kept in a vessel, pervades the atmosphere of the whole house, and gives pleasure, not only to those near it but also to others in the vicinity; similarly, the fragrance of a holy soul, beloved of God, when given out through all the senses of the body, conveys to those who perceive it the holiness that lies within."
>
> (St. Theodoros the Great Ascetic, *A Century of Spiritual Texts*, 88, p. 33, Vol. 2, Philokalia)

Through this inner perspective of things, we can perhaps understand better the real notion of strength, hope and determination. When our attention is directed to an outer work of offering which remains meteor and unconnected to the inner work of Love, then it's unavoidable to be tired and disappointed at some point. On the one hand because we won't draw energy from the Source of all energy, and on the other because our concepts of usefulness and happiness will be completely distorted, since they will be turned outwardly.

On the contrary, when there is the *necessary inner foundation* in relation to our outer offering, then all *external disappointment* can always be *transformed* into *internal determination*.

The disappointment is born without us knowing it when our attention is transferred from inside to outside. This happens when we forget that our first concern is the Kingdom of God, that is, our inner work of Love, and so its outer result and manifestation become our main concern. This imperceptible change of perspective from inside to outside is soon followed by the sense of disappointment.

Yet, as soon as we realize or remember the cause of this feeling of disappointment, then we will be able to return with more fervor, certainty and determination to our main concern, to our inner work. So the *external disappointment* is an *alarm-clock* which can bring about a *renewal* and *reinforcement* of our *inner efforts*.

In this point, it's important to determine once again the objective value of our inner Divine work in contrast to the relevant value of any external subjective work of ours. Otherwise, the circumstances and events of the external world will claim and divert our attention and in that way keep disorientating us.

We have been given a gift: life, existence. And it has been given to use it wisely and prudently for the benefit of our soul and everything around us, and not just for the sake of life itself. In other words, we do not live to "live," but to Live.

Real Life is inspired by God and so provides Abundance, and creates and works miracles, as long as her Derivation and Destination is Love.

"In everything that we do God searches out our purpose to see whether we do it for Him or for some other motive."

(St. Maximos the Confessor, *Four Hundred Texts on Love*, 36, Second Century, p. 71, Vol. 2, Philokalia)

So it's not so important *what we do* and how insignificant or great this seems, *as long as* we do it out of the truly creative and transforming action of God's Love.

"I come to you, my child, God assures us, in the smallest things, in the most humble details. Every gesture you make can give expression to Love without limits.

You wash a plate, then you wipe it dry. Make of that simple act an act of love toward those who have eaten from that plate, and toward all those who will eat from it.

A housewife walks out the back door. She hangs out the wash on a clothesline so it will dry. Does this rapid gesture of service remind you of anything? Do her two arms, extended for just a moment, make you think of two other arms that were stretched out on a sacred Tree?

All things can become sacred, if they are transfigured by love. That Love is forever with us, as one who serves."

(Lev Gillet, *Love Without Limits*, Ch. *I Come to You in the Little Things*)

Our path of life becomes truly unique and extraordinary when we follow the footprints of the One to whom we owe our existence. That is why each one of us must discover his own objective inner path which will lead him to Life, so we will be able, through our own subjective outer destination, to become another source of Love for everything around us.

And then we will discover, feeling a newly found joy and exultation, the perfection of the Divine Plan which was designed on the basis of an ideal Harmony, according to which all and everything have their *proper* place, in order to create all together a puzzle of indescribable Beauty.

When we find our own place in this puzzle, we will experience an immense relief. We will be relieved from all this sense of upset, anxiety and expectancy that appears when we feel *uncoordinated* and *pendulous within our own life*. All feelings of jealousy and envy for what the places of others might involve will be dissolved, since having found our own place in this Divine Plan, we will receive and experience the utmost satisfaction from all that constitutes our own journey in life.

When God's Will is fulfilled for us, regarding both our inner and outer destination, our main sensation is one of Perfect Harmony and Completion. What is given to us is the best we could ever ask for and at the same time *surpasses* anything we could have imagined. Everything takes its proper place, from the smallest things to the largest. All aspects of our existence are constantly arranged within their right boundaries according to the supreme wisdom of the Divine Will of Love.

Yet, in order to enter into this inner state of Fullness which will also set us toward our proper external place in life, we *first need it to be placed properly within us*. The inner work we should perform is to *become* Love, to our possible extent, so that all external offerings of real Love might also become feasible.

> "(Paul Evdokimov 1901-1970): 'It is not enough to *possess* prayer: we must *become* prayer – prayer incarnate. It is not enough to have moments of praise; our whole life, every act and every gesture, even a smile, must become a hymn of adoration, an offering, a prayer. We must offer not what we *have* but what we *are*.' That is what the world needs above all else: not people who 'say prayers' with greater or lesser regularity, but people who *are* prayers."
>
> (Kallistos Ware, *The Power of the Name*, p. 19)

However, we will never be able to bring this seemingly impossible inner work of Love to fulfillment as long as our efforts and motives are either egocentric or anthropocentric. Essentially, the only way to perform this huge inner work of Love is *through* God and *for the sake* of God, since in reality its inspirer is God Himself.

In this inner journey, the motive of our "self" might constitute only the starting-point of our journey, the motive of others can take us as far as to its middle, but only the motive of God sets everything in its proper place and leads us to the endless end of this journey.

If this final and perfect motive isn't there, everything will fall apart or end up at an absolute dead-end. For if we don't eventually tread our inner path, with its corresponding outer manifestations, for the sake of Love Herself, how can we expect to reach Her perfect destination? The only way to reach Her is to want to be taught, humbled and patient; wanting to travel, grow, *Live* and *Be* for *Her Sake*.

The Inner Restoration of Christianity

"For Your Sake"

It is true that Love draws us, and that's why after we have *tasted* Her for awhile, having at the same time been disappointed by our former "loves," we turn to Her and begin seeking Her, feeling that it is in Her where our real interest lies.

"Theologians call the divine sometimes an erotic force, sometimes love, sometimes that which is intensely longed for and loved. Consequently, as an erotic force and as love, the divine itself is subject to movement; and as that which is intensely longed for and loved, it moves towards itself everything that is receptive of this force and love."

(St. Maximos the Confessor, *Various Texts*, 84, Fifth Century, p. 280, Vol. 2, Philokalia)

Sooner or later, however, we realize that in this path of Love, our "self" constitutes, in reality, a heavy burden which doesn't let us go very far; as well as that our interest *doesn't* consist of a sufficient motive for traveling this entire rough road opening before us towards the heights or the depths of Love. For seeing the (inner) road we need to travel, we might feel that we were better before: yes our joy was ephemeral, but it was also effortless; our happiness was fleeting but we were "free" to do whatever we liked; we might have felt incomplete, but we also had our "pleasures." So the initial motive of our self will begin shaking and falling apart, and then we will either want to go back and worship our former idols or we will have to find some additional motives in order to die to our first, gross aspects of our egoism and march towards a new land, the one of Love for our neighbor and God.

Our *first real freedom* from our oppressing self is experienced when we start caring *essentially* more for others than ourselves; when we want to endure all trials, hardships and temptations, not only for our sake, but also *for the sake of others.*

This stage usually appears long before the stage where we want to travel for the sake of Love Herself, to be sacrificed for God Himself, since, *"For he that loveth not his brother whom he hath seen, how can he love God whom he hath not seen?"* (1 John 4:20).

Later on, however, we will realize that only if we love Love Herself exclusively for Her sake, will it be possible to truly love everything else as well, either ourselves or anyone and anything else, since, *"God is love; and he that dwelleth in love dwelleth in God, and God [Love] in him"* (1 John 4:16).

Yet, in the beginning we walk the path of Love out of "love" for our self and for the sake of ourselves. So it's inevitable to carry the hard-to-bear burdens of vainglory and pride along with us until we realize that as long as we carry them on our back, we won't be able to ascend to the Mountain of Love, nor enter through the strait gate of the Kingdom of Heaven.

That's why, in order to get rid of these burdens, it's necessary that we do not disclose to people our inner efforts and do not seek to be liked by men, but rather, to attribute every good thing to the Maker of Good so that humility can keep our soul's soil fertile.

> "Self-esteem is eradicated by the hidden practice of the virtues, pride, by ascribing our achievements to God."
>
> (St.Maximos the Confessor, *Four Hundred Texts on Love*, 62, Third Century, p. 93, Vol. 2, Philokalia)

At the same time it is equally necessary not to disclose, even to our own self, anything regarding our inner struggles and our course to Love, *"But when thou doest alms, let not thy left hand know what thy right hand doeth"* (Matthew 6:3). For when our false self learns (from us) that we struggle for virtue, it comes to misappropriate our efforts, in this way trying to remain alive and also collect any possible profit from our virtuous acts. This inner deviation is always possible until we perceive that we cannot truly progress in this inner journey of Love as long as we are motivated by anything else than Love Herself.

When we experience this objective reality, we will be freed from many bonds and impediments which hinder our inner ascent or deepening. We will be freed from our compulsive need to *unfailingly* defend ourselves; from our permanent and unbearable burden of the opinion others have about us; from the unpleasant taste of fair or unfair accusations; from the pleasant taste of justified or unjustified praises; from the exhausting effort to preserve our nice and imaginary pictures of ourselves; from the destructive pride which cuts us off from everything Good; and also from the foolish vainglory and the vain effort to be liked by men.

"He who has been granted divine knowledge and has through love acquired its illumination will never be swept hither and thither by the demon of self-esteem. But he who has not yet been granted such knowledge will readily succumb to this demon. However, if in all that he does he keeps his gaze fixed on God, doing everything for His sake, he will with God's help soon escape."

(St. Maximos the Confessor, *Four Hundred Texts on Love*, 46, First Century, p. 57, Vol. 2, Philokalia)

Yet, this total freedom comes only when we surrender completely to Divine Love, aiming and looking forward only to pleasing Her, *"Do I seek to please men? For if I yet pleased men, I should not be the servant of Christ"* (Galatians 1:10).

So if we, who are so small and insignificant, but with the potential of existing as Children of God, feel the inner call of Love and decide to begin on this journey which spreads in perpetuity so we can meet Her and be united with Her, we should realize that in order to contain even one of Her sunbeams we ought to be emptied from the things of our "self," even from *our own* will to be united with Her!

"If Thy desire is that I should be at rest in Thy knowledge, I shall not refuse. If it is that I should experience temptation so as to learn humility, again I am with Thee. Of myself, there is absolutely nothing I can do. For without Thee I would not have come into existence from non-existence; without Thee I cannot live or be saved. Do what Thou wilt to Thy creature; for I believe that, being good, Thou bestowest blessings on me, even if I do not recognize that they are for my benefit. Nor am I worthy to know, nor do I claim to understand, so as to be at rest: this might not be to my profit.

"I do not dare to ask for relief in any of my battles, even if I am weak and utterly exhausted: for I do not know what is good for me. 'Thou knowest all things' (John 21:17); act according to Thy knowledge. Only do not let me go astray, whatever happens; whether I want it or not, save me, though, again, only if it accords with Thy will. I, then, have nothing: before Thee I am as one that is dead; I commit my soul into Thy pure hands."

(St. Peter of Damaskos, *Book I – How to Acquire True Faith*, p. 165, Vol. 3, Philokalia)

As strong as our desire is for a beautiful, paradisiacal Life; as intense as our aversion is for the ephemeral and vain "life," for the Babylonian life; at some point, what will lead and urge us should be the voice, the desire, of the One calling us.

We must want to travel for His sake, to endure all sufferings, be exposed to all the dangers, for His sake, not for "ourselves," not only for the sake of others, but *in essence* because He calls us; because He wants us.

In order to walk the path of Love we must surely learn to love. And we know from our human loves that when we love deeply, we put others before ourselves, and the ones who truly love us do the same. For every real human love starts where our excessive occupation with our "self" stops – when we transcend the "self" which always stands *between* us and the object of our love.

> "Love [Eros], whether we speak of Divine, or Angelic, or intelligent, or psychical, or physical, let us regard as a certain unifying and combining power."
>
> (Dionysius the Areopagite, *On Divine Names*, Caput IV, Sec. XV, p. 50)

So how much truer will this be in relation to the Divine Love? To She who surrenders Herself completely to us, making it impossible for us not to surrender ourselves completely to Her?

> "But Divine Love is ecstatic, not permitting (any) to be lovers of themselves, but of those beloved. [...] Wherefore also, Paul the Great, when possessed by the Divine Love, and participating in its ecstatic power, says with inspired lips, "I live no longer, but Christ lives in me." As a true lover, and beside himself, as he says, to Almighty God, and

not living the life of himself, but the life of the Beloved, as a life excessively esteemed."

(Dionysius the Areopagite, *On Divine Names*, Caput IV, Sec. XIII, p. 48)

When we begin experiencing all this Love of God, the Divine Love which warms our heart, there is born in us an intense sense of *gratitude*, which as it grows makes us very strong and truly happy, ready to transcend everything in order to be deeper united with Love. And at the *same time*, it will make us feel deeply contrite, bringing tears to our heart, as we realize how ungratefully we constantly respond to the miracle of God's Love and how easily we forget both God and all His benefactions. Then our gratitude will bring forth internally (and perhaps externally as well) tears of joy and sadness. We will feel indescribable joy for the Love we receive and unimaginable sadness for the love we don't offer.

"Why Don't You Cry, My Heart?"

"My eyes are dry, why?

Isn't my heart crying enough?

Is she still so hard?

Do I still believe in myself?

Do I still not believe in You?

Break her, our Father!

Break her!

Tear her apart into pieces!

Empty her from all her false gods,

all the things of herself,

all her false loves.

Make room in her for You!

Open her wide,

and fill her with Your Light!"

Why doesn't our heart seek only You?

You who are the Heart of our hearts.

You who are the everlasting and firm source of Love, Beauty and Fullness.

Why does she turn to false gods, chimeras, vain desires and longings? Why does she become a prodigal? In all our journeys, in all things, activities, relationships, in our whole lives, what do we seek? It is *You* who we seek, our Lost Paradise, Love.

We might say, or even feel, that we have returned to You like the prodigal son and wonder why don't You welcome us. But the truth is that we are still far from You, our longing for You is still weak; we still worship idols. When our Divine longing for You flames up, only then we will return. We will turn to You and You will run to welcome us.

We often have the impression that You are not accepting us back, whereas in reality, *we cannot return* because of our way of life, because of what we have become. You are constantly calling us, but *we* do not hear. And then we say: "But why do You turn away from me? Why don't You talk to me? Why do You abandon me?" Yet, it is we that have cut off the communication with You, because we desire other things than You. And then we complain that You don't pay attention to us, when we are indifferent to the perfection of Your Love. Our own deafness and blindness are cutting off our communication.

Our heart has become like a hard shell and needs many blows to break and open. We imagine, however, despite our hard-heartedness that we can love You. We don't understand that the relationship with You is like all relations of Love and Eros. We cannot grasp that to fall in Love with You and Love You, our heart needs first to be cleansed of our other "loves."

We do not want to renounce our foreign and false loves, even though they keep betraying us and letting us down. Despite their bitter taste and vainness, we remain faithful to them. Yet, we keep disbelieving You, even after we have tasted Your greatness, beauty and perfection; we soon get used to it and like bored husbands and wives we seek for new thrills or return to our former loves, even when they have let us down innumerable times. So we taint our heart and don't realize that *this is Your* residence, the sacred dwelling of Your Love. Our heart has hardened and we have lost all contact with her.

> "People often complain that their heart is hardened, and this is not surprising. Man does not collect himself within, and so is unaccustomed to inward self-awareness; he fails to establish himself where he should, and does not know the place of the heart."
>
> (*The Art of Prayer – An Orthodox Anthology*, pp. 178-179)

That is why we ignore the Treasure contained inside us and are enchanted by all kinds of outer treasures. We ignore the gift which we have been given inside us and our inner wealth, so, feeling empty and poor, we labor and struggle for all kinds of external riches.

> "You seek the Lord? Seek, but only within yourself. He is not far from anyone. The Lord is near all those who truly call on Him. Find a place in your heart, and speak there with the Lord. It is the Lord's reception room. Everyone who meets the Lord, meets Him there; He has fixed no other place for meeting souls."
>
> (*The Art of Prayer – An Orthodox Anthology*, p. 187)

So what is our real *sin*? Our real *miss*?

The Inner Restoration of Christianity

It is the fact that we turn *outside* from our internal, seeking all kinds of gods to erect in the sanctuary of our heart and worship them there, forgetting the real God, Love, which we dethroned from His rightful place within us.

> "The kingdom of heaven is within you. Insofar as the Son of God dwells in you, the kingdom of heaven lies within you also. Here within are the riches of heaven, if you desire them. Here, O sinner, is the kingdom of God within you. Enter into yourself, seek more eagerly and you will find it without great travail. Outside you is death, and the door to death is sin. Enter within yourself and remain in your heart, for there is God."
>
> (*The Art of Prayer – An Orthodox Anthology*, pp. 181-182)

Yet, even if we eventually decide to return within us, it is very easy being so unfamiliar with our inner world, to be misled and think that we have entered into our depths when we have only wandered to the surface of our internal, the borders of which are inhabiting imagination, delusion and our former idols.

> "In the natural order of things, when we try to bring our spiritual powers under control, the path from without to within is blocked by the imagination. To arrive successfully at our inward objective, we must travel safely past the imagination. If we are careless about this, we may stick fast to the imagination and remain there, under the impression that we have entered within, whereas in fact we are merely outside the entrance, as it were in the court of the Gentiles. This, in itself, would not matter so much, were it not that this state is almost always accompanied by self-deception."
>
> (*The Art of Prayer – An Orthodox Anthology*, pp. 182-183)

Still, we shouldn't be discouraged because in there, within our heart, we can discover what is most sacred.

"The heart is the place where God is revealed as love and light."

(Metropolitan of Nafpaktos Hierotheos, *Orthodox Psychotherapy – The Science of the Fathers*, p.163)

Even though we all recognize the decisive part that the physical heart plays in our life, most of us don't recognize the part that the deeper spiritual heart plays.

"The heart is the primary organ of our identity, it is our inner-most being, 'the very deepest and truest self, not attained except through sacrifice, through death.' According to Boris Vysheslavtsev, it is 'the centre not only of consciousness but of the unconscious, not only of the soul but of the spirit, not only of the spirit but of the body, not only of the comprehensible but of the incomprehensible; in one word, it is the absolute centre.' Interpreted in this way, the heart is far more than a material organ in the body; the physical heart is an outward symbol of the boundless spiritual potentialities of the human creature, made in the image of God, called to attain his likeness."

(Kallistos Ware, *The Power of the Name*, p. 21)

So we can spend our whole life without ever suspecting what is hidden inside us, without ever turning towards our internal to begin a long journey, aiming to penetrate into our heart's abyss.

"The heart has a double significance in the spiritual life: it is both the centre of the human being and the point of meeting between the human being and God. It is both the place of self-knowledge, where we see ourselves as we truly are, and the place of self-transcendence, where we understand our nature as a temple of the Holy Trinity, where the image comes face to face with the Archetype. In the 'inner sanctuary' of our own heart we find the ground of our being and so cross the mysterious frontier between the created and the Uncreated."

(Kallistos Ware, *The Power of the Name*, pp. 21-22)

Yet, the door of our spiritual heart is the only real door for the Kingdom of Heaven. And fortunately, this door is as close to us as, unfortunately, we cannot even imagine.

"Enter eagerly into the treasure-house that lies within you, and so you will see the treasure-house of heaven: for the two are the same, and there is but one single entry to them both. The ladder that leads to the Kingdom is hidden within you, and is found in your own soul. Dive into yourself and in your soul you will discover the rungs by which to ascend."

(*The Art of Prayer – An Orthodox Anthology*, p. 164)

Around our heart, however, there has been formed a hard mass of impurities, which have lingered over her and made our heart seem *heartless*. Our heart is filled with imaginations, desires, passions, thoughts, foreign and false loves; so she is constantly daydreaming unsubstantial and temporal paradises which soon turn into hells.

So our heart needs to be cleansed from all her impurities and our acquired hard-heartedness must be dissolved. Prayer, *metanoia*, humility and above all the *inner* tears of the heart, cleanse, heal, open and broaden her.

"God gave you tears of contrition. These are good. But the tears of the heart are even better. For the tears that the eyes shed, feed the worm of pride, while the heart's contrition, known only to God, feeds humility."

(St. Theophan the Recluse, *Guidance in the Spiritual Life*, p. 180)

Yet, we need to be careful in this point as well, because our heart is used to hypocrisy, deceit and pretense.

"But try to combat the stoniness of your heart through intensifying your humility, not through calling forth tears; these are a special grace and should not be striven after."

(Starets Macarius of Optino, *Russian Letters of Direction*, Letter 191)

The inner tears of the soul are necessary for our cleansing, but only when they are coming from Love who is wounding our heart and are shed exclusively for Her sake.

'Only one tear has been shed in years and years... and this wasn't mine, it was my egoism's... it was wounded... and it shed a tear... that was all... in years and years.'

It was a man who wanted to cry. He wanted to cry lest his heart softens, lest she is cleansed, lest she breaks and opens... for a little light to enter. He wanted to cry, not because he was moved by some sight, not for something that happened to him, not even for his mistakes... but because he was so inadequate towards God; he had betrayed Him so many times, he was forgetting Him so often, he was constantly setting Him aside. He wanted to cry for his ungratefulness, his ingratitude, his pettiness; he wanted to cry *for the sake of God*. But nothing... his heart remained closed, hard and unmoved; she couldn't shed even one tear.

'So what do you want?' asked the holy man.

'I want to cry.'

"Why?"

"For the sake of God."

"Then you have to pray... so God will give you His tears. Your tears are for yourself... God's tears are for His sake... and even though your eyes are dry, your heart needs to cry deeply and one should be her prayer: "Our God, forgive us."

Without contrition, without our deep *metanoia*, without the *redirection of our attention* to our internal, to Love, it's not possible for the Divine flame to be born inside us which will initially cleanse all the impurities and soften our heart, and then enlighten her with Her Divine Light.

"Your inner remaking will begin properly from the time your heart becomes warmed with the Divine warmth. The little flame within you melts down everything and refines it; in other words, everything will begin spiritualizing until it is entirely spiritualized."

(St. Theophan the Recluse, *The Spiritual Life*, pp. 210-211)

Yet, we should remember that our heart's contrition is again, in essence, necessary for us. For if we don't ache, if we don't break loose and cry, we do not appreciate, we do not love, we do not thank; in fact it's the opposite: we disbelieve, we are filled with ungratefulness, we consider everything a *given*. That is why our heart's tears are again bestowed by God. He offers us in reality *His own tears* for our benefit.

For in the end God doesn't need any tears, nor does He want to see us in pain and sorrow. The only desire of God for us, which is related exclusively to *our* utmost benefit, is to be united with Him; it is our return to His Love, to our inner Lost Paradise.

The Inner Restoration of Christianity

The Inner Restoration of Christianity

The Lost Paradise

"Seek Paradise lost, in order to sing the praise
of Paradise regained."

(*The Art of Prayer – An Orthodox Anthology*, p. 180)

What do our souls search for?

What do we seek? ... the Lost Paradise.

What was Paradise?

You and the communication with You.

You and the contact with You, the *relationship* with You.

So the Lost Paradise *Is* You.

We all seek the Lost Paradise,

and we still don't grasp,

that the Lost Paradise Is You.

How tragic!

What vain pain!

We still cannot hear Your voice *inside us*.

And even if we hear it, we give no heed to it and do not return to You, we do not return to Paradise but we continue to be prodigals searching for other paradises... since we have forgotten You... and only when we get too low; when we taste every vainness; when we begin thirsting, and starving spiritually, only then we might wake up, "come to our Self" (Luke 15:17) and remember... the dwelling of Love, the Lost Paradise... You.

For in You there was, there is and there will be all Goods, Abundance, Everything. In You we will find our completion, our fullness.

When we decide to return, You always run to meet us and offer us more than before (Luke 15:20-24), for You Are Love. But we come and go, so you keep calling us: "Come back to Me my children" but we do not listen...

We continue searching for "paradises" because our heart is hardened and cannot feel Your Paradise; our mind is full of chatter and we cannot hear Your Voice. Our soul is in delusion and our *soul's soul*, our *spirit*, is starving... and dies away with the remembrance of a Lost Paradise. If we pay *attention* to it, we might hear it sighing and confessing:

"Really and truly I am not interested in anything anymore; only in You.

For You Are Love. How could I be interested in anything else?

You Are our Derivation and Destination.

You Are Paradise... the Lost Paradise."

"To Be My True Self"

"I am your Lord, the Lord of Love. Do you want to enter into the life of Love? This is not an invitation to some realm of tepid tenderness. It is a calling to enter into the burning flame of Love. There alone is true conversion: conversion to incandescent Love.

"Do you wish to become someone other than you have been, someone other than you are? Do you wish to be someone who lives for others, and first of all for that Other and with that Other who calls all things into being? Do you wish to be a brother to all, a brother to the entire world?

Then hear what my Love speaks to you.

"My child, you have never known who you really are. You do not yet know yourself. By this I mean that you have never really known yourself to be the object of my Love. As a result, you have never known who you are in me, or all the potential within yourself.

"Awake from this sleep and its bad dreams! In certain moments of truth, you see nothing in yourself but failures and defeats, set-backs, corruption, and perhaps even crimes. But none of that is really of you. It is not your true "me," the most profound expression of your true self.

"Beneath and behind all that, deeper than all your sin, transgressions and lacks, my eyes are upon you. I see you, and I love you. It is you that I love."

(Lev Gillet, *Love Without Limits*, Ch. *To You, Whoever You may Be*)

Let's stop being afraid and let's begin sacrificing the old, false and limited, so we can accept our Metamorphosis, the Gifts of God, Love. Let's allow our spirit to be heard inside us, until its voice is so strong that it will spring from our Divine Depths and reach to the Heavenly Heights:

"I need to be my Real Self.

I need to be with You.

I need to be in You.

I *want* to *Be* in *You*; which is to be in the state of prayer, stillness, humility, silence, solitude, fullness and Love.

To be our Real Self means to be genuinely relaxed, beautiful, humble, kind, incorruptible, dispassionate, simple, not cunning and calculating, or full of desires and wishful thinking, but silent, complete and smiling. It means not to be self-limited, not to be scattered, dependent, not to be lost, but to *Be*: Simple, Here, with You, One with You and thus with All. Without masks, anxiety, longings, but free, completely independent from everything and absolutely dependent on You.

Thank You for claiming us.

What can be more excellent than being claimed by Love!

Shouldn't we then surrender to Her?

That is why I have to Be my Real Self.

For *I am* what You Want me to Be.

I am what You have made me to Be.

I am what deep down *We All Are*.

We all *are* charismatic.

We are wholly a Gift.

I *want* to be my Real Self: I want to *be* in the state of Love.

But I am nothing, and cannot be anything, without You.

Inside You I am Nothing and so I Am Everything.

Outside of You I am "everything" and so I am nothing.

I do not exist without You.

My Real Self is You.

For You Are the Spirit of my spirit.

You… and I are One."

"I and my Father are one" (John 10:30).

The Inner Restoration of Christianity

The Inner Restoration of Christianity

"You... and We"

"Therefore doth my Father love me, because I lay down my soul [psyche-ψυχή], that I might take it again." (John 10:17)

"What can we attribute to ourselves?

For what can we be proud?

All is Yours; all *Is* You.

Silence though is needed... *stillness*,

even if we keep losing ourselves in whatever

imaginations.

For all worries are imaginations,

all anxieties, fears and wants,

all the things of ourselves are imaginations.

Only *You Are* Real.

The only thing needed (Luke 10:41-42)

is association with You, the union with You,

where there is duration, joy, light and *Meaning*.

When we are with You, we are in the Present,

there is silence, *hesychia*, rest.

When we are with You, we have everything,

gratitude, forgiveness, guidance.

When we are with You, all is good,

there is patience, relaxation, fullness.

When we are with You, all is magic,

there is beauty, eternity, miracle.

When we are with You, there is Life,

Unity – Love.

When we are with You, *We Are* our Real Self,

we are what you created us to *be*.

When we are with You,

there is perfection, harmony, completion,

everything is perfect for You *Are* Perfection.

When we are with You, we *Exist*, we are *Free*,

We Are because *You, Are*.

We want... yes, we want... but let us have *one* want... may we want to be *full* and *complete*, that is, *to be with You*. May we want Your Kingdom and nothing else; may we want You. Yes, let us want... You.

And the law is known; it is known that in this way we can have all: "*Seek ye first the kingdom of God [...] and all these things shall be added unto you*" (Matthew 6:33), but let us not want You in order to have everything; let us want You only for You.

Forgive us! Our hearts belong to You!

Thank You eternally for all Your Love!

When the highest ideal in this world is Love; when everyone is seeking to love and be loved; when our life is futile and unjustified without Love... how is it possible to be interested more in the creations of Love, than Love Herself? Let us have only one desire: You.

For when we don't desire only You, we become small, we do not hear You, we do not do Your Will, and so we create disharmony. We become rapacious, quarrelsome, negative, and whatever dreadful thing one can imagine. And then again, when we want You *for our sake*, we might retreat and step backwards, we might desire again something else out of You. We might want both Your Will and the things of ourselves. We might demand to use You for our profit, for the gratification of our desires. Nevertheless, when we want You only for Your sake – for only You deserve all our love (which is born from Your Love) – You still give us whatever else we desire, or better, *need*. For if this is not the case, we will become spoilt, greedy, arrogant and proud; we will consider Your gifts as *a given,* and won't value them enough, so they will slip from our hands and hearts without us even noticing it.

So Only You, for everything else is futile. As long as we keep believing in various gods, we cannot have faith and hope in You; we cannot love You, despite the fact that only You love us *unceasingly* and *unalterably*.

This Is the Truth: You *Are* Love.

Free us from our "self,"

teach us to *be* Love,

regenerate us in Your Light.

Our Real Self Is You.

You Are our Beginning and End.

We exist From You and for You.

You Are the Meaning and Purpose of our being.

You Are All. There is nothing outside You.

You Are the One Source.

Without You, we have nothing.

Without You, we can do nothing.

Without You, we are nothing.

May we have *one* desire... You.

You and we to be... *One*."

The Inner Restoration of Christianity

"So that they all may be one, just as You, Father, are in Me, and I in You; that they also may be one in Us" (John 17:21).

The Inner Restoration of Christianity

Epilogue

"He is indeed within us, but we ourselves do not stand before Him in His presence. Therefore we must return within ourselves, and find Him there. We have read enough, now we must act; we have watched enough how others walk, now we must walk ourselves."

(*The Art of Prayer – An Orthodox Anthology*, p. 196)

If you derived even a little benefit from this book thank God who is calling us all to come close to Him and offers us the necessary help for this *Return* to be possible.

"For Thine is the kingdom, and the power, and the glory, forever. Amen."

The Inner Restoration of Christianity

Acknowledgments - Bibliography

Wholehearted thanks are due to Alice, Theoharis, Vasilis and Ioanna, for their decisive contribution to the final shaping of this work; and also to Theodore J. Nottingham for his invaluable editorial work in this English version, as well as to Father Modestos who constituted a significant motivation for this work to be translated in English. Warm thanks are also due to all who contributed to the creation of the following spiritual works which were a necessary foundation for the present work; yet, above all, let us thank again *Love* – the Creator of Everything – and may *She* always be the Divine Inspiration for all of us: *"For Thine is the kingdom, and the power, and the glory, for ever. Amen."*

Abba Ammonas, *Useful Servanthood – A Study of Spiritual Formation in the Writings of Abba Ammonas*, Bernadette McNary-Zak, A Cistercian Publications title publ. by Liturgical Press

Abba Zosimas, *The Reflections of Abba Zosimas*, translated by John Chryssavgis, publ. by SLG Press

Anthony Bloom, *Courage to Pray*, publ. by Darton, Longman and Todd Ltd

Anthony Bloom (of Sourozh) with Marghanita Laski, *God and Man*, publ. by St. Vladimir's Seminary Press

Anthony of Sourozh, *Living Prayer*, publ. by Darton, Longman and Todd Ltd

Anthony of Sourozh, *School for Prayer*, publ. by Darton, Longman and Todd Ltd

Dimitri of Rostov, *Spiritual Alphabet,* publ. by Holy Monastery of the Paraclete, Oropos, Attica, Greece (translated from Greek)

Dionysius the Areopagite, *The Works of Dionysius the Areopagite,* translated by Rev. John Parker (1897), published by James Parker and Co (can be found posted on the website of Christian Classics Ethereal Library)

Evagrius of Pontus, *The Greek Ascetic Corpus,* Robert E. Sinkewicz, publ. by Oxford University Press

Ignatius Brianchaninov, *On Miracles and Signs,* Orthodox Life, Vol. 45, Nos 2-4, publ. by Holy Trinity Monastery (can be found posted on the website of Orthodox Christian Information Center)

Ignatius Brianchaninov, *The Arena: An Offering to Contemporary Monasticism,* publ. by Holy Trinity Monastery

Irenaeus of Lyons, *The Ante-Nicene Fathers, Vol. 1, The Apostolic Fathers, Justin Martyr, Irenaeus* compiled by Arthur Cleveland Coxe (1885), publ. by The Christian Literature Company (can be found posted on the website of Christian Classics Ethereal Library)

John G. Bennett, *Witness: The Story of a Search,* publ. by Bennett Books

John Climacus, *The Ladder of Divine Ascent,* publ. by Paulist Press

Kallistos Ware, *The Orthodox Way,* publ. by St. Vladimir's Seminary Press

Kallistos Ware, *The Power of the Name – The Jesus Prayer in Orthodox Spirituality,* publ. by SLG Press

Lev Gillet, *Love without Limits,* translation from the French, *Amour Sans Limites,* Éditions de Chevetogne, Namur, Belgium (1971), by

Fr. John Breck, posted on the site of the Orthodox Church in America

Lev Gillet, *Our Father... Lord Jesus Christ*, publ. by Akritas, Athens, Greece (translated from Greek, for further study see, Lev Gillet / Un Moine de l'Église d'Orient, *Notre Père – Introduction à la Foi et à la Vie Chrétienne*, publ. by Éditions du Cerf)

Mersine Vigopoulou, *From I-ville to You-ville*, publ. by Uncut Mountain Press

Metropolitan of Nafpaktos Hierotheos, *A Night in the Desert of the Holy Mountain*, publ. by Birth of the Theotokos Monastery

Metropolitan of Nafpaktos Hierotheos, *Orthodox Psychotherapy – The Science of the Fathers*, publ. by Birth of the Theotokos Monastery

On the Necessity of Constant Prayer for all Christians in General, From The Life of St. Gregory Palamas, by St. Nikodemos of the Holy Mountain, translation by St Gregory Palamas Monastery (can be found posted on the website of Orthodox Christian Information Center)

Paisius Velichkovsky, *Field Flowers or Lilies of the Field (Gathered from the Divine Scripture concerning God's Commandments and the Holy Virtues)*, publ. by Holy Monastery of the Paraclete, Oropos, Attica, Greece (translated from Greek – for further study see, *Little Russian Philokalia, vol. IV: St. Paisius Velichkovsky*, publ. by St. Herman's Press)

Philokalia: The Complete Text, Four Volumes, publ. by Faber & Faber

[The Sentences of] Sextus, from the *The Nag Hammadi Library* by James M. Robinson, publ. by HarperCollins, San Francisco, 1990

Sextus the Pythagorean, *The Golden Verses of Pythagoras and Other Pythagorean Fragments*, selected by Florence M. Firth (1904)

Sophia Antzaka, *Hieros Gamos (Sacred Marriage)*, 12 Volumes, publ. by Spageiria, Greece (translated from Greek)

Starets Macarius of Optino, <u>Russian Letters of Direction 1843-1860</u>, publ. by St. Vladimir's Seminary Press, posted (as *Letters of Elder Macarius of Optina*) on the website of St. Vladimir's Russian Orthodox Church in Edmonton, Alberta

Starets Parthenios, publ. by Holy Monastery of the Paraclete, Oropos, Attica, Greece (translated from Greek)

The Art of Prayer: An Orthodox Anthology compiled by Igumen Chariton of Valamo, publ. by Faber & Faber

Theophan the Recluse, *Guidance in the Spiritual Life (Extracts from Letters)*, publ. by Holy Monastery of the Paraclete, Oropos, Attica, Greece (translated from Greek)

Theophan the Recluse, *Preaching Another Christ*, publ. by Orthodox Witness

Theophan the Recluse, *Selection of Letters*, publ. by Holy Monastery of the Paraclete, Oropos, Attica, Greece (translated from Greek)

Theophan the Recluse, *The Spiritual Life and How to Be Attuned to It*, publ. by St. Paisius Serbian Orthodox Monastery

Tikhon of Zadonsk, *Journey to Heaven – Counsels on the Particular Duties of Every Christian*, publ. by Holy Trinity Monastery

www.ingramcontent.com/pod-product-compliance
Lightning Source LLC
Chambersburg PA
CBHW071959150426
43194CB00008B/925